Contents

SETTING THE PRISONERS FREE

1. James Ramsay, 1733-1789 10
FRIEND OF THE SLAVES

2. Sir Charles Middleton, 1726-1813 18
THE MAN BEHIND TRAFALGAR

3. John Newton, 1725-1807 29
A NAVAL DESERTER

4. William Wilberforce, 1759-1833 38
THE LITTLE LIBERATOR

MAKE THE FOULEST CLEAN

5: Robert Raikes, 1735-1811 46
RAGAMUFFINS' UNCLE

6. Elizabeth Fry, 1780-1845 52
LADY OF NEWGATE

7. Sir George Williams, 1821-1905 60
FATHER OF THE YMCA

8. 7th Earl of Shaftesbury, 1801-1885 69
NOBLE LORD

SOLDIERS FOR CHRIST

9. Sir Henry Havelock, 1795-1857 80
THE SOLDIERS' GENERAL

10. Sir Herbert Edwardes, 1819–1868 98
HE TAMED THE TRIBES

11. Thomas 'Stonewall' Jackson, 1824-1863 102
STONEWALL

ASSIST ME TO PROCLAIM

12. Brownlow North, 1810-1874 110
RAKE'S PROGRESS

13. D. L. Moody, 1837-1899; 118
Ira D. Sankey, 1840-1908
MEN OF GOD, MAN OF SONG

14. Reuben Archer Torrey, 1856-1928 127
FAILED SUICIDE

15. Bramwell Booth, 1856-1929 134
CHIEF OF STAFF

16: Lord Radstock, 1833–1913 140
LORD APOSTOL

INTO ALL THE WORLD

17. William Carey, 1761-1834 152
ALL MY FRIENDS ARE BUT ONE

18. Adonirum Judson, 1788-1850 159
JUDSON'S DARKEST HOUR

19. Hudson Taylor, 1832–1905 166
YOUNG MAN WITH A PIGTAIL

20. James Chalmers, 1841–1901 174
CANNIBAL EASTER

21. Mary Slessor, 1848-1915 181
LASSIE QUEEN OF CALABAR

22. Rosalie Harvey, 1854-1932 191
THE LAME COW'S FRIEND

23. Stanley Smith, 1861-1931 206
C.T. Studd, 1860-1931: Test Cricketer
THE CAMBRIDGE SEVEN

24. Rowland V. Bingham, 1870-1943 235
LEFT IN LAGOS

25. Mildred Cable, 1878–1952 241
Eva and Francesca French,
1869–1960 and 1871–1960
THE GOOD GOSSIPS OF GOBI

26. John and Betty Stam 252
1916–1934, 1917–1934
VICTIMS OF THE LONG MARCH

27. Ernest Presswood, 1908–1946 259
TUAN CHANGE

28. Sir Wilfred Grenfell, 1865–1940 266
SANTA CLAUS OF LABRADOR

PREFACE

One fascination of Christian biography is its variety. Men and women come to Christ in different ways. Their faith grows and they respond to different calls; some in this book were primarily reformers, others evangelists, and I begin with four whose imperishable service was to confront and defeat the Slave Trade.

Some who are sketched here spent their lives based in their homelands. Others went far from home. In the last years of the eighteenth century the Christian faith was virtually confined to Europe and part of the Americas, with small pockets surviving in North Africa and Asia. Two hundred years later almost every country of the world has a Christian church, and the faith grows fastest in Africa and China. Under God, a prime cause of this vast expansion was the willingness of men and women to leave the security of Europe or North America to become pioneers.

Three of those described became martyrs. One, 'Lord Apostol', is forgotten in his own country yet his life story is a key to the events which unfold in Russia in the last decade of the twentieth century.

Most of these sketches were collected in two companion volumes, *A Fistful of Heroes* (1988) and *On Fire For God* (1990), published by Marshall Pickering. Many had appeared originally in periodicals which are listed, with other acknowledgements, in the earlier books. I am grateful to Christian Focus and especially to William Mackenzie and Malcolm Maclean for bringing these stories together for a new readership.

I have written full length biographies of several of these heroes. Titles, with names of the publishers of the current editions, will be found on page 8.

The men and women who are recalled here are just a few from a great multitude. They differed from each other in character and achievement but their dedication shames a softer age.

John Pollock
Rose Ash
Devon

For further reading

Books by John Pollock,
listing publishers of current editions.

Way to Glory: the Life of Henry Havelock
(Christian Focus)

Moody Without Sankey (Christian Focus)

Hudson and Maria (Christian Focus)

Amazing Grace: John Newton's Story (Lion)

Wilberforce (Lion).
(and for Ramsay and Barham)

Shaftesbury: The Poor Man's Earl (Lion)

The Cambridge Seven (IVP)

SETTING THE
PRISONERS FREE

1. James Ramsay, 1733-1789
FRIEND OF THE SLAVES

The *Arundel* was cleared for action. The West Indian sun beat down on the tanned bodies of the crew at the guns, and a light breeze filled the canvas as the frigate closed on the strange sail ahead.

Down in the cockpit the young Scots surgeon, James Ramsay, laid out his instruments while the surgeon's mate covered the midshipmen's sea chests with sail cloth; the rush of water below the keel told that she moved fast towards the enemy. Ramsay paused for a moment and prayed – not for himself but for the captain, Charles Middleton, that whatever occurred he be a true witness to Christ.

The *Arundel* was an unusual man-of-war. Alone among the captains on the West Indies station Middleton was an active Christian, and James Ramsay owed his conversion to his captain. Together, on this 20th November, 1759, northwest of Antigua, they were once more going into action.

A single gun fired. Ramsay taughtened, waiting for the enemy's reply. None came. He heard the shout of orders, a scurry of feet, the sound of the whaler being lowered. He wondered how many of the boarding party would return with shattered limbs or faces shot away. The minutes dragged by. Suddenly a midshipman clattered down. 'Captain's compliments, sir, and would you please go to him at once?'

'It's a British slaver, Mr. Ramsay,' said Middleton when Ramsay reached him. 'The French prize crew have surrendered. She was only taken yesterday, but there is plague aboard and the captain begs help. You will be good enough to do what you can. The whaler awaits you, Mr. Ramsay.'

The surgeon was soon clambering up the side of the *Swift* of Bristol, bound from the Guinea coast for Barbados. Slavery was an accepted part of West Indian life, and though Ramsay and other naval officers were sometimes disgusted at the cruelty of owners and overseers, and had a low opinion of planters' women who were depraved by absolute authority over slaves, it no more occurred to them to question slavery itself than the use of the cat-o'-nine-tails on a man-of-war.

But when Ramsay stepped on board the slaver he was appalled. He saw the crowded holds of naked slaves chained row by row, with ankles and wrists chafed and raw; the callous indifference of the captain, who was concerned at the financial loss which plague would cause yet cared nothing for the slaves as human beings; and the glee with which the crew showed off the brutal instruments used to coerce or punish. Ramsay felt sick.

He gave such treatment as he could, and left medicine and instruments. Meanwhile the *Arundel* had taken the slaver in tow, and Ramsay returned to his ship. All that morning his thoughts and eyes reverted to the ship they were towing. At noon the hawser broke. An hour later the two ships parted, and the *Arundel* increased sail and was away. By evening the slaver with her cargo of misery had dropped below the horizon, but not out of Ramsay's mind. He vowed that he would henceforth do his utmost for the slaves. What, however, could be done by an insignificant naval surgeon? God knew the answer.

Three years later Ramsay was a West Indian parson – and a slave-owner himself. A serious fall on board ship and a badly broken leg had incapacitated him for sea service. He had decided to take Holy Orders and dedicate his life to the slaves, and in 1762 he had been appointed through Captain Middleton to a living in the little West Indian island of St. Kitts. He married a settler's daughter and bought ten slaves, without which he could not have run his household, resolving to prove to his fellow owners 'how much might be done by one in earnest'.

Thus, on any evening in the following years, a passerby might have noticed an unwonted sight on the rectory verandah. The ten slaves, their wives and children, stood humbly in a group before their master, lisping the Lord's Prayer at his dictation and listening open-mouthed to the story of Jesus. No slaves could expect to be happier. Work was light, punishment was not severe, and they had every medical attention. But though the slaves were soon 'plump, healthy and full of spirits', Ramsay found at the end of ten years that he 'possessed not a single slave on whom he could place confidence'. Not one had become a true Christian, and two had been sold off as intractable.

Nor were his efforts among the slave-owners successful. When, as surgeon to the plantations, Ramsay was called to attend recalcitrant slaves who had been flogged to an inch of death, or branded on chest, face, or arms, he was cursed for interference if he attempted to protest. On asking that slaves should be allowed Sunday rest and religious instruction he was roundly told not to encourage idleness. His efforts to gather together the slaves of his parish for public instruction received 'bitter censure'. At last there came an awful Sunday morning in the parish church when Ramsay was bold enough to insert in the Bidding Prayer a petition for the conversion of the blacks. Immediately there was a rustle in the pews. Two or three planter couples stalked out.

When it became known that the rector actually had visions of the eventual abolition of slavery, St. Kitts was enraged. The Churchwarden presented Ramsay with a formal protest against 'neglect of his parish'. He was deprived of his magistracy, attacked in the island's newspaper, and ostracized. Depressed and aged by the violence of the storm, Ramsay was tempted to doubt and despair. God seemed to have set him against a brick wall.

War broke out again, and when Ramsay took a naval chaplaincy, St. Kitt's was delighted. He never saw the island again, and by the end of 1781 he was rector of Captain Middleton's little village in the English countryside of Kent.

The cry of the slaves haunted him. Often in the evenings he would sit in the drawing room of the great house, Barham Court, and tell Lady Middleton and the two spinster friends who lived with her, 'Mrs' Bouverie and 'Mrs' Twysden, of the horrors of slavery. Ramsay was only forty-eight, but his grey hair, sad eyes, and lean face seemed to reflect the sufferings he had seen in the Negroes. The agony of the 'Middle Passage', the indignities of the slave warehouse, and the brutal manner in which human beings were bought and sold like cattle; the crowded sickhouses with their nauseating stench and filth, the overlong hours of labour under a tropical sun and the overseer's whip – all this he told in graphic terms, arousing in the ladies' hearts a determination to protest.

Lady Middleton was the most outspoken of the three, and one day she sat down at her escritoire and wrote him a long letter, begging him to set before the world the temporal and eternal needs of the slaves. The letter was handed to Ramsay the next morning by Nestor, the Negro who had served him since shortly before the return to England, whose 'neat dress, chaste sober life and inoffensive manner subdued the prejudices his colour raised', and who 'from his humble station fixed his faith in Christ and looked up to heaven for happiness'.

The letter threw Ramsay into a turmoil. He longed to

act on Lady Middleton's advice, but feared to face again the 'censure and abuse' it was sure to bring. But, as Ramsay said later, 'her importunities were great respecting it'. Behind her he could sense the quiet insistence of Christ, who for Ramsay's sake, and for the slaves and all men had 'endured the cross, despising the shame'.

The book was begun. Then the folly of attacking 'the interest and majesty of plantership' once more overcame him, and he laid the manuscript aside. The Bishop of London, who had a country house nearby and was a warm friend to the slaves, urged him to resume, and at long last, on a summer's day in 1784, James Ramsay sat anxiously in his study at Teston Rectory, knowing that his mild and constructive book was in the hands of the public.

The storm burst. 'Fie! Fie! Mr. Ramsay,' cried the West Indian press, 'you ought to blush indeed! Ill-natured, wicked, mistaken – deserves punishment for such a libel.' 'Gross misrepresentations ... absurdest prejudices,' claimed the planters' representatives in London. But if he was abused, to his acute pain and distress, Ramsay was encouraged also by the many hitherto scattered who made themselves known to him as friends of the cause.

Men whose names were to resound across the world as abolitionists found their way to Teston, and the rectory guest-room was in continual use – Granville Sharp, young Thomas Clarkson fresh from Cambridge, Ignatius Latrobe, the gentle and musical Moravian. Each had written or spoken against slavery but had never met the others.

The months dragged by. Ramsay no longer felt useless and frustrated, a hostage to faith, although the slaves continued to live in misery and die in spiritual darkness, and every trade wind brought fresh cargoes of human cattle. The next step, however, was near.

Ignatius Latrobe stayed at the rectory. Ramsay took him one morning through the park gates, past the new orangery and up to Barham Court for breakfast. In the manner of the day the party sat round the table long after the plates were cleared and the last cups of coffee drunk. As was inevitable, the conversation turned to slavery. Lady Middleton was waxing indignant – 'Some very animated expressions of her feelings,' recalled Latrobe, 'on considering the national guilt attached to the continuation of such a traffic.' Ramsay listened, grateful that his seed had borne such fruit in her mind.

She turned to her husband, then in Parliament, and said, 'Indeed, Sir Charles, I think you ought to bring the subject before the House.' Her words startled the whole table. Occasional resolutions against the Slave Trade had received short shrift. To marshal support until the Commons appointed an inquiry would be a long and thankless task needing eloquence, yet Middleton had only made four of the briefest of speeches and was busy with his work at the Admiralty – he was the man whose faithfulness and persistence prepared the Royal Navy for Trafalgar.

Ramsay waited, praying in his heart, for Middleton's answer, 'You are right, my lady,' Ramsay heard him say at last, 'but the cause would be in bad hands if committed to me. But I will strenuously support any able member who will undertake it.' They fell to discussing possible leaders. Mrs Bouverie suggested one, Ramsay another, and timid Mrs Twysden ventured on a third, but all lacked the ability required. And then someone – they could never remember who – suggested a young *beau*, the Member for Hull, who had been so splendidly converted a short while before: William Wilberforce.

Sir Charles promised to write to him. A few days

later Ramsay and Latrobe were again at Barham Court and heard Lady Middleton read Wilberforce's reply. Though some months were to pass before a firm decision, James Ramsay's cause had found a leader.

In the hectic times that followed, Teston was the centre of the abolition campaign, and Ramsay its unofficial secretary. The appointment of a Privy Council Committee of Enquiry through Wilberforce's friendship with Pitt enormously increased his work, and Mrs Ramsay watched anxiously as he pushed his frail body to its utmost. But their hearts were bright as the spring of 1789 drew on, for victory seemed in sight.

'Mr. Wilberforce and whole junta of Abolitionists are locked up at Teston,' wrote Hannah More in the early spring of 1789, 'they are up *slaving* till two o'clock every morning.' The path between the rectory and Barham Court was in constant use, while as the days grew warmer the discussions continued in the garden under the cedar tree which stands today. And from time to time they would gather for prayer in the tiny parish church beyond the rectory wall.

On May 12, 1789, Wilberforce introduced his Bill for the Abolition of the Slave Trade, and Ramsay was in the happy little party which waited in the Wilberforce house in Palace Yard, their hearts high with praise to God. He did not stay for the debate and was back in Teston when it began to bog down as the slave-owners' friends attacked the Bill with every weapon they could muster. Ramsay's old fears returned. The victory for which he had prayed seemed to recede, until on May 21st a blow fell which he was unable to parry: a Member lampooned him in one of the bitterest speeches of the session, raking up every slander and cruel jibe that had been flung in St. Kitts. Middleton sprang to his rescue, but when Ramsay read the speech at Teston his nerve broke. Depression was made worse by weariness of body.

The Middletons pressed him to go for a holiday. After delays and hesitations he set out, but at the Middletons' London house, the first stage of his journey, he died.

Forty-three years later, when slavery was abolished throughout the British Empire and the dying Wilberforce received the great praise which was his due, few remembered Ramsay, who in the course of his ordinary duties had heard God's call to attack a great injustice which everyone took for granted.

2. Sir Charles Middleton, Lord Barham, 1726-1813
THE MAN BEHIND TRAFALGAR

Sir Charles Middleton, who as Admiral Lord Barham was First Lord of the Admiralty at the time of Trafalgar, has been called the greatest naval administrator since Samuel Pepys.

A Lowland Scot, born in 1726, Charles Middleton joined the Navy before he was fifteen. His early service in the Atlantic patrols of the French wars gave him little excitement. He had, however, a taste of adventure when he, his captain and a dozen others were stranded overnight on a desolate African beach, while a mutinous crew took their ship, the *Chesterfield*, out to sea. The captain, who had gone ashore to cure his rheumatism, fortunately saw his ship again the next day, a loyal mate having quelled the mutiny. The captain was later court-martialled for unwarranted absence from his command, but somehow managed to prove that he had been busy on a survey.

Some years later, in 1755, Middleton saw his first real action, two French ships being captured by the *Anson* after sharp engagements, several months before any declaration of war. In 1761, after being promoted captain, he won a measure of fame in command of the frigate *Emerald*, suppressing West Indian pirates. He continued to climb the slow ladder of promotion, until in 1778 he exchanged command of a first-rate ship for what proved to be his life work; he succeeded Nelson's relative and patron, Maurice Suckling, as Comptroller of the Navy.

When Middleton arrived at the Navy Office the American War of Independence was about to become a more general conflict, France and Spain having decided to make good use of the rebel successes. This war was certain to be almost entirely naval, but the Navy had never been so derelict or unprepared. False economy, added to perennial corruption and misuse of funds, had reduced the British Fleet to a farce. A sudden demand for ships, supplies and men to fight the new war had added pandemonium to the prevalent apathy. Admiral Keppel, one of the most brilliant seamen of his day, was sent with a string of unseaworthy hulks to do battle, and was beaten off Ushant. Kempenfelt, who replaced him found himself expected to intercept a heavily guarded convoy with a wholly inadequate force, and only good luck and brilliant tactics gave him a measure of success. The state of affairs was vividly brought home to the nation, a little later, when the *Royal George* sank with all hands at Spithead, part of its bottom having fallen away through sheer neglect.

The First Lord of the Admiralty and the Comptroller, who was chief executive assistant and head of the Navy Office, were the two upon whom affairs principally depended. The First Lord in 1778, the Earl of Sandwich, was a public scandal in an age when corruption and jobbery were normal. Fifty years old and a peer since he was eleven, a patron of art with a charming manner to offset his ugly gait, he frankly made national business subservient to the interests of his party. He used his extensive naval patronage to enlarge his political influence, and though he himself is not known to have taken bribes, his mistress, an opera singer, did a brisk trade in all contracts and commissions.

Maurice Suckling, whom Middleton replaced as Comptroller, was neither vicious nor ill-meaning. He was a typical man of his age and during his four short years of office trod the well-worn path of departmental inefficiency and corruption. In consequence, soon after Middleton took over, the Navy was found to be short of three hundred thousand pounds of bread besides beef, pork and other provisions, while supplies were contracted, with somebody's friend or relative, for as much as forty-five per cent above market price. Had Suckling even wished to make reforms his four years were too short. But he had no such desire; he kept in the swim, increased his income with commissions, and made no effort to purge his office of its customary rottenness. It was expected that his successor would do the same.

Charles Middleton, however, saw his responsibilities in a different light. In 1761, at the age of thirty-five, he had married Margaret Gambier, whose brother was with him on the West Indian station and later died an admiral. Margaret Gambier had an old school friend, Elizabeth Bouverie, a lifelong spinster of fortune and property, and after their marriage the Middletons made their home with her at Barham Court at Teston in Kent. Elizabeth Bouverie and Mrs Middleton had been drawn into the orbit of the great evangelist George Whitefield, and his patron the Countess of Huntingdon; a set which later included John Newton, Hannah More and William Wilberforce. They had thus learned to live to the glory of Christ, and in his strength.

They became noted as well for their generosity and the high level of their lives in the loose-living society of Georgian England as for their wit and happiness. Beilby Porteus, Bishop of London, wrote of Margaret Middleton that 'the great and distinguishing feature of her character was an active and indefatigable spirit of benevolence, which extended even to the brute creation, and which kept her mind so constantly on the stretch in seeking out opportunities of promoting in every possible way the ease, the comfort, the prosperity, the happiness temporal and eternal, of all within her reach that she seemed to have no time left for anything else and scarce ever appeared to bestow a single thought upon herself ...' A room in Barham Court was kept for sick cottagers, tramps, discharged sailors or anyone in distress who passed that way.

When Charles Middleton married, he followed his wife, bringing his affectionate nature, bluff good humour and considerable talents to the service of the Saviour: he was not ashamed to say that he owed 'to her perseverance all I possess of religion'. The precise steps are obscure, but certainly during his later years at sea he was a Christian. There was little enough in the Navy at the time. At its best the Christianity of the officers was shallow. Nelson could write of 'the great God whom I adore', but his treatment of his wife is in strange contrast to his dying words to the chaplain, 'I have not been a great sinner, doctor.' The seamen had little beyond a superstitious faith in 'A sweet little cherub that sits up aloft to keep watch for the life of poor Jack.' Captain Middleton, however, in command successively of the *Arden*, the *Prince George* and the *Arundel*, constantly showed himself a 'friend to religion' on board. He always made certain of a supply of Bibles 'and other good books' for his men, he did the duties of a chaplain when none was available, and saw to it that 'drunkenness and swearing never found room in any ship that I commanded'.

When, therefore, he came to the Admiralty as Comptroller in August 1778, his approach to office was thoroughly untraditional. As he once put it, 'I know myself to be amenable to a much higher tribunal than any on earth.' He was not interested in lining his pockets, and wished to obey God's command. 'Whatsoever thy hand findeth to do, do it with thy might.' Others therefore could employ underlings to scrape through their work, but he must stick to his desk. 'To skulk from duty,' he wrote some years later, 'instead of meeting it fairly would have secured to me the tranquillity which others enjoy, without the risk of their censure.' But he preferred to please God rather than man. As a result the Navy, which stumbled through the American War, its sordid failures relieved by the splendour of Rodney's victory in 1782, was overhauled and re-equipped in the ten years' peace which followed, despite the false economies of the Government. Without Middleton's work at the Admiralty the Fleet actions and the blockade of the ensuing Revolutionary Wars would scarcely have been possible.

His first problem was Lord Sandwich himself. He dealt with him frankly, risking dismissal. 'All I can do at the Navy Office will avail for little if the Admiralty continues what it is at present,' he told the First Lord. He asked him how he hoped to win the war when his habit was to come to the Office one day and spend the next two on 'amusements or private concerns'. He attacked his 'political system of management', which put the claims of service second, and told him roundly, 'the fleet is terribly managed – it is in a dreadful condition' (though he crossed out this later phrase before despatching the letter), 'the men are daily deserting in scores and those that remain are inclined to mutiny.'

Meanwhile Sir Charles Middleton – he became a baronet in 1781 – was endeavouring to reform and reorganize. He improved the system of contracts and supplies, thereby saving large sums of public money; he busied himself with ship repairs; he overhauled the manner of appointing dockyard commissioners and sought to drive out corruption by ensuring them higher pay; like Pepys before him he wrote memoranda on the duties of captains and issued minutes on every conceivable naval matter. His task was slow and disheartening. 'The past summer has been unprofitably spent,' he wrote in 1782 while Gibraltar was under siege and the relief expedition dallied at home; 'we have undertaken everything and executed nothing.' He worked under handicap, lacking a permanent secretary – his parson, James Ramsay, did much of the work – and struggling against both the ingrained corruption of his subordinates and the inactivity of his superiors. For although Sandwich resigned in 1782 and was followed by Keppel, Howe, and Pitt's brother Chatham, Sandwich was in fact 'more zealous for the improvement of the service' than his successors, in Middleton's estimation.

Towards the end of the 'eighties full success seemed in sight. The Government appointed a commission to enquire into naval administration, and when its report was presented early in 1790 Admiral Middleton's worst complaints were proven just; but the Government never moved. To his disgust, Middleton learnt that the report was not to be studied, nor the abuses it revealed rectified. His hands were therefore tied and he saw no choice but to resign.

'The fleet is left in the best possible state,' wrote Middleton to Pitt in his resignation letter, and it was true. Arsenals almost empty twelve years before were now full. Large numbers of ships were ready for the war that could not be far off. Although when mobilisation came in 1793, it was distressingly slow, the Fleet was in a position to wage war, and the first major battle was the Glorious First of June. Few realised how much was due to Middleton, but those few knew that his untraditional integrity was rooted in faith.

Middleton, now sixty-four, retired to Teston on his resignation, but was not idle. He was continually consulted on naval matters – the Prime Minister called him 'the best man of business I know' – and he had many other interests. He farmed his land – or rather Miss Bouverie's, for it did not become his until her death in

1798 – and improved his villages. He was for a while a Member of Parliament and had been one of the earliest opponents of slavery. 'Indeed, Sir Charles,' Lady Middleton had said at breakfast that day in 1786 when James Ramsay, Middleton's old shipmate and now their rector, had described slavery's horrors, 'You ought to bring the subject before the House.' It was he who wrote to Wilberforce.

Middleton was forward in every good cause. He supported the Proclamation Society, which had an abiding influence on English morals; and his own home life and attitude as a landlord were both untypical of his age and a foretaste of mid-nineteenth-century integrity. He wished to see the end of the press-gang, although a strong disciplinarian. He was generous in the use of his money. Hannah More was rapturous at what she called 'the zeal you are animated for doing good'. His portraits – one was painted by his wife, an accomplished artist and the pupil of Reynolds – show him a cheerful, kindly man; Teston was noted for warmth and hospitality, and Dr. Johnson, Garrick and Reynolds had often stayed there. He had his faults: he liked to be consulted on everything, and there was a streak of vanity of which, when it came to the point, his angling for a peerage was proof. But his faults were nothing to his virtues.

Both character and action were moulded by love for Christ. He delighted to hear of men who 'preached redemption by a Saviour', and he was 'interested in the meanest attempt to spread Christianity'. He used to describe his activities to Hannah More, who wrote of her great pleasure at 'the spiritual prosperity of your villages'. His faith was seen in its truest light when Lady Middleton died in 1792. No human could give him adequate comfort, wrote a friend, 'but thank God Almighty you know where to look for it'; and after the funeral he told Wilberforce that though he felt much as he paced behind the coffin, yet on entering the church he 'found a holy contentment and composure which was scarce ever disturbed'.

Thus the years passed. In 1794, a year after the outbreak of war, he was made a Lord of the Admiralty and did good service again at the Board. His tenure of office, however was brief, for in 1795 the First Lord, Chatham, ordered the recall of the Commissioner in the West Indies, Sir John Laforey, on wholly political grounds and without even expressing a reason for the dismissal. The signatures of the Lords Commissioners were naturally required. Admiral Middleton immediately wrote 'No consideration on earth will induce me to concur in what I think is an unjust measure,' and therefore retired once more into private life.

In April 1805 he was over seventy-eight and had been ten years in full retirement, although continuing to take close interest in the war and to seize occasional opportunities of advising Pitt. To the world at large his name meant nothing, and even the Navy was too conscious of its victorious captains to remember the man who had made their victories possible. It was a critical time. Invasion was imminent: the Grand Army was at Boulogne, and Villeneuve, whose combined French and Spanish Fleets were to put Napoleon across the Channel, had slipped the blockade and was at sea. At home Pitt's plans, both for defence and for a secret attack in the Mediterranean, were in jeopardy to the fractiousness of the opposition. For Lord Melville, First Lord of the Admiralty and Pitt's most trusted counsellor, had been exposed for malpractices in a previous office, and forced to resign. The most vital post in the Cabinet was vacant, when wise judgment and a steady hand were needed more desperately every day.

Society gossip expected Admiral Hood or Lord Castlereagh to succeed Melville. Pitt, however, although already in a politically perilous position, risked the break-up of his Cabinet by a choice of which he almost alone could see the wisdom. He sent for Sir Charles Middleton. To the world at large it seemed absurd, or a mere sop to Melville's wounded pride, for Middleton was his cousin. The Prince of Wales (telling the Speaker that the new First Lord was eighty-two) 'ridiculed the idea'. Lord Sidmouth 'objected very strongly' and sought to resign. Wilberforce, however, was so delighted that during the Navy debate he bubbled forth that even the prosaic pages of *Hansard* described as 'the highest panegyric' on the new First Lord. It was not empty praise. Wilberforce knew Middleton's worth. 'His opinion weighs with me beyond that of any other naval man,' he had written shortly before, 'because besides his providence, his experience, his integrity, he is less of a party man by far than any other.'

Middleton did not relish office. 'I would rather be without it,' he wrote. But with an old man's vanity he wanted the peerage recently promised him, and this seemed its price. Furthermore, he had been highly critical of affairs and here was his chance to translate armchair theories into strategy. On 30 April 1805 he therefore became First Lord, and a day later Lord Barham. Now that his mind was made up, he approached his task in the old spirit, seeing not only his country's desperate need but hearing a call to service from the God he loved. 'The task is a very arduous one,' he wrote to Wilberforce; 'I shall hope for the prayers of my friends and do the best I can in the post wherein God has through His providence placed me.' Although posterity was slow to honour him, it is recognized that the great Comptroller made also a great First Lord.

The next seven months, from May to November 1805, were the most glorious in naval history since the Armada. They began with Nelson's chase to the West Indies and ended with Trafalgar and the return of the battered but triumphant British Fleet, saddened only by the death of Nelson. The story needs no repetition; but the part played by Barham was not appreciated at the time. Before victory came and fear of invasion was scattered to the winds, months of uncertainty, with Nelson lost in the blue, set tongues wagging. But Barham, clearheaded and cool, sat at the Admiralty directing the movements of fleets and squadrons. He knew what was wanted, and he worked on quietly, weighing each scrap of intelligence received and seeking to anticipate each move of the enemy. On the morning of 9 July, for instance, he was woken early with news of the Combined Fleets' return. While shaving – the incident became famous – he thought out his plans. Before dressing he sent off orders, without waiting for discussion at the Board, and in due course Sir Robert Calder was fighting the French and Spanish off Finisterre 'in a fog at night'. All that summer and autumn the campaign of Trafalgar was developing, culminating in the great battle of 21 October.

In the providence of God, England had at the Admiralty a man who not only knew his job but was unaffected by the ebb and flow of popularity, or by the claims of party and ambition. Again and again Barham took decisions which to the uninitiated seemed dangerous risks. Without his cool brain and wide experience the various strands of sea defence could scarcely have been woven together. Off Cape Trafalgar Nelson reaped the harvest of Barham's constant, unwearied planning at the Admiralty. Neither could have won the campaign without the other.

When it was all over, Barham retired once again, on

the reorganization of the Government after the death of Pitt in January 1806. He lived seven more years, dying at Teston in June 1813 at the age of eighty-six, content to have gathered as First Lord the fruits of his own vital years as Comptroller.

He had not only helped to save England in her hour of peril; he had left an example which imperceptibly became a tradition. More than any other man he was ancestor of the incorruptible public servant. 'Where there is no religion there can be no public principle,' he had once written. The principle he stood for became so unquestioned that it could exist without the religion; but that would not have been enough for Barham: he believed that a man could neither be truly happy nor fully useful to his country unless, like himself, he possessed 'the deep consolations of true and genuine Christianity'.

3. John Newton, 1725-1807
A NAVAL DESERTER

The battered fleet of Admiral Pocock, bound for the East
Indies, lay in Plymouth Sound after being damaged off
the Lizard by the great storm of March 1745.

From one man-of-war, HMS *Harwich*, a longboat
put off and was rowed to Plymouth quay. It was commanded by a nineteen-year-old midshipman called John
Newton. The sailors began to load vegetables and other
stores. Once they were hard at work Midshipman Newton looked to left and right; then he slunk away – a deserter, despite his Captain's strict instructions to keep a
sharp eye on the men lest any 'run' (the naval term for
deserting).

Young Newton climbed away from Plymouth into
the Devon countryside, determined not to go with his
ship for five years on the East India station, far from
Polly, the girl he hoped to marry. On the second day he
walked straight into a naval patrol, who arrested him.
Back at Plymouth, chained like a felon, he was returned
to his ship, where Captain Carteret had him stripped and
flogged, then reduced him from midshipman to ordinary
seaman.

At that point, no one could have forecast that John
Newton would live to write some of the world's best
loved hymns, to be a preacher and evangelist, and one
of the liberators who destroyed the Slave Trade.

Born in 1725 near the Tower of London, son of a
rather ridiculous sea captain who had been educated by
Jesuits in Spain, and a pious Dissenter mother who
brought him up on Isaac Watts, but died when he was
seven, John Newton's early youth had swung between
self-conscious piety and rowdiness.

He lived with his stepmother at Aveley in Essex until

he went to sea at the age of eleven in his father's ship. This sailor lad could not quite escape his dead mother's early teaching. When, in a bookshop at a Dutch port, he came across the works of the deistic moralist Shaftesbury he thought he had found a doctrine to reconcile a sensitive conscience with an increasingly sensual and self-willed nature.

Meanwhile he had met and fallen in love with young Polly Catlett, then a mere thirteen years old. Through all his sexual adventures before conversion his heart remained true to her whatever his body did.

It was because of her that he missed the ship which would have taken him to Jamaica and a good job as a slave-overseer. Instead his father sent him to sea again, this time before the mast. After another voyage, his lingering with Polly led to being caught by a press gang from HMS *Harwich*; Captain Carteret entered 'John Newton' as A.B., along with John Cullpack and other choice names; but after a month's misery Newton was made midshipman through his father's influence.

Another midshipman destroyed his last link with the Christian faith. The next few years, between the ages of eighteen and twenty-two, turned Newton not just into a foul-mouthed, fornicating tough, but into a militant atheist.

He fought in an action with the French. He went absent without leave at Deal in order to ride to Chatham for a few days with Polly; and now, at Plymouth, he had become a deserter, to be caught, flogged and degraded.

A few weeks later at Madeira he managed to exchange out of the Navy to serve in a slaver on the west coast of Africa, taking his pleasure on defenceless slave girls. Then he fell on evil days, the period he afterwards described as being 'a servant of slaves in Africa'. When things got better, he got worse.

Yet it was not his viciousness that would appal him in retrospect. 'My obstinate contempt of the glorious gospel,' he wrote at the age of twenty-eight in the earliest manuscript account of his conversion, 'and the horrid effrontery with which I treated it, distinguished me even among freethinkers themselves ... and so industrious in propagating my tenets that I believe for some years I never was in company without attempting to corrupt them.'

During his captivity on an African island he had smuggled home a pitiful letter to his father, though he had offended him again and again. His father asked a shipowner to help and the *Greyhound*, sailing from Liverpool, had been asked to find him. By an amazing coincidence her captain met him on a distant shore, but Newton's fortunes had turned again. He nearly refused to come.

The hard-bitten captain and crew soon wished they had never taken him on board. As they traded up and down the coast (not in slaves), they disliked him as not merely the hardest swearer but a ribald, blaspheming atheist. Then came a violent storm. All were used to storms but the ship was rotten after a long voyage in the tropics. Soon her sails had gone, part of her side was stove in, great seas washed over her. Most of the crew of twelve believed that the ship must soon go down and all would drown, on this terrible 10 March 1748 in the North Atlantic.

As John Newton laboured at the pumps, facing death if she broke up or foundered in the exceptional seas, a chance remark suddenly faced him with an appalling awareness that God, whom he despised and denied, might exist after all; if so, John Newton was about to face judgement.

Up from the depths of his mind came the long forgotten teaching of his devout mother, to confront his terrible past, as a blasphemer who would wreck the faith of any man he met; as a lecher whose body raped the black girls in his power, although his heart was given to that pure English maiden in Kent called Polly, a girl he scarcely hoped to win. All this overwhelmed him until, in deep contrition, he sought forgiveness of the God he had scorned.

When the storm abated and they had survived, he began to believe that God might grant his request, although doubts of God's existence still assailed him.

In the days which followed he struggled to believe. His crew mates quickly forgot their prayers but John Newton spent his off duty hours trying to grasp the gospel. No pastor or Christian brother was present to help, but the fog of unbelief gradually dispersed. When, weeks overdue, the battered ship dropped anchor in an Irish harbour, Newton had surrendered to God and believed that Christ had died for his sins. Yet so hazy was his understanding that he saw himself as like a galley-slave, labouring to offset the wickedness of his past.

For the rest of his life Newton honoured 10 March 1748 as the 'hour I first believed', when amazing grace had saved 'a wretch like me'.

The owner of the *Greyhound* offered him command of a slaver, for Newton was a skilled and experienced seaman. He asked to go first as second-in-command, and sailed from England, secure in the knowledge that Polly had not rejected him though her hand was not yet his.

He resolved to be true to her and worthy of Christ, but he had forgotten what he afterwards described as 'the dreadful effects of the Slave Trade' on the morals of those engaged in it.

With no fellow Christian on board his new ship, *Brownlow*, he slackened in prayer, forgot to read his

Bible, and cooled his gratitude for past mercies. By the time he reached the slave coast of West Africa 'I was almost as bad as before,' except that he no longer swore. When the slaves came on board, and he saw the salacious grins of the sailors as they each chose a black girl to rape, his good resolutions dissolved, his blood surged, and he went down into the hold where the girls lay naked and chained.

After that he 'followed a course of evil of which, a few months before, I should not have supposed myself any longer capable.' Temptation proved stronger than conscience, or thoughts of Polly, or of Christ. Then Newton fell ill with fever while staying on the very island where he had suffered as a slave but now was honoured as a guest. Debauchery had weakened him and he knew he might die. His heart smote him as he recalled his solemn vows and his sincere gratitude at the time for deliverance in the storm. Having crucified the Son of God afresh he believed that he had shut and locked the door of hope. Then he remembered that his Judge was also his Father, of infinite mercy.

Weak, almost delirious, Newton dragged himself to a remote corner of the island and cast himself on the mercy of God. No particular text flashed into his mind, but very humbly and sincerely he laid hold of his crucified Saviour. Peace returned to his conscience. Within two days he was fit again, to resume his work as officer on a slaver.

The experience was decisive. He never backslid violently again. All his life he would be keenly aware how often he failed the Lord, but now he genuinely sought to know him better. The *Brownlow* made the 'middle passage' across the Atlantic. The slaves were sold at Charleston, South Carolina; the ship was in harbour, loading with tobacco and cotton. Newton would slip away into the woods to pray and meditate. 'My views of Christian truth were very imperfect and my conduct inconsistent. Spiritually I chiefly depended on myself, I knew I had been very bad. I had a desire to be better, and thought I should in time make myself so.'

In May 1754, six years after the Atlantic storm and 'the hour I first believed', Captain John Newton, aged twenty-nine and in command of the slaver *African*, from Liverpool, brought his cargo of slaves safely to the small West Indian island of St. Kitts. Newton had commanded two earlier voyages and had transported hundreds of his fellow beings to slavery and hard labour for life. He tried to be humane but no voice had been raised against the Slave Trade; it was considered honourable and necessary. Newton said afterwards that had he realized its wickedness he would have stopped at once. He thought it an unpleasant occupation, like that of a jailer, but he had a wife, his adorable Polly, to support. His prayers, as he had sailed towards St. Kitts that spring, were dominated by two petitions: that he might be freed from this distasteful calling; and that he might know God better.

At St. Kitts Captain Newton was popular at the planter's evening parties, served by house slaves, for he was amusing, could write verse, and had a fine singing voice. At one party he met another captain, not in the Slave Trade: one Alexander Clunie, a lively, cheerful Scot in his late thirties. Some 'casual expressions in mixed company' revealed to both men that they, alone among hosts and guests, loved God. They walked back to the quayside together and soon became inseparable, preferring to spend their evenings in one or other's cabin, talking of the things of God, than to idle away the hours at parties.

Clunie, who lived in London, was a well taught Christian. He opened Newton's understanding. The Bible became like a new book. Newton realized at last that the distant God whom he had served in fear and humble gratitude, but without joy or intimacy, could be a Friend, walking at his side. The name of Jesus became sweet to his ear. 'The knowledge of His love to me produced a return of love to Him. I now adored Him and admired Him.' John Newton made an unreserved surrender to Jesus, 'My Lord, my Life, my way, my end.'

A few weeks later, back in England, Newton suffered a sudden illness which prevented him taking a new command to sea. Further amazing coincidences caused him to obtain a respectable post in the Customs Service in Liverpool.

Soon after settling at Liverpool with his 'dearest sweetest dear Polly', he heard George Whitefield preach and caught the vision of evangelism. His zeal scared the bishops; he sought Holy Orders in 1758 only to find 'I am rejected as an improper if not a dangerous person,' and it was not until 1764, sixteen years after the storm in great waters when he had cried unto the Lord in his trouble, that he began his ordained ministry, at Olney, preaching 'amazing grace'.

Whimsical saint, with his sailor songs, sense of humour, and deep passion for his Redeemer, John Newton is proof that the most militant atheist may be converted. A sexually depraved youth may become a powerful evangelist. Newton is proof too that slow growth in Christ, with setbacks and struggles, may yet lead to Christian service which makes an indelible mark.

For John Newton became not only one of the best loved hymn writers of the day, with *Amazing Grace*, *How Sweet the Name of Jesus Sounds*, *Glorious Things of Thee are Spoken*, and many others; but a powerful influence on the age. Reading a pamphlet newly written by his friend John Wesley, his eyes were opened to the wickedness of the Slave Trade. 'My heart shudders that I was ever engaged in it.'

By the time he moved to London in 1779, to become rector of the Lord Mayor's parish church, he was appalled by the Trade. He grew intense in his opposition, bewailing this crime against humanity at every opportunity, button-holing any who would listen to his stories of the horrors, and to his dreadful concern that he should have continued in it when a Christian.

The Slave Trade would not vanish because an ex-slave trader repented. Only an Act of Parliament could bring in Abolition, and no one could expect a majority for that, in either Commons or Lords, while other nations continued the Trade. Newton could see no prospect of success until one day in December 1785. Among the requests received at his vestry for interviews lay a note signed by a name which made his heart leap: William Wilberforce.

The world knew William Wilberforce as a brilliant, amusing young man of fashion and Member of Parliament, bosom friend of the Prime Minister, William Pitt. Newton knew him as the nephew of his dear friend Hannah Wilberforce, née Thornton. When Wilberforce was eight years old he had lost his father and gone to live with his uncle and aunt in Wimbledon. The boy became John Newton's ardent disciple, listening wide eyed to his sea stories, laughing at his jokes, joining in his songs –and coming, as it seemed, to share his faith.

Wilberforce revered John Newton almost as a parent. But the boy's mother became alarmed that he was turning into a little 'methodist', and removed him from the Wimbledon household and thus from Newton's influence. When Wilberforce was twenty-three and already a Member of Parliament, Newton referred to his lost disciple: 'I am aware religious appearances in so young a subject are to be regarded with caution. The strongest and most promising views of this sort I ever met with were in the case of Mr. Wilberforce when he was a boy – but they seem now entirely worn off, not a trace left behind, except a deportment comparatively decent and moral in a young man of large fortune.'

Four years later in December 1785 Newton received the note at his church begging for the strictly secret interview.

Wilberforce's conversion (or wholehearted re-dedication) belongs to his own story, but by Easter 1786 Newton could write of him: 'I judge he is now decidedly on the right track ... I hope the Lord will make him a blessing both as a Christian and a statesman. How seldom do these characters coincide!! But they are not incompatible.' The old ex-slave trader and the young statesman became firm friends, and Newton used to harp on his shame about the Trade. He was undoubtedly one of the several influences which led Wilberforce to take up Abolition and agree to lay the subject before Parliament.

Once the campaign began, Newton was in the inner circle of the Abolitionists, the only one with personal knowledge of the Trade. He wrote a devastating pamphlet, saying that it would be criminal of him not to reveal the horrors he had seen and abetted. Old and stiff, the ex-slave trader went to St. James' Palace to give evidence before the Committee of the Privy Council. The Prime Minister met him at the door and all in the room rose to their feet.

The Abolitionists fought the Slave Trade for twenty-one years. When Wilberforce triumphed at last, in 1807, John Newton was blind and dying. He lived just long enough to see the Trade abolished on both sides of the Atlantic which he had sailed with his cargoes of slaves.

4. William Wilberforce, 1759-1833
THE LITTLE LIBERATOR

A few years before the French Revolution an ugly little Englishman, with a delightful character and a great sense of humour, sat squeezed in a post-chaise which bumped and swung along the roads of France. Beside him, taking up most of the seat, was a huge, jolly bear of a man with one of the most brilliant minds in England.

The smaller of the two, William Wilberforce, M.P., was rich and of political importance, although only twenty-five years old, for he had recently won Yorkshire for Pitt, the young Prime Minister, his bosom friend.

Wilberforce's widowed mother and his sister had wanted to winter in the South of France, taking also a delicate cousin, Bessy Smith. As the ladies would fill the family carriage, Wilberforce sought a travelling companion for the chaise, and happened to meet his former schoolmaster, Isaac Milner, now a tutor at Cambridge University.

Unknown to Wilberforce, Milner had become an Evangelical Christian. Wilberforce when a boy had enthusiastically followed Christ while living with an uncle and aunt after his father's death. These had been Whitefield's converts and friends of John Newton, once a sailor and slave trader, now the great hymn writer and preacher. The boy had looked on the whimsical Newton, with his incredible but true tales of the sea and of Africa, as his hero. Then his mother, alarmed that her son was fast becoming a 'little methodist', removed him, and scrubbed his soul until nothing was left of his fervour except a more moral tone than usual among men of fashion. And he went to church weekly, though his choice was Unitarian.

In the chaise, a religious topic came up. Wilberforce

fired off some Unitarian notions and ridiculed John Newton's views. Milner replied gravely: he was 'no match for you in this running fire', he said, but he would try to explain the true Christian gospel. Wilberforce showed little interest.

They had not been long on the Riviera when the Prime Minister wrote begging Wilberforce to return to support him on Parliamentary Reform. As the two travellers prepared to set out again, leaving the ladies in the sunshine, Wilberforce casually picked up a book belonging to Bessy Smith; *The Rise and Progress of Religion in the Soul*, by Philip Doddridge (author of the hymn, 'O happy day that fix'd my choice.') and leafed through it. He asked Milner's opinion. 'It is one of the best books ever written,' replied Milner, seizing his chance. 'Let us take it with us and read it on our journey.'

The effect, as they drove northward, was dramatic. By the time Wilberforce arrived at 10 Downing Street, he had reached intellectual assent to the biblical view of Christ as Son of God and Saviour of man. He thrust it to the back of his mind and plunged back into politics and social life.

The next summer, 1785, he and Milner set out again to rejoin the ladies and bring them back through Switzerland. This time, for mile after mile, the two men read and discussed the New Testament, until intellectual assent became profound conviction, that unless Wilberforce repented, and trusted Christ, 'I should perish everlastingly.' But Evangelicals were despised and derided; coming out as a believer might ruin his political future. Struggling to yield his stubborn will he turned gloomy and sad and decided that his only hope was to withdraw from politics and become a clergyman.

Back in England the conflict continued, until Wilberforce felt that unless he could confide in a spiritual counsellor he would go out of his mind. Covering his tracks, lest his fashionable friends discover, he secretly visited his boyhood hero, John Newton. Newton's own slow conversion from lecher and slaver to humble Christian made him an understanding adviser. Moreover he convinced Wilberforce that God could use him mightily in the counsels of the State.

Wilberforce walked out of Newton's study that December day of 1785 with a less burdened conscience; yet it was not until Easter that he reached joyful assurance that he had been redeemed from the slavery of sin by a Saviour who had paid the price with his own blood.

He began immediately to serve God in political life, making tentative attempts to right some of the wrongs of eighteenth-century England. Then he received a letter from one of the only two other Evangelicals in the House of Commons, Captain Sir Charles Middleton, a naval administrator who later, as Admiral Lord Barham, was the supreme strategist of the Trafalgar campaign. Before the American War Middleton had served in the West Indies, where all labour was done by slaves imported from Africa. He now urged young Wilberforce to lead a Parliamentary campaign to stop the Atlantic Slave Trade.

Almost all England believed the Slave Trade to be an economic necessity. In Parliament a strong West Indian lobby would violently oppose any attempt at Abolition. Only a few voices, such as John Wesley's, had been raised against the Trade.

Wilberforce travelled down to Kent where the Middletons lived. He already knew Sir Charles and his wife, an accomplished artist and a woman of great benevolence who longed to rouse the country's conscience. They took him to their rector, James Ramsay, formerly a surgeon and clergyman in the West Indies, who had been forced out of his parish by irate slave owners after he had protested at brutal punishments inflicted on the slaves. Wilberforce met Nestor, Ramsay's delightful black servant, whom he had bought as a slave and set free.

The Middletons had learned much about slavery from a young Moravian missionary, Benjamin La Trobe, who now lived in London. Wilberforce paid him a visit but arrived to find the living room being spring cleaned. The two men sat in the bedroom where the fire smoked but Wilberforce would not let La Trobe open the window: 'I can bear smoke better than toothache!'

Fact by fact, Wilberforce was learning the horrors of the Slave Trade; and all the time John Newton, bitterly ashamed of his own part in it, which had continued for some years after he had become a believing Christian because no-one had then spoken of it as evil, urged Wilberforce to take up the cause. Wilberforce wondered whether he had the strength or the faith to change public opinion and force Abolition through a reluctant Parliament. He hesitated – until one night, poring over a mass of papers and statistics by the light of guttering candles, he suddenly realised how high was the death rate of slaves in the ships engaged in the Trade. 'From that moment, so enormous, so dreadful, so irremediable did its wickedness appear, that my own mind was completely made up for Abolition. Let the consequences be what they would, I from this time determined that I would never rest until I had effected its Abolition.'

He soon found that he had stirred up a hornet's nest. Never strong physically, he was overwhelmed by the work of preparing his case to lay before Parliament, especially as he was also engaged in the moral reformation of England. Pitt, as Prime Minister, helped him by ordering an investigation of the Slave Trade by a standing committee of the Privy Council: this increased Wilberforce's load as he briefed counsel and members until, in February 1788, he collapsed. He fell so ill that his political opponents prepared for the by-election which his death would cause.

The doctors saved his life by prescribing opium, then considered a pure drug; but as he reached convalescence, he fell into a Dark Night of the Soul, perhaps partly through the side effects of the medicine. He cried to God to 'restore me to rest, quietness and comfort, in the world; or in another by removing me hence into a state of peace and happiness'.

He dreaded the Abolition battle ahead. 'Give me grace to trust firmly in Thee, that I may not sink under my sorrows nor be disquieted with the *fears* of those evils which cannot without Thy permission fall upon me.' Fears closed in from every side, but at length his experience of Christ's power outweighed them. Wilberforce slowly returned to calmness, and a determination to persevere.

Physically frailer, spiritually stronger, with a deep love of the Bible, Wilberforce went back to the Commons. On 11 May 1789, in a great speech of three and a half hours, he asked the House to vote for the Abolition of the Slave Trade.

The House refused. Thus began a Parliamentary struggle of eighteen years. One opponent complained that Wilberforce 'is blessed with a very sufficient quantity of that Enthusiastic spirit, which is so far from yielding that it grows more vigorous from blows.'

He preserved his humour and charm; he loved his enemies while never letting them forget their guilt; and throughout these long and painful years each partial success or renewed failure taught him more of the love of God, until at last, on a February day of 1807, the

Commons voted by a large majority for Abolition. Almost the whole House rose to its feet and cheered Wilberforce, who sat, head bowed, with tears streaming down his face.

From that night he was not only the saviour of the slaves but the moral leader of the Western World.

His great moral authority enabled him to push numerous good works. He encouraged Elizabeth Fry in her prison relief and Jeremy Bentham, the prison reformer. He fought poverty and hunger wherever he found it, and no contemporary libel pained him more than the jibe that he cared nothing for the 'wage slaves' of Britain. This libel was circulated by radical politicians whose schemes he rated as positively harmful.

The radicals hated and excluded Christianity. Wilberforce believed that Christ must be at the heart of social progress. While still a young man, much occupied with Abolition, he spent weeks driving all over England in his carriage to stir up nobles and great landowners – the trend setters of the day – to support a campaign for the moral and spiritual reform of England. His success may be gauged from the change in the tone of British public life 'before' and 'after' Wilberforce.

In his later years he made much use of the Bible Society, which he helped to found. He set up 'auxiliaries' everywhere, headed by prominent people; and many who had sat lightly to their faith and morals were shamed or encouraged to give a good example now that they were vice presidents of the Bible Society. In some instances this led whole families in their great country houses to become shining witnesses to Christ.

In 1807 Wilberforce had supposed that Abolition would lead to Emancipation; that as the supply dried up, the West Indian proprietors would turn their slaves into a free people. Instead, slaves were still driven by the cart whip to work in the fields and punished horribly. Wilberforce grew more and more distressed until he actually believed that only the blood of Christ saved him from eternal punishment for his failure.

He declared open war on slavery. By now he was old and feeble in body and feared he would lack strength to lead until victory. He therefore chose a younger man to be his successor. The campaign was long and hard until at last in July, 1833, Parliament voted to set the slaves free throughout the British Empire. Friends hurried to the London house where Wilberforce lay gravely ill. They were in time to tell him that the case was won.

MAKE THE
FOULEST CLEAN

5: Robert Raikes, 1735-1811
RAGAMUFFINS' UNCLE

The proprietor and printer of the weekly *Gloucester Journal* was annoyed. Every Sunday evening Mr. Raikes must make up his page from the printed columns already set by his men, but he was continually distracted by the noise of urchins playing, screaming or fighting in the gutters and paths of the lane outside the window of his house in the city.

Mr. Robert Raikes was a benevolent citizen whose newspaper, by the year 1780, had considerable circulation and prestige in the West of England. Raikes, now forty-five years of age, had inherited it when young from his father, the founder, and had built up its importance. The Raikeses had come from Hull – the Wilberforces were distant cousins – and perhaps originally from Denmark, but the world of Robert Raikes was centred on Gloucester: he seldom went anywhere else.

Raikes was quietly religious; he had attended the Cathedral that Sunday and would attend on weekdays too: on weekdays the streets might be full of coaches, carts, horses, and foot passengers of every kind but not of shouting children, for all the children of the poor would be labouring in the cottages or the small factories of Gloucester, wearily helping to make pins or sewing hempen garments. Only on Sundays were they free to roam; and they had nothing to do except make mischief.

Raikes, who loved children and had a large family, knew how often the boys and girls of the poor passed from mischief to crime, for one of his special benevolences was to visit the two prisons of Gloucester.

Years earlier his father had begun a campaign, through the pages of his *Journal*, to awaken the citizens to the miseries of prisoners. Robert Raikes the younger had followed his father's concern and would raise subscriptions to help prisoners who were unable to buy food; who were almost naked because other prisoners had seized their garments; or were held in prison for small debts. Youths and girls were thrown in with older prisoners and kept in the crowded rooms until their cases came before the magistrates or the assize judge.

The more Raikes went among prisoners, or discussed improvements with well meaning but impotent prison governors, or with travelling reformers like the great John Howard, the more he realised that crime started young. If he could improve the children of Gloucester he would help to empty its prisons.

The children of the poor had no opportunity to learn their letters, for they had neither the time nor the schools. The tradesmen could send their children to the grammar school where Raikes himself had learned. The school's most famous scholar had been George Whitefield, recently dead in America. Charity schools had been founded for the poor in some parishes but as soon as the children could earn, at the age of seven or eight, they were taken away by their parents. Sunday was the only day on which they were free to learn, yet no school opened on a Sunday.

Raikes' benevolent heart was torn between the noise of the gutter snipes under his window, making his Sunday hideous, and the noise of the prisoners in the gaols whenever he went to help where he could.

One morning the affairs of the paper took him to an outlying slum, where whole families earned a pittance by making pins in their tumbledown cottages or in the factories. He saw a group of ragged children, unemployed. Their scanty clothing contrasted with his own plum-coloured elegant suit and they were playing in the mud.

He gazed at them, then accosted a woman who stood at a cottage door. Raikes remarked on 'their misery and idleness'.

'Ah, Sir,' she replied. 'Could you take a view of this part of the town on a Sunday, you would be shocked indeed. For then the street is filled with multitudes of these wretches. They are released from their employment that day, Sir, and they spend their time in noise and riot. We have a worthy clergyman in this parish, Sir, and he puts some of them to school; but on Sunday they do what they like.' She complained that the parents had no morals themselves and did nothing to train their children.

An idea began to form in Raikes' mind. Early in the mornings, when he began his day with prayer, he prayed for the children. A week or two later on a Sunday he happened to turn into a mean back street in the centre of the city, lamenting to himself the buying and selling, the drunkenness, and gambling, the revels and wakes, which he had seen on all sides as he walked through the city on Sunday morning. Here in the backstreet were ragged children playing wild. The 'destitution of the children and the desecration of the Sabbath by the inhabitants of the city,' as he described it afterwards, made him stop. He stood still. 'Can nothing be done?' he asked aloud.

A voice, as it seemed, answered clearly, 'Try!' Whether he had heard a human voice or a voice in his mind, it was as clear as the voice which Saul of Tarsus heard on the Damascus Road or Saint Augustine heard in the garden. Then and there he determined to start a school for Sundays.

He walked on. Raikes passed the rectory of the parish. At that moment the young rector, Thomas Stock, was coming out of his door. Stock was rector of St. John's and headmaster of the Cathedral school: Raikes had come to know him well since Stock's arrival in the city a year or two earlier. Raikes at once told him of his call to help the children.

Stock replied that some such idea had crossed his own mind. He suggested that they go together to some of the streets on the parish. 'We immediately proceeded to the business,' recalled Stock a few years later, 'and, procuring the names of about ninety children, placed them under the care of four persons for a stated number of hours on the Sunday.'

At first the rector took the superintendence as the schools were in his parish, but Raikes soon branched out into other parishes. He was tireless in persuading parents to send children; one father tied a block of wood round his boy's ankle to prevent him running away. Raikes would also tempt possible recruits by offering combs and sweets to ragamuffins, but he was not sentimental: he gave rewards for good behaviour or learning, but he imposed discipline on any urchin who joined a school. A boy who caused too much uproar might find himself summarily marched back to Raikes' home to be birched.

Raikes' schools were not primarily to teach religion, though his motive was Christian. The term Sunday School would later come to mean a class for children, held before, during or after a church service, to teach the rudiments of the faith. To Raikes, however, a Sunday School was a weekly day school, held on the one day in which the children were not employed. He had them taught to read and write. Some of his schools taught crafts to the boys and sewing to the girls. All the schools included simple Bible teaching.

Raikes insisted that the children come to school well scrubbed, and thus he began to influence their general well-being, especially in Sooty Lane where the sweeps lived. He called on parents in order to check whether the children now behaved better at home.

In the first years Raikes was experimenting. Failures were soon outweighed by successes. In one lane where he had set up a school he was delighted to be told by a local woman that 'the place is quite heaven upon Sundays compared with what it used to be'. The mistresses taught the children in the morning, then walked them to church in an orderly crocodile in the afternoon. If Raikes were present they would flock round him afterwards and make their bows, often rewarded with little presents from his pockets, for he loved to be uncle to them all.

'What is more extraordinary,' he wrote, 'these little ragamuffins have taken it into their heads to frequent the early morning prayers at the Cathedral.'

By 1783 the results in Gloucester were sufficiently encouraging for Raikes to describe them in his *Gloucester Journal*. The effect was startling. The idea caught on rapidly across England. As Raikes knew, attempts had been made in some towns and villages to instruct children who did not go to Dames' Schools or Charity schools; but the majority of the children of the poor, throughout the kingdom, had been left illiterate and unschooled. After 1783, as the *Gloucester Journal* was read, or its reports were copied into other newspapers, Sunday Schools sprang up. In 1785 an enthusiastic admirer in London formed a Sunday School Society, encouraging new schools and distributing Bibles and spelling-books. In 1788 the veteran John Wesley, from his vast experience of Britain, remarked in a private letter to a friend: 'I verily think these Sunday Schools are one of the noblest specimens of charity which have been set on foot in England since William the Conqueror.'

In Raikes' own city and county the crime rate dropped sharply. At the Easter Quarter Sessions of 1786 the magistrate passed a unanimous vote of thanks: 'The benefit of Sunday Schools to the morals of the rising generation is too evident not to merit the recognition of this Bench and thanks of the community to the gentleman instrumental in promoting them.' And at the Autumn Assizes of 1792, not one single criminal defendant was produced before the judge, who thereupon received the rare perk of a pair of white kid gloves. Raikes rejoiced, saying that ten years earlier an assize judge at Gloucester might expect to try at least five, and any number up to a hundred, criminal cases. 'That was the period when Providence was pleased to make me the instrument of introducing Sunday Schools and regulations in prisons – Not unto us, O Lord, but unto Thy name be the glory.'

Raikes became famous, honoured by the Royal Family; and, for all his fussy ways and vanity, admired and loved in his native city. And every Christmas he would give a great feast at his house to the children of his schools.

Shortly before his death in 1811 he welcomed Joseph Lancaster, the Quaker educationalist, to his home. They went to the back street where Raikes had walked, thirty years before. 'Pause here,' said the aged Raikes. He uncovered his head and closed his eyes and stood for a moment in silent prayer. Then he turned, with tears rolling down his cheeks. He said to Lancaster: 'This is the spot ...' And he told the story again.

'Try!' the voice had said.

'I did try,' old Raikes went on. 'And see what God has wrought! I can never pass by the spot where the word "Try!" came so powerfully into my mind without lifting up my hands and heart to Heaven in gratitude to God for having put such a great thought into my heart.'

6. Elizabeth Fry, 1780-1845
LADY OF NEWGATE

Some eighteen months after the battle of Waterloo, on a cold January day in 1817, a visitor to Newgate, the grim, windowless prison beside the Old Bailey, might have noticed agitated turnkeys talking to a dignified, plainly dressed lady who had evidently made a difficult request. Elizabeth Fry, the Quakeress, was asking admission to the woman's section.

The gaolers knew and respected her, and saw the governor's permit in her hand, but stark fear for her safety deterred them. They could hear the noise of the women prisoners – screams and swearing interspersed with coarse laughter; cries of children and sounds of sobbing on a background of ceaseless chatter. Through the grill they could see them. Conditions were appalling. In a cramped covered yard and two or three small rooms 300 women were herded together, a milling, fighting mass.

All ages were there – small children, and young mothers, hardened old hags and the middle-aged. All sorts and conditions – thorough-going felons, tried and condemned; respectable maidservants, awaiting trial for offences of which they might be innocent; a girl who had tried to rescue a husband condemned to death and who now was in prison herself; pick-ups from the slums; cast-off mistresses who had sunk to crime. Some were half-naked, many were starving, most were drunk and all were filthy. They had no bedding at night and no occupation by day: nothing to do but gamble, quarrel and drink. The noise they made was deafening, the stench disgusting. 'The filth, the closeness of the rooms, the ferocious manners and expressions of the women towards each other and the abandoned wickedness are quite indescribable,' said Elizabeth Fry later. And yet she was asking to be left alone with them.

She had visited Newgate before. In 1813, with several of her friends, she had helped to ease conditions in the infirmary, a hospital which differed from the rest of the prison in little but name. Elizabeth Fry had never forgotten her experience, and in the course of her busy, humdrum life as a merchant-banker's wife and mother of ten children, her thoughts had often returned to Newgate, while she had several times visited other prisons.

In the winter of 1816 reform was in the air. Several of her friends had been organizing a Society for the Reformation of Prison Discipline. Her brother-in-law, Fowell Buxton, later to be Wilberforce's successor in the war against slavery, was writing of his longing to 'assist in checking and diminishing crime and its consequent misery'. Mackintosh and Romilly were already planning to move Parliament. Elizabeth Fry, however, thought of Newgate as one among the many calls on her charity. As a Quaker minister, tested and approved according to the rigid and yet curiously free regulations of the Society of Friends, she was as much used to doing works of compassion as to speaking words of comfort. Thinking about the women prisoners, she had begun to see a way to help them in their immediate needs.

Thus she stood that January morning, coaxing the gaolers to obey the governor's order and let her in, a solitary woman in her plain Quaker dress, to that 'den of wild beasts' where they never went themselves except in pairs.

Elizabeth Fry entered, and not only came out uninjured but stayed several hours. When she left it was with a promise to return, and a certainty of welcome when she did. She had stilled the raging mass of women by her very presence. She had fondled the children, made the mothers sit down, had read to them from the Bible and spoken to them of Christ. It was their first touch of human kindness since they had entered Newgate, and they responded to it. She then outlined her idea of starting a school for the children within their prison, and the mothers agreed with all the scant vigour of which they were capable.

In the following days her plan was made a reality stage by stage. She won the half-hearted acquiescence of the prison authorities, who were certain she would fail though they wished her well; she made the women appoint one of their number schoolmistress, and for Mary Connor, the prisoner chosen, who had been gaoled for stealing a watch, it meant interest and occupation and later a free pardon. Several of Mrs. Fry's friends joined her, and within a month the school was flourishing, a corner of quiet and order within the 'boisterous violence' of the women's prison.

Although Elizabeth Fry had no long-range plans when she began, the school led her on step by step. As the ladies made their way through the 'dreadful proceedings' of the women's yard to reach the school room, they determined to do something more. Thus in course of time Mrs. Fry revolutionized Newgate and, to her own surprise, became a household word and the confidante of princes. Her reforms hinged on three principles: classification of prisoners according to age and sentence, employment – 'reformation is impossible without employment' – and religious instruction. She wanted these principles to become the practice of every women's prison. Governments, however, move slowly, and at first, therefore, success followed only her personal touch.

But Newgate was transformed. By the end of 1817 the women prisoners had willingly submitted themselves to Mrs. Fry's rules, and where once was 'begging, swearing, gaming, fighting, singing, dancing, dressing up in men's clothes', were now classes of women, each under its own monitor chosen by themselves, meeting regularly during the day to knit and sew for wages and coming together at nine in the morning and six in the evening for Bible reading. The ladies determined to 'use nothing but kindness', and with trifling exceptions their trust was rewarded. The naked were clothed, the starving were regularly fed. Self-respect and hope began to reappear and the one-time 'wild beasts' would now 'flock upstairs after me' when Mrs. Fry came to read the Scriptures.

This was not all. She helped those who were to be transported to Botany Bay, and in course of time her Association arranged work for them there. The convict ships were worse than Newgate. Her efforts had some effect and instead of being chained in gangs and left to fend for themselves during the voyage, with their babies taken away and their future prospects black, the convict women found themselves each with a set of gifts (ranging from a Bible to scissors, thread, an apron and a black cotton cap), a parson or missionary to take care of them, and a promise of fair treatment when they arrived.

She had particular concern for women condemned to death – of which there were scores. She would make every effort to win their reprieves if possible, bearding the stiff, mediocre Home Secretary, Lord Sidmouth, who grudgingly did what he was asked on every occasion but one. She would go and sit beside those awaiting execution ('this tried me a good deal') and her calm words to some poor thing 'distressed and tormented in mind, her hands cold and covered with perspiration, and in a universal tremor' would give courage to face the gallows in peace and, often enough, with quiet assurance for eternity.

She added her weight, and her dogged, stuffy and selfless perseverance to the current agitation for the reform of criminal law, which at that time could send men and women to the gallows for trivial thefts. Her activities in Newgate had made her name a symbol, and where diehards could resist the reforming efforts of Parliament men, they were powerless against the tide of a public opinion enthused by the self-sacrifice of a woman.

In some ways Elizabeth Fry's success was slight. Some twenty years later, in 1835, prison inspectors could say that the 'female side' of Newgate was still bad, and the prisoners' language 'shocking'. But they admitted that thanks to Mrs. Fry's Ladies Association the women's side was better than the men's. Overseas, however, she had given a spur to the reforms which her predecessor, John Howard, had first stirred. She was invited to visit France and parts of Germany, examining and advising. Her principles were adopted in prisons built by the Tsar, who also had Bibles given to every prisoner. The King of Prussia paid her a visit and showed her most deferential respect. She received queens and princesses, and whenever she travelled as a Quaker minister in Britain she would visit prisons, preaching to the convicts and urging reforms to the governors.

Although she could describe her life as 'a little like being in the whirlwind', she never hurried; when fussed, she kept it to herself; when she fretted, it was in the pages of her journal where she regularly tapped her spiritual barometer – 'tossed in mind', 'weak in body', 'clouds permitted to rises', 'in the storm', 'deep exercise and travail of spirit'. In spite of rebuffs and humiliations, despite her husband's bankruptcy in 1828, she achieved an immense position among her contemporaries. And not only did she help prisoners; whenever some fresh call came she managed to do something. At Brighton she became interested in the lonely coastguards, whom she saw pacing the cliffs when she stood at the window of her lodgings. Supplies of Bibles and a library followed, not only at Saltdean but, in due course, to all other parts of the coast.

In 1820, during a hard winter, an urchin was found frozen to death on her door step. Nightly shelter for the homeless in her district followed. She visited the sick, and in her old age started hospital reforms and the training of nurses, fourteen years before Florence Nightingale went to the Crimea. She established village schools and encouraged others to do the same. Her various other philanthropies ranged far and wide, from the education of Dartmouth shepherds to providing Bibles for sailors, and all along she had her family to care for and her task as châtelaine of Plashet in Essex.

Elizabeth Fry's work has a secure place in history. It did not, however, arise from any determination to do great things for her fellow men, nor from the superficial condescension of a busy woman of the world. She saw it a natural response to 'my conviction of the mercy and loving kindness of Him who loveth us'. In her early days, carefree and gay in the Gurney home at Earlham, new Norwich, she had little time even for the easy-going Quakerism of her family. 'How I long to get a broom and bang all the old Quakers, they do look so triumphant and cross', wrote one of her sisters, and Elizabeth would have written the same. They disliked the Sunday meetings at Goats Lane, Norwich; 'rather goatifying and cross' neatly expressed their feelings in their school room slang.

As she grew older Elizabeth Gurney, tempestuous and wilful, began to look for a firmer anchor than any of the pleasures which London and Norwich could give. Spurred on by the preaching of William Savery, an

American Quaker whom she first heard when she was eighteen, she slowly felt her way, with many ups and downs – 'my mind in a whirl' – and much probing of conscience to a deep faith. By 1800, the year she married Joseph Fry, she could write of her 'most deep wishes that I may do to my utmost the will of God'. For her this meant subscribing to the discipline and principles of 'plain Quakers'. She adopted their dress, their turns of speech and their outlook on the world – she would not even stand for a royal toast – and that detachment from normal life which they combined with a thorough-going efficiency in matters of business.

She was a Quaker, but as a Quaker she was first and foremost a Christian. 'It is only through the redeeming power of Christ that we can look for salvation,' she could write, and she knew that 'Christ in me is my *only hope* of glory'. She built her life on the Scriptures. 'That sacred Book,' wrote one of her friends in the formal phrases of the time, 'was the Fountain whence she derived all that strength and grace to do her work of faith, and labour of love'. Her way was not easy; when she believed that she must speak publicly for Christ, 'her fright was extreme'. She had to screw herself up to the effort, and her diary of 1809 is filled with self-reproachings. But had she not 'dared to open my mouth in public' the world would have lost a voice as singularly beautiful as it was effective.

Because she sought to be a 'devoted follower of the Lord Jesus' her work cannot be measured in terms of prison reform and public achievement alone, but in the countless lives which she touched. Thus, to take one instance, a woman who rushed out, 'yelling like a wild beast', tearing her hair and clawing at the other women's caps, later became a firm Christian and after her release, as one of Mrs. Fry's ladies put it, 'a well-conducted person'. Perhaps the most poignant and impressive testimony to Elizabeth Fry's influence is in the letters of Charlotte Newman and Mary James, condemned to death for forgery in February 1818. A few hours before execution Newman wrote to Mrs. Fry 'expressing my gratitude for your very great attention to the care of my poor soul'. When this woman affirmed, 'I trust through the Saviour's blood my sins will be washed away', and when Mary James, two hours before death, wrote to her fellow prisoners 'Oh, lay hold of Jesus. He is my refuge and strength', they were long past mouthing empty phrases. They knew what they meant.

Elizabeth Fry died in 1845 at the age of sixty-five. Her Quaker principles allowed no Westminster Abbey funeral, but the crowds who pressed to the Baking burial ground symbolized national feeling. Detached and apart from the common run of life, yet affecting multitudes by her acts of mercy and her clear-headed grasp of the needs of prison reform, Elizabeth Fry lived simply and solely, as she constantly wrote in her journal, 'for Thy service ... in Thy love, Thy fear and Thy light'.

'Oh my dear Lord, help and keep Thy servant' were her last words. That prayer was answered then, as it had been all the long years before.

7. Sir George Williams, 1821-1905
FATHER OF THE YMCA

It is fascinating to trace the world-wide growth of the Young Men's Christian Association from a remark made by a twenty-two-year-old draper's assistant to a friend, as they walked across Blackfriars Bridge one Sunday evening in the early summer of 1844.

The draper's assistant, George Williams, had come up some two and a half years earlier from the West Country and had found a post in a Ludgate Hill shop. Charles Dickens had been faithfully picturing that part of the city in his new book, *Oliver Twist*: 'a dirtier and more wretched place he had never seen', wrote Dickens of one of the warrens behind St. Paul's. 'The street was very narrow and muddy, and the air impregnated with filthy odours ... the sole places that seemed to prosper amid the general blight of the place were the public houses ... Covered ways and yards which here and there diverged from the main street, disclosed little knots of houses where drunken men and women were positively wallowing in filth.'

Shop assistants, bound by convention to black coats and white ties, were never far away, in feeling or in fact, from the slums behind the buildings where they slept, ate and worked. Hours were long in a draper's shop, fourteen being usual in summer; boys and youths were herded in dormitories, and horseplay and obscenity would often reign unchecked; they could be dismissed at a moment's notice, and unless a man's luck was in, the sack could lead straight to the slums. In many businesses sharp practice was commended by promotion, and since there was little opportunity for any amusement except in the nearby clusters of taverns, private morals were often on a par with public. Thus a well-meaning young man who started behind the counter in the eighteen-forties, might be forced, by sheer pressure of his surroundings, to discard high ideals and sink to the easygoing, dissatisfied existence of the average run of his fellows.

George Williams, however, entering Messrs. Hitchcock and Rogers in 1841, did not sink. Not only did he work his way honestly into the confidence of his employer, but he succeeded both in resisting temptations and in helping others to do the same. From his achievement sprang the YMCA. Behind it lay an experience four years earlier.

The country farm near Dulverton, where he was born, gave him nothing but a strong constitution. The draper's shop in Bridgwater, where he was apprenticed, gave him something more. He was fourteen when he began there. Small in size, he made up for it by quick wit and breezy efficiency; he was honest, but no plaster saint. Yet before he left Bridgwater for London, 'God helped me to yield myself wholly to Him.' The draper was a dissenter and obliged his boys to attend chapel. Resentful at first, young Williams owed both his immense fortune and his fame to this clause in the indentures. For in course of time the minister's preaching showed him, a boy of sixteen, that in life there is an upward and a downward road. He saw that he was himself heading downward, although outwardly as good as his fellows, if not better. He began to search for a way of escape, and in the winter of 1837 he found it. 'They told me in this very town of Bridgwater how to escape,' he said many years later; 'confess your sins, accept Christ, trust in Him, yield your heart to the Saviour.' This he did. Returning one night after sermontime, he knelt down at the back of the empty shop. 'I cannot describe to you the joy and peace which flowed into my soul when first I saw that the Lord Jesus had died for my sins, and that they were all forgiven.' What to others might be empty phrases were to George Williams solid experience.

When eventually he left for London he had tested and proved his faith. By reading and prayer he had been grounded in truth and experience, and had learned to love others for Christ's sake. It was therefore a strong-willed young man who started work at Ludgate Hill in 1841, but the will was not his own. 'O Lord, wilt Thou keep me and preserve me to the end ... guide my judgment and keep me in the right way' was the theme of the constant prayers he scrawled across his diary.

He made an immediate success of his work – his story has an unavoidable touch of Hilaire Belloc's Charles Fortescue, who 'always did what was right and thus accumulated an immense fortune' – and was soon promoted. He worked hard and was scrupulous in business details. All along he sought to be of service to others; since he believed he had a message of which they were in desperate need, he not only helped them in their jobs but tried to bring the thoughts of the most frivolous down to earth and up to heaven. He was, however, popular; high spirits went with high ideals and he lacked any trace of the prig.

His Sundays he spent slumming, visiting in the St. Giles rookeries, teaching in Ragged Schools and Sunday Schools, and going twice in the day to hear a famous Nonconformist divine. Meanwhile he was educating himself in music and literature, 'that I may be better able to work with Christ'. The core of his life was prayer, and companionship with Christ. 'What ought I to do?' he once asked in his diary, 'Constantly repose on God.' He prayed more for others than for himself and as a result longed to win them for Christ. He would write names of his fellow assistants in his diary, and would add, 'let me plead with Thee until I prevail'. When he joined the firm there was one other Christian among the one hundred and forty assistants. Within two years the number was over twenty – nearly all the result, on the human level, of George Williams' prayers, example and personal approach.

It was not an easy time. To the normal stress of long hours and hard work were added the strains peculiar to a young and lonely Christian. But temptations were slowly overcome. His character developed, moulded by his deep desire 'to glorify Him', and what is more, by 1844 he had seen a transformation in his shop. Regular meetings for prayer were held, Bible readings and services took place, and Mr. Hitchcock, head of the firm, who appeared all along to have a slumbering faith, became as active as any.

George Williams had for a while an ambition to be a foreign missionary. Friends, however, persuaded him to throw this overboard and devote himself to the mission field of his trade. In May 1844 the idea came to him that something ought to be done in the other large shops.

'Teddy, are you prepared to make a sacrifice for Christ?' he asked his fellow assistant, Beaumont, that Sunday evening as they walked across Blackfriars Bridge to chapel. He then outlined his plan for 'a few earnest, devoted, self-denying men' to pray and work their way together. The idea grew; they found that the manager of another shop, and their own employer, were equally in favour. On 6 June twelve of them met in Williams' bedroom in the shop-buildings to form a society. Their aim was simple: 'to spread the Redeemer's kingdom amongst those by whom they are surrounded.'

They went a step at a time. They hired a room in a nearby coffee house and drafted a letter which was sent to every drapery business in the city. Various clumsy names were suggested for the new association, and that finally chosen was not always used at first. But the movement caught on. Lonely Christians in other shops, working behind the counters or as clerks in the offices upstairs, or as buyers like Williams himself, found encouragement and companionship. By November, having moved its place of meeting to a hotel in Blackfriars (which, however, forbade the singing of hymns), they had about one hundred and fifty members. Within a year of the talk on the bridge, the Young Men's Christian Association had a paid secretary, a regular programme and a steadily increasing following.

They met weekly. At first the meetings were not open and were restricted to prayer and the exchange of news. Soon they were opened to everybody, of any trade and whatever his views, and talks and Bible readings were given. 'God was there; His blessing filled the place,' said one of the first members some years afterwards, as he described (with an enthusiasm of reminiscence) 'souls renewed, backsliders reclaimed, evil prevented, weak brethren strengthened, friendships made ...'

The whole movement was rooted in prayer. 'In answer to prayer, the Spirit of God was present and we had conversion after conversion,' wrote Williams of the earliest days in his own firm, and that atmosphere continued unabated. They believed also that the Bible would do its own work, and it did. But they knew that without personal contact prayer would not be used, and they sought to crown their social friendship by straightforward talks, one by one alone, with those to whom they wished to pass the secret of Christ. They came to realise also that a hot-house spiritual atmosphere would not bring lasting results, and they therefore, after some hesitation, encircled their message with the provision of reading rooms, a library and a coffee room.

They bought a building for such purposes in 1849, and arranged winter lectures at the Exeter Hall in the Strand. No such benefits had been offered before to young London men in trade. New opportunities of recreation, leisure and education began to oust the loneliness and boredom which had led them straight to vice and drink. Thus George Williams, like Lord Shaftesbury, who became his close friend, and like Barnardo in the next generation, found that his spiritual purpose was making him also a social reformer. But like them, he never lost sight of that primary spiritual aim.

By the year of the Great Exhibition George Williams was thirty and the YMCA seven. Henceforth Williams' life runs in two parallel strands, interweaving and supporting one another, and each dedicated as much as the other to God. First there is the man of business. He rose steadily in his firm and, unconsciously true to tradition, married his employer's daughter and became a partner. When his father-in-law died in 1863 he became sole owner of the fast-growing business. His clear-headed grasp of affairs, and the Free Trading prosperity of the times enabled him to amass a fortune. Like Samuel Morley, who inherited a small draper's shop in the city and died the head of a vast textile combine and a millionaire, he gave a great deal away. Taxation and the cost of living was low, but such philanthropy was not as easy as it sounds. Both Morley and Williams 'erected benevolence into a business' which they ran as efficiently as their trade. Williams' firm was also in the van of trade reform, and the movements for early closing and shorter hours owed much to him. He lived in the full glare of publicity as a Christian leader; but neither his methods nor his business morals ever earned him a hint of such criticism as Keir Hardie, the labour leader, made on another philanthropist of the period, when he declared that 'men who make so much profession of Christianity as Lord Overtoun makes' should first of all give 'some evidence of the faith that is in them by their treatment of their work-people'.

Each day this genial businessman, with his immaculate clothes, his stumpy frame and his whiskers, which followed fashion and later became a beard, went from his house in Woburn Square to work. George Williams lived happily, combining his innumerable interests with the steady, punctilious grind at the office. Permeating all his activities was his zeal for extending the joys he himself possessed. 'What are *you* doing for the Master?' he would constantly ask his friends, while he himself had the rare knack of speaking acceptably of Christ to thousands whom he met in the normal push and pull of life, cabbies and porters, servants and fellow guests, applicants for jobs and business acquaintances; an embarrassment or annoyance for some, but of known value to many others.

The dominating concern of Williams' life, however, continued to be the YMCA. 1851 was a year of great growth, for opportunities were taken to reach the thousands who came to the Great Exhibition, and as a result associations were started in other countries and in other parts of Britain. In 1855, during the Crimean War, the first general conference was held in Paris. Independent but closely linked associations developed in city after city and country after country, bound together by their basis: 'to unite young men who, regarding Jesus Christ as their God and Saviour according to the Holy Scriptures, desire to be His disciples ... for the extension of His kingdom among men'. They passed through financial difficulties but remained unscathed.

They made their mistakes; much ribald Press comment, for instance, arose from the pious decision of one association to ban *Punch* for a joke which had, as it turned out, been misread by the committee. Slowly, however, the YMCA established itself high in public estimation. In spiritual work the association kept diversity in unity, avoiding the restrictions which would follow absorption in any one church or sect. In cultural activities they steadily extended their range, becoming taken for granted by hosts of young men ignorant of the bad old days before.

Year after year George Williams played a dominant part in YMCA affairs. In his spare time he travelled up and down the country, starting fresh associations or reviving decayed ones. He gave liberally. Often when a branch was in debt he would offer to give one half of the sum needed if they raised the other half. When Exeter Hall in the Strand was put up for sale he determined to buy it for a central headquarters, and within two days he had raised the necessary £25,000, he and four friends each giving £5,000. By letters and chats he would encourage committee men and secretaries, and frequently spent time with ordinary and obscure youths who would call with their problems. He held a regular Bible reading on Sunday afternoons at his house, and was a constant attendant at the noon prayer-meeting in the Aldersgate Street offices.

He lived to see the Diamond Jubilee of the YMCA in 1904, dying the following year at the age of eighty-four. After his death his aims and ideals continued to inspire the YMCA. But a subtle change was occurring. In 1906, less than two years after his death, one of the leading men in the movement could write, 'There is a danger that the spiritual work of the Association may be placed in a secondary position.' In 1914 the test came, when the war made a vital choice necessary. To meet the social needs of the troops the YMCA expanded its facilities and recruited large numbers of workers, to some of whom, inevitably, the spiritual side was secondary.

But Sir George Williams' last message remained apposite. 'I would,' he said, 'urge upon all young men to give themselves body, soul and spirit to the Saviour who died for them, and to spend their lives in seeking to extend His kingdom.' Behind that urge was George Williams' own consciousness of 'the peace and joy which have come to me through my Lord and Saviour, Jesus Christ'.

8. 7th Earl of Shaftesbury, 1801-1885
NOBLE LORD

Dogs, horses, shooting parties, stately waltzes in stately homes – this was the background of the 7th Earl of Shaftesbury when he was in his twenties.

'Very handsome and captivating,' a great Whig hostess described Lord Ashley (as he was known during his father's life) in 1822. All the ladies fell in love with him. Down from Oxford, quickly into Parliament for one of his ducal uncle's boroughs, and before long a junior minister, he seemed to the casual eye like other young lords, except that his personal character was more upright than usual among George IV's aristocrats, and he was shy, studious, and never seen at the gambling tables of clubland.

Deep inside, not yet detected by his intimates, stirred hidden fires. Through the early friendship of a lovable, elderly housekeeper in a hard, bleak home (his parents disgracefully neglected their children), Ashley had known what few of his class in that age knew: the abiding sense of Christ's presence as Saviour. Since boyhood too, when he had seen a pauper's coffin dropped and broken open at his feet because the bearers were drunk, he had held a resolve to dedicate his life to the poor and miserable, though at first he did little about it.

Ashley developed late. He was in Parliament before his intellect took wings, and this had to compete with a streak of laziness until his life's work found him. He was twenty-five before his simple faith became more than a personal private comfort.

When the smouldering spiritual flame caught fire at last, he awoke to the realities of his position. Belonging to a class that considered formal religion proper but enthusiasm vulgar, he was unlikely to meet sympathy or understanding. The heir to a great estate, he must live in a style far from apostolic poverty. By birth, position, prospects, he was a man of the world.

'I must now choose my line of life, and stand to it manfully.' Had he withdrawn from his world into a private paradise of piety, or renounced his background to immerse himself in a patently spiritual labour, perhaps abandoning his title to devote his years to some northern slum, the suffering millions would have had to wait for another champion. Ashley, unaware of his great future, took the more difficult part of accepting that he must serve God where he was. 'I see nothing but a political career, for every one must take that in which his various circumstances will give him the best means of doing good,' he wrote in 1827; 'I am bound to try what God has put into me for the benefit of old England.'

More than five years passed, years when he sometimes wondered if he would ever find a true vocation. Then, on a February day in 1833, a Yorkshire clergyman called on him in his Mayfair home, to beg that he take up the parliamentary leadership of the agitation to reduce the labour of factory children to ten hours a day – and less if possible.

'I can perfectly recollect my astonishment and doubt and terror,' Ashley wrote later. He had been moved by the recent revelations of child slavery, and was prepared to aid reform by doing small services; but to *lead* the agitation ...! He was no speaker, he thought. He would forfeit hopes of high political office; might he not one day be Prime Minister provided he refused such mad causes? And it would take him much away from his beautiful, young wife, Minny, and their baby. Ashley prayed. He sought the Word of God. He consulted Minny. Her words were decisive. 'It's your duty, and the consequences we must leave. Go forward and to Victory!'

The call had come. It was unexpected and unlikely, for he knew nothing personally about the murky hills of Lancashire and Yorkshire where children lived short brutish lives, or of the mines where soon he was to discover untold horrors. It was the start of fifty years' crusade for children, for the poor, the oppressed, the exploited.

Much of what he did would have been impossible had he not continued to move with assured ease in the world of power, wealth and title that then ruled Great Britain. He could chat about a point with the Prime Minister at the Queen's ball; he could deftly win the support of a political hostess who would whisper of her sympathy to an opposition leader. Whatever government came to power, he or his wife would be relatives of half the ministers and know the other half socially.

The cause young Lord Ashley had adopted ran counter to the beliefs of his world. It was commonly supposed that to interfere with economic liberty, even to reduce the working hours of little children, would imperil the British Empire. To encourage the lower orders in any way might lead to revolution. 'There,' murmured Melbourne to the young Queen Victoria, looking at Ashley, 'goes the greatest Jacobin in your dominions.' The Prime Minister's gentle joke about the husband of his niece Minny was taken seriously by many of their equals.

Some thought Ashley a bore, though admitting his personality to be delightful; others, a nuisance or a menace, a traitor to his class. 'Some few sympathised,' he wrote after five years of it, 'more ridiculed, as many resisted and far more were indifferent.' It was because he was one of them that he had to endure their gibes, cutting deep into a sensitive nature. As he rose in the Commons in 1842 to make his great speech for children in the mines, 'just before I opened my mouth, the words of God came forcibly to my mind: "Only be strong and of a good courage..."'

The achievements of Shaftesbury (as he became on succession to the earldom in 1851) are written fair in the history of nation and church.

His most famous fights were indeed the ones for reasonable working hours in factory and mine. He accepted leadership in 1833 – 'it seems no one else will undertake it, so I will' – and fourteen years passed before the Factory Act of 1847 reduced the hours of women and children to ten daily. During the following thirty years he continued to assault the current doctrine of *laissez-faire* until in 1878 'we find ourselves at last in possession of what we prayed for at first', a ten hours' limit for all factory workers. Shaftesbury never dreamed of pretending to all the merit, but his was the continual inspiration, the leadership and a great deal of the personal labour which brought victory.

Meanwhile he was vigorous in other causes. In 1842, after the shocking revelations of the Royal Commission, he won the exclusion of women and children from the horror of the coal mines. He worked hard on behalf of the Climbing Boys, who were sent naked up chimneys by sweeps. He often paid for their release, prosecuted brutal masters at his own expense, and in 1875 finally managed to steer a bill through Parliament to end the evil. Among his other interests were emigration schemes for the poor, housing improvements in towns and villages (in which he was at first handicapped by the disgraceful state of the cottages owned by his own indifferent father); education in factories and the provision of Ragged Schools in the slums; training ships for orphans and street-arabs; and the control and improvement of common lodging-houses, which were bug-infested harbourers of disease and notorious sins of iniquity.

He made friends with the costers – his famous donkey was their gift to him in gratitude. Flower girls, paupers and merchant sailors found their lot eased through his efforts. When others started a crusade, whether Plimsoll for sailors, George Williams for young shopmen, or Barnardo for destitute children, he would give time and money to their cause. Even animals had reason to thank him: he was one of the earliest and strongest supporters of the RSPCA. Nor did his concern stop at home: he attacked the opium traffic and supported the suppression of the Arab slave trade in Africa.

At the same time he was a strong supporter of the Bible Society and of missionary societies; he laid so many foundation-stones of churches and chapels, that a wag suggested that archaeologists six centuries on would suppose him the last king of the dynasty. He continually spoke on church questions in Parliament.

Throughout his life were constant acts of charity and kindness, large and small, whenever a need met his eye: the rescue and education of 'the wretched sweep behind my house in London'; food for the famished in a hard winter; a ride for an old tramp woman whom he passed on his way to a review, at which he therefore arrived in full lord lieutenant's uniform, sitting on the box with the old woman safe and comfortable inside; a couple of beds given to a children's home in response to a little girl's request; drives into the slums with his carriage full of toys for neglected children. These were a few incidents in nearly fifty years of practical sympathy for the lonely and downtrodden.

Although in later life acclaimed and honoured on every side, he was continually thwarted and opposed. Even his working-men colleagues had abused him when he had courage to compromise temporarily in order to win their battle in the end. Such opposition of the rib-aldry of men such as Melbourne or the implacable en-mity of Cobden, made Shaftesbury smart in his youth: 'met Melbourne at dinner – a good deal excited by his language and opinions and spoke strongly. Will hence-forth never say anything to him ...' In later life, more gentle and unruffled, he was still acutely distressed by criticism and opposition for he was, as Lord Bathurst remarked to him, 'mighty sensitive'.

Shaftesbury thrived on sympathy, and this was often denied him. He knew his own cause to be just and found it hard when political friends would give 'no assistance, no sympathy' when he was attacking some 'foul stain' in industrial or urban life. He was fortunate in his de-voted wife, 'the purest, gentlest, kindest, sweetest and most confiding spirit that ever lived', who shared all his burdens for forty years until her death in 1872. By na-ture Shaftesbury was a lonely man, and thus sometimes unaware of others' sympathy. 'Who is with me?' was a frequent theme of his diary in old age, although thou-sands believed in him and the toiling millions loved him.

The famous portrait of Millais, painted in old age, suggest that Shaftesbury was a dreary, humourless, anx-ious man. This was far from true, though long years of work and constant feeling for the misery of others had made his face mournful in repose. He had in fact a strong sense of humour. In youth he was renowned for the spar-kle of his talk. To the end he kept his love of fun – a 'solemn sense of humour', wrote his granddaughter 'which bubbled forth at times and betrayed itself in a remote twinkle in his great blue eyes'. When once he arrived to take a chair at a meeting, to find that he had been told the wrong day, only one person, a reporter, was present in an empty hall. On the stroke of the hour Shaftesbury rose. 'At this large and distinguished gathering ...' he began. The reporter looked up astonished. 'Why not?' said Shaftesbury. 'Am not I large and are you not distinguished?' And with that they both walked out.

His mind had an ordered and practical bent. He was no armchair philanthropist. His first-hand knowledge of conditions, the fruit of constant tours of inspection, lay behind much of his success in agitation and debate. He saw men and women as individuals, not as pawns in the economic or political game. The poorest, most friendless person was sure of sympathy and a hot meal on calling at his town house for advice or help. He often went off to filthy lodging-houses in search of some insignificant girl or young man who had run away from home, and would not rest until he had them reconciled to their parents. He sat by sick beds, comforted the bereaved, spoke to the lonely. 'His magnificent and rather melancholy figure, six-foot tall' was well known and well loved in hovels and warrens in every part of London.

Shaftesbury loved people as individuals. One of his intimates said that he 'hardly ever passed a ragged child in the street without the desire to stop and talk to it' – and in Victorian London a ragged barefoot child was a normal sight. For his own kind Shaftesbury cared too. In no instance is his influence more remarkably shown than in his close friendship with that sprightly old pagan, Lord Palmerston.

Palmerston, a bachelor till late middle age, married Minny's widowed mother. Shaftesbury brought to his lovable, cynical stepfather-in-law a warmth of affection. Broadlands, Palmerston's Hampshire seat, became a second home and Pam 'my dear, true and private friend'. They were devoted to each other.

British religion owes much to this friendship, for when Palmerston became Prime Minister in 1855 he made Shaftesbury his bishop-maker. Recognising that the religious feelings of the country were 'as strange to him as the interior of Japan', he gave his son-in-law an almost free hand in ecclesiastical appointments. Until then no Evangelical had ever been promoted to the bench of bishops except Henry Ryder, back in 1815, who owed his elevation to being the younger son of an earl and Cabinet Minister. Shaftesbury, while taking care not to be partisan, made several gifted Evangelicals bishops, placing them where they could do good, choosing 'men who would preach the truth, be active in their dioceses, be acceptable to the working people, and not offensive to the Nonconformists.' Of non-evangelicals, no clerics could hope to be given bishoprics by Palmerston unless 'moderate and decent in their language to Nonconformists'.

In October 1865, Shaftesbury received a wire to warn him that the aged Prime Minister had fallen dangerously ill. On reaching the house, Shaftesbury was told of all hope abandoned, 'yet I could not quite abandon prayer'. As the end approached Palmerston's stepchildren gathered round the bed. One of the doctors had said that the dying statesman had actually spoken of trust in Christ three days before. Minny's brother William repeated familiar passages from the Prayer Book and then asked Shaftesbury to pray. 'Inwardly I implored God's grace and then I did so. I spoke of sin, of forgiveness, and of sin being washed away only by the blood of a crucified Saviour.'

Palmerston seemed to murmur assent, certainly not to make signs of denial, 'and he never would have passed in silence, still less have apparently admitted anything his spirit rejected'.

The doctors became certain Palmerston had clearly understood and had joined in the prayers fully conscious.

Shaftesbury's heart welled within him. His years of loving and praying for the old worldling had borne fruit at last. 'We may joyously believe that God of His free and unbounded mercy revealed to him His Son Jesus Christ.'

To Shaftesbury, Jesus Christ was his 'unchanging friend'. What a comfort it is,' he once said, 'to know Christ as a personal Saviour ... My Saviour.'

His whole life was rooted in prayer. The day began with prayer, and in the spirit of prayer it continued. After his first important speech in the Commons, he 'hastened home to throw myself on my knees in gratitude'. When in 1855 Palmerston had been determined to make him Chancellor of the Duchy of Lancaster, and Shaftesbury, in great distress of mind, was reluctantly preparing to go and kiss hands at the Palace, 'while I was waiting for the carriage I went down on my knees and prayed for wisdom and understanding'. Almost immediately a note came from the Prime Minister releasing him. In the House, or walking along the street he would silently turn in prayer to the Lord whose promise he remembered, 'I am with you alway.'

The Bible, 'that source of our safety and our greatness' as he called it, 'our life, our light, our joy' was his inspiration and guide from his earliest days until the end. He would 'never go in action or belief where the Scriptures would not guide me'. He knew the Bible from end to end. Where he did not understand he was prepared to trust, and he always set himself against 'milk and water dilutions of the saving truths' it contained.

With this deep-rooted faith in God he was not content with material reforms alone. 'The sole, the sovereign remedy is to do what we can to evangelise the people ... in the grandest cathedral and at the corner of the street, in the royal palace and in the back slums, preaching Christ to the people.' For him practical relief and the message of Christianity went hand in hand. He wanted the church to 'drive into the recesses of human misery and bring out the wretched and ignorant sufferers to bask in the light and life and liberty of the gospel'.

Once in the George Yard Ragged School in Whitechapel, a magic-lantern show was in progress. The room was crowded – 'four hundred people in the room, and the police told me that four or five hundred were turned away.' The slides were of the crucifixion story and Shaftesbury was explaining them. His audience was ragged, illiterate and of the lowest level of poverty. His last picture showed our Lord standing outside a closed door, and the text was 'Behold I stand at the door and knock'. 'The effect was startling,' said Shaftesbury, 'it seemed to bring the story home to every heart.' 'What you see there,' he explained, 'is going on at the door of every house in Whitechapel.' Men and women began to weep.

'When I told them,' he went on, 'that if they would throw open the door, Christ would "come in and sup with them", there was something so cosy and comfortable in the idea of it that they came pouring round me and thanking me.'

SOLDIERS
FOR CHRIST

9. Sir Henry Havelock, 1795-1857
THE SOLDIERS' GENERAL

In the early months of 1823 the East Indiaman *General Kyd* was sailing southwards off the west coast of Africa, on its three-month voyage from England round the Cape to Bengal. Among the junior officers on board was an obscure subaltern, Henry Havelock. He was aged twenty-seven, and after nearly eight years on home duties, having missed the battle of Waterloo by a month, he had exchanged from the Rifle Brigade into the 13th Light Infantry, being anxious to see some active service in India.

He was small, thin and wiry, but remarkably good-looking. Having, however, neither family influence nor a long purse, he was determined to rise by sheer professional efficiency, a somewhat thin hope in the early nineteenth century except for time of war. Encouraged by his company commander, the redoubtable and famed Harry Smith, he had burrowed deep into textbooks and drilled and disciplined his men with enthusiasm.

At the same time he had tasted the pleasures of his garrison towns, where good-looking young officers were much in demand at balls, routs and romps, and pretty girls loved bright uniforms. He also read widely, and having been educated at Charterhouse and then having tried his hand at the law, until a family quarrel threw him on his own resources, his mind was supple and active.

Henry Havelock found himself welcomed on the *General Kyd* as one of the few officers who had troubled to learn both Hindustani and Persian. With India not far away others welcomed his tuition. Among them was another subaltern of his own regiment, James Gardner, with whom he struck up a warm friendship.

Gardner was a Christian, with the courage of his convictions. Havelock, though occasionally stirred by memories of a Bible-reading mother, long dead, and of precocious sermon-making with future bishops and archdeacons in the dormitory at Charterhouse, possessed nothing but the lip-service religion typical of his contemporaries in the service.

As the friendship developed Gardner sought to bring Havelock to face the claims of Christ, but he was not particularly interested. Slowly, however, he saw that the Spirit of God, as he later wrote, was coming to him 'with its offer of peace and mandate of love'. He consented to read, and Gardner lent him a life of Henry Martyn, the brilliant Cambridge don who had thrown his life away in the East a dozen years before, preaching Christianity to Hindus and Mohammedans. He read a compendious volume of Christian evidences, compiled by a contemporary Northamptonshire parson. These, and Gardner's own words, convinced him of his need.

Before the *General Kyd* reached Cape Town, therefore 'love had prevailed'. Havelock had opened his life to Christ and, in his own words, a 'great change in his soul which has been productive of unspeakable advantage' had occurred. He was not slow to 'make public avowal' of his Christianity by seeking to live as he felt a Christian should, whilst Gardner and he regularly read the Bible and prayed together during the rest of the voyage. When Havelock reached Calcutta his determination to shine as a soldier had thus been linked to and absorbed by his determination to carry out the dictates of the Epistles to 'shine as a light in the world'.

August 1826 was hot and steamy in the Irrawaddy valley of Burma, where British forces, their scarlet uniforms contrasting with the dark jungle green, were pushing their way slowly against the brutal and well-trained troops of the king of Ava.

Henry Havelock had joined the army in the field after the fall of Rangoon. He had shown himself an efficient officer and stiff disciplinarian in his three years in India. He was, however, somewhat unpopular with his brother officers, being both too rigid in his morals and too abrupt in his comments for their liking. But the path he had taken was hard; though his men might appreciate his efforts to convert them, loose-living officers had little time for his ways. He was, therefore, lonely and often on edge. Such hardships merely spurred him on, though somewhat subduing his humour. But he knew already that spiritual warfare could be as rough as a soldier's battle.

In captured Rangoon he had continued the training of his men. He found also that no chaplain had been appointed. From this followed the experience of a brother officer, sightseeing in a Burmese pagoda, who was somewhat surprised to hear psalm-singing in such an unexpected place. He tracked down the sound, entered an inner sanctum of the temple and found Havelock leading a group of soldiers in an informal service, while round the room were small stone Buddhas with oil lamps perched rakishly on their laps.

When eventually Havelock was sent up to the front the hot season was at its height. Enemy forays were increasing. Bodies of sentries caught unawares would be discovered shockingly mutilated. Sir Archibald Campbell, the Commander-in-Chief, found his men jittery and occasionally out of hand, and matters were not improved by the appearance of three wild prophetesses in the Burmese ranks, whose frenzied screams heard at night through the jungle were too eerie for joking. Nights and days were harassing. It was then that an incident occurred which became something of a legend in the Army: an outpost was set on at night and a runner came back to headquarters for instant support. Campbell sent an orderly to the next company on the roster. The orderly reappeared with the company officer, who had to confess that half his men were drunk.

Campbell swore roundly and turned to his aide-de-camp. 'Then call out Havelock's saints,' he roared, 'they are always sober and can be depended on and Havelock himself is always ready.'

In 1828 Henry Havelock, back from the war in Burma but still a lieutenant, was Adjutant at the depot at Chinsura on the Hoogly not far from Calcutta.

He spent much of his leisure at Serampore, the nearby Baptist missionary settlement presided over by the great William Carey, where one of his greatest friends, John Marshman, lived with his mother and youngest sister, nineteen-year-old Hannah Marshman, a gay young lady fresh from schooling in England. On June 14th Havelock wrote a long letter to Miss Hannah asking for her hand.

In reply he received a note, 'short and penned in a spirit of *very exemplary caution*', but sufficient to give 'much encouragement and consolation'. Mrs. Marshman also wrote encouragingly, but referred to his poverty and said she could not allow a definite engagement until Dr. Marshman returned from Europe. Havelock thought this 'a little cruel' and wondered why John Marshman could not act on his father's behalf.

The following weekend Havelock was able to get down to Serampore and knew without a shadow of doubt that his love was fully returned and that whatever Dr. Marshman might say the family looked on the two as engaged. 'I would not exchange for half the years which I have lived, the evening of Sunday last,' he wrote to

Hannah when he had returned to his damp and lonely bungalow at Chinsura. 'It is necessary that you should first have seen and felt all the calamity and vicissitude which I have witnessed; and been conversant as I have been with jealousy, calumny, strife, debate and turmoil before you comprehend as I did in that happy hour the joy of having peace and consolation and love spoken to me by one nurtured in the purest piety, and of feeling that the affection and fidelity which was then promised me was not that which could cease with time but such as would survive and continue to bless into eternity.'

In 1829 they were married.

Two years later Havelock rejoined the 13th Light Infantry, bringing Hannah and their little boy, Harry, to Dinapore. Although his duties were slight he was determined to be the best soldier in the regiment, and for a definite purpose. 'It was,' he recalled in later years, 'the great object of my ambition to be surpassed by none in zeal and determination in the path of my duty because I was resolved to put down the vile calumny that a Christian could not be a meritorious soldier.'

With men living under the awful moral conditions typical of every British regiment then in India, Havelock re-started his Bible meeting. A few survived of his earlier group, the chief being a sergeant George Godfrey. Not unnaturally Godfrey and his fellows followed their leader into Baptist allegiance, and built a makeshift chapel.

The small group of thoroughgoing Christians met each morning and evening in their chapel for hymn singing, Bible reading and prayer. The building also provided an opportunity not otherwise allowed for in a military cantonment, of 'small places for retirement for private devotion, to which many resort,' as Havelock wrote to his father-in-law Dr. Marshman. On Sundays, after the men had attended the obligatory parade service, 'there is public worship before noon, and in the evening. I think,' continued Havelock, 'the congregation on the latter occasion fluctuates between fifty and sixty, sometimes however exceeding this latter number; and it is admitted by those who, without any prepossession in favour of the faith, have the best opportunities of judging of the fact, that instances of immorality or neglect of duty among this body in the course of a year are very rare. The frequenters of this chapel are reckoned among the best behaved men in the regiment.'

And thus, in those days of the early 1830s at Dinapore, young privates who had almost forgotten childhood attendance in an English country church, or who since earliest days in slum streets had never had the chance of hearing the Christian gospel, would risk the ribaldry of their friends and take a seat at the back of the chapel on a Sunday evening.

When the singing and prayers were done, Havelock preached. He knew what they needed, and could speak it in clipped, simple phrases: 'Time is short, and eternity at hand,' he would say, and the men remembered the dozen or more of their comrades buried in the past six or nine months, 'so I must not delay to speak to you on the most important of all subjects – the care and prospects of your immortal souls ....'

When the service was over he would, if a man so desired, speak with him individually, showing from his Bible the way in which he might 'have Jesus for your friend.' For those moments the relationship of officer and ranker was forgotten, to be resumed inexorably when they left the chapel.

All this was done, so Havelock wrote years later, 'in the very teeth of ridicule and opposition.'

One couple alone stood quietly for Havelock – Robert Sale, the commanding officer, and Florentia, his masterful and determined wife. Hannah gave all support in her power. 'I trust,' she wrote in August 1831, 'that my dear Henry will be spared to continue to use all his efforts to be useful to the soldiers, among whom he is greatly beloved.'

Late in 1834 the adjutancy of the 13th, now at Agra, was vacant, and Havelock applied, without much hope of receiving the appointment.

Hannah was away at Serampore. One day she boldly wrote a letter to Lord William Bentinck the Governor-General and sent it across to Barrackpore. Shortly afterwards a red and gold liveried servant called at the mission house with a request from Lord William that Hannah should do him the goodness to call. She stepped into the Governor-General's barge and was carried swiftly across the river to the fine park with its zoo and artificial hills.

Lady William Bentinck received her. Lord William entered, smiling, and carrying a bundle of letters. 'About that letter you wrote me, madam,' he began, 'I am going to read you a few other letters I have received on the subject from your husband's regiment.' Hannah was all of a flutter. Lord William then said, 'Before I allude to this correspondence I give you the assurance that I have bestowed the adjutancy of the 13th on your husband because he is unquestionably the fittest man for it.'

Hannah subsided with relief, and Lord William began to read out from the letters. One called Havelock a methodist and a fanatic. Another begged the Governor-General to realise that Havelock's 'character as an officer was lowered by familiar intercourse with the men,' and a third respectfully intimated to his lordship that strong religious views would destroy an Adjutant's impartiality.

Lord William said he had made enquiries and was convinced that Havelock's men were the most sober and well disciplined in the regiment. 'Give your husband my compliments and tell him he must continue his religious exertions, and if possible convert the whole regiment. He can baptise the lot if he likes. But,' he added with a smile, tapping the letters, 'the *Adjutant* must not preach.'

Whatever the critics' disgust at Bentinck's choice, Havelock quickly won their loyalty and an inspecting General later in 1835 reported that 'the greatest unanimity seems to prevail among the officers of the regiment.'

The work in the chapel continued, not without sacrifice, for Hannah who told her mother that 'Henry is at his office all the morning and I do enjoy his society so much when he comes home that I am quite jealous of the time he spends among the soldiers.' Hannah herself was busy teaching her own boys and putting in time among the children of the regiment who she found had no religious instruction in their school, and helping men of the chapel to learn to read.

In their home, each day began with family prayers, by no means yet common even in England, and on one such occasion an Irish servant, daughter of one of the men in the regiment, provided a tale long current among the Havelocks. The Adjutant's extempore prayer had reduced the girl to tears and as she rose from her knees she blurted out, 'Oh Misther dear, you're not fit for a soldier. It's too tinderhearted you are. Sure you was born a praist, and a praist you ought to be.'

At the Regiment's next station, Karnal, Henry Havelock, now a brevet-captain, began a new work. Though he had won men to faith and character, he had failed to break the worst habit of the regiment. The Divisional General at his last inspection in Agra had commented on the 'many courts marital which proceeded from habitual drunkenness...'

In the garrison Havelock met an old friend, Edward Wakefield of a Native regiment. They discussed this problem together and Wakefield mentioned an abortive attempt in a battalion of the Buffs at Fort William in 1833 to form a Temperance Society, a British and Foreign Temperance Society having recently been formed in England. The idea struck Havelock as he passed it to Sale, remarking, 'We've tried everything else.' Sale approved and a Regimental Temperance Association was formed, of men pledged to abjure alcohol. But to expect them to honour such a surprising and original pledge was impossible unless a counter attraction was provided. Sale therefore secured the Commander-in-Chief's permission to allocate £90 from the Canteen Fund for the building of a Coffee Room, such as had never been seen in an Indian cantonment.

When it was built, Sergeant Godfrey, who was advanced in years, was placed in charge. 'We put him at the bar of the Coffee Room,' recalled Wakefield, 'his wife made the coffee and he distributed it. We gave them a cup of good coffee for about three farthings. We gave them the *Penny Magazine* and other papers to read, and we had meetings.' 'By pure moral persuasion,' as Wakefield put it, the 13th soon had strong membership for their Regimental Temperance Association. Within a few months General Duncan officially reported its strength at 'two hundred and seventy-four persons'. 'Havelock's crotchet', as the men called the Temperance drive, had caught on.

The scheme gradually expanded. A Savings Bank was established. 'Mrs. Sale joined in and we had our monthly meetings for the wives of the men and their children, and we gave them buns and cakes, and they enjoyed themselves.' Havelock wrote to Adjutants of other British regiments in India, and in the course of the next two years some thirty units formed Temperance Societies; reports from them were read out at monthly meetings in the 13th. By June 1838, when General Duncan again inspected the regiment, he reported a definite improvement. 'Courts martial continue to be numerous, but they appear all to be held on the same set of men for habitual drunkenness.'

In January 1842 the British garrison of Jalalabad, a small fortress-town beyond the Khyber Pass, realized that they were isolated. A few days before they had been shocked by the arrival of a solitary horseman, unarmed, wounded and exhausted, the sole survivor of the garrison of the Afghan capital, Kabul. Dr. Brydon's arrival, and the three hopeless days of beacon-lights and bugle-calls that followed had convinced General Sale and his command that the whole British force, which an unwise Government had risked in a futile attempt to occupy Afghanistan, had been wiped out by treachery in the Khurd Kabul pass.

Siege was inevitable. Far to the east a relieving force was slowly pushing its way through mountainous and hostile country. The question was whether famine and the Afghan army would combine to eliminate Jalalabad before General Pollock could arrive to relieve it. The garrison was merely an under strength brigade. They had six weeks' provisions.

Havelock, now a full captain but nothing more, was attached to the staff of his former colonel. When the trouble with Persia and Afghanistan had broken out in 1838, Sale had left to a command and Havelock to be Persian interpreter to General Elphinstone, the martyr to gout in whose incapable hands the expedition had been placed.

During the next two years of battles, shady diplomacy and uneasy occupation, Havelock had his full of excitement. By the time the British envoy had been murdered and Elphinstone, his gout now excruciating, had sealed the fate of his troops by capitulation, Havelock had rejoined Sale and thus was in Jalalabad.

The arrival of Dr. Brydon, 'remnant of an army', threw the British garrison into gloom.

The whole force was awed and shaken by the proximity of a disaster unparalleled in British Indian history. The next Sunday Havelock, who had maintained his informal Bible meetings with such men as were off duty, suggested a partial cessation of work in order that divine service might be held. Sale invited him to read the service.

The European officers and men assembled in a square of Bala Hissar, with the Union Jack fluttering overhead from the tower. 'Everyone came as usual, with sword and pistol or musket and bayonet,' wrote one officer, 'and with sixty rounds in pouch, ready at a moment's notice to march to battle. To me it was an affecting sight to see those great rough fellows of the 13th, with their heads bowed, humbly confessing their sins before God, and acknowledging their dependence on His goodness and mercy.' The familiar Church of England morning service sounded moving and impressive as Havelock read, in his clear, rather abrupt voice. For the Psalm of the day he substituted Psalm 46 'which,' he remarked, 'Luther was wont to use in seasons of peculiar difficulty and depression,' and the men all joined in the words of it: 'God is our hope and strength, a very present help in trouble ...'

In that spirit they fought the siege, which began a fortnight later on 15 February 1842. An untimely earthquake nearly put an end to their efforts, and by mid-

March famine was 'staring us in the face'. A courageous little sortie from the walls, however, seized a convenient flock of sheep and saved the situation. The rank and file were admirable and Havelock gleefully, and accurately, ascribed their morale to the convenient loss of the rum supply some months earlier. The weeks passed, and the relieving force under General Sir George Pollock[1] seemed as far away as ever. Then came a report that Pollock had been defeated. Havelock urged Sale to attack.

Early in the morning of 7 April Akbar Khan, the Afghan general, who was preparing for final victory, found himself vigorously attacked instead. A few days earlier Havelock had written, 'I am relying fully on the merits of the Redeemer and will be well pleased, if it be His will, to end my days in so honourable an enterprise'; and in the mêlée he was thrown from his horse and nearly killed. But by the time the sun was fully up Akbar's camp was in ashes and his army in flight. Four of Elphinstone's guns were back in British hands, much plunder had been taken, and the siege effectually raised.

The honours of the day, as no one doubted or grudged, were with Havelock. And to the end of his life he kept the anniversary of this 'crowning mercy'.

Nine days afterwards Pollock's relieving army, which had not been defeated, marched into Jalalabad (under whose walls they had expected a famous victory) while the garrison band played *Oh! but ye've been long o'coming*.

Ten years later, in 1852, Lieut.-Colonel Havelock, C.B., had arrived back in India after two years' leave in England – his first for twenty-six years. He had held staff

1. The present writer's great-great uncle. Afterwards a Field Marshal.

appointments and had taken part in the various minor wars of the later 'forties, but promotion was dishearteningly slow. Although Lord Hardinge could call him 'every inch a soldier and every inch a Christian' he could not take 'the path of popularity, the broad way ... Principles alone are worth living for.' Thus, as he wrote at the age of fifty-nine, he 'could not hope to be a major-general before seventy-one'.

He was so poor that the education of his family worried him. He found himself, to his own disgust, touting for influence and recommendations. 'How can I help it? I have soldiered with heart and soul for thirty-nine years and my country's generals neglect me.' But he did not waver in his faith. His philosophy is neatly expressed in a letter to his small son: 'Take care that you have Jesus for your friend ... be a credit to your name and country.' His spiritual life was no longer so lonely, for his own quiet efforts had combined with the changing atmosphere in England to increase the number of wholehearted Christians in the Indian civil and military services. Thus Sir John and Sir Henry Lawrence, John Nicholson and James Outram, all famous names of the period, were strong Christians; and so were many others.

But the unkindest cut of all, in his return to India, was the need to leave his wife in England for the children's sake. 'If you knew what I endured since I parted from you ...' he wrote on the way back, 'but my God will support me. I have Jesus Christ to trust and His presence to comfort me.'

The early 'fifties were lean years for Havelock. But, though he did not know it, his day was coming.

June 1857 in Calcutta. The general consternation at the Sepoy mutiny, which had burst out at Meerut in early May and was now blazing throughout the Bengal army, had been absorbed by the general preparations for its suppression. The Governor-General, Canning, refused to realize the gravity of the position; the commander-in-chief had most inconveniently died; India was denuded of troops, for a war with Persia was only just over; an army must be raised to besiege Delhi, but a mobile column, it was thought, was enough for the mutineers in Oudh.

Havelock, full colonel and acting brigadier-general, was on his way back from Persia, where he had distinguished himself. Before the battle of Mohumra he had written to his wife, 'I have good troops and cannon, but my trust is in the Lord Jesus, my tried and merciful friend.' After the victory he wrote again, 'the cannonade was warm ... I felt throughout that the Lord Jesus was at my side.' And now the new commander-in-chief appointed him to command the mobile column.

Havelock was obscure, 'an old fossil, dug up and only fit to be turned into pipe-clay'. He was 'not in fashion', as Lady Canning wrote, 'but all the same we believe he will do well. No doubt he is fussy and tiresome,' she added, 'but his little old stiff figure looks as active and fit for use as if he were made of steel'.

On 24 June 1857 he took command at Allahabad. There followed two months of splendid, impossible victories which made Havelock's name a household word in India and England. His force was absurdly small, and the heat was intense, yet an inefficient Government had left his Highlanders to fight in winter woollen uniforms. The one advantage he had was the new Enfield rifle.

The first task was to recapture Cawnpore and rescue the women and children prisoners. His little column trounced the rebels at Fatehpur and Havelock wrote home, 'One of the prayers oft repeated throughout my life has been answered, and I have lived to command in a successful action.' His Order of the Day attributed the victory to 'the Enfield rifle ... British pluck ... and the blessing of Almighty God'. The last phrase was unusual for the times, but Havelock had deliberately chosen it.

Just short of Cawnpore his force was on the verge of defeat, held up by heavy gunfire which caused one regiment to waver. As Harry Havelock, the General's eldest son, described the moment of danger, in a letter home: 'It was the turning point of the day and of our campaign. If we had receded one inch not a hundred of us would ever have got back to the shelter of the walls of Allahabad. I must confess that I felt absolutely *sick* with apprehension, and if I looked calm, I never was before and hope never to be again in such a funk in my life. The enemy thought we were lying down from fear.

'Just then the dear old Governor rode bareheaded to the front, spoke half a dozen words – and at the magic of his example up sprang the line, and advanced. And that advance *saved India*.'

Havelock had seen the waver. He had sent an urgent message to the guns but realised he could not wait. He rode round, Harry said, to the front of the prostrate Highlanders, calmly smiling while bullets and shells whizzed and whined within an inch of his face. 'With increasing darkness the shadows lengthened,' wrote Major North, 'which added to the imposing effect of the rebel line. General Havelock, who had just had his horse shot under him, now appeared boldly riding a hack, the only man who dared raise his head – so close and thick was the fire that rained upon us.' He reined up with his back to the fire, facing the line, and spoke clearly, firmly and without a trace of excitement, and still smiling: 'The longer you look at it men, the less you will like it. Rise up. The brigade will advance, left battalion leading.'

'Hardly were the words spoken,' wrote North, 'when

a feeling of confidence inspired every breast and displaced the overwhelming weight and uncertainty and doubt engendered by inaction. Up sprang our thinned line ... the odds being fearfully against us. But to this act of intrepidity in our general his troops worthily responded.'

In the action which followed, Harry himself won the Victoria Cross by an act of incredible bravery.

On 17 July Havelock entered Cawnpore too late. Nana Sahib, the rebel leader, had massacred his prisoners and thrown their bodies down a well. When Havelock's soldiers found the well and the bloodstained room of butchery, they were maddened. Only his firmness prevented a ghastly revenge on the Cawnpore inhabitants. He promptly bought up all looted wines and spirits. Otherwise, 'I should scarcely have a sober soldier in camp'; there had been drunkenness enough already.

He forced the Ganges and pressed on towards besieged Lucknow. His fifteen hundred men fought four more battles against overwhelming odds. 'I have fought seven fights with the enemy and by God's blessing have beat him in every one. But', he added, 'things are in a most perilous state.' Every casualty mattered, for he had no reserves, they were in hostile country and Lucknow's need was pressing. On 31 July, to the Lucknow garrison's despair, the victorious Havelock was forced to retire and await reinforcements. His column had no more than a thousand men still fit, and even they looked 'ragged, woebegone, bearded ruffians'. Havelock shared every hardship and often slept on the ground with his horse saddled beside him. His column, with Lucknow, was being sacrificed on the altar of Government ineptitude.

In September, back at Cawnpore, he was joined by fresh troops under Outram, his senior officer. With memorable chivalry Outram waived his rights of command, to give Havelock the glory of relieving Lucknow. This action was splendid but unwise, for Outram continued to advise (and expected to be listened to), sometimes against Havelock's better judgment.

They pressed on together. At the end of September they fought their way into the besieged Lucknow residency, after violent battles. 'Rarely has a commander,' wrote the Governor-General in a General Order, 'been so fortunate as to relieve by his success as many aching hearts, or to reap so rich a reward of gratitude as will deservingly be offered to Brigadier-General Havelock and his gallant band, wherever their triumph shall be known.'

His force was too weak either to withdraw the garrison or drive off the enemy. But though the siege continued, his action and earlier victories, his personal courage and the endurance of his troops had made his name a household word.

He was promoted major-general and knighted. His wife at home found herself suddenly launched into high society. Not least, Victorian England revelled in the glamour of the 'old puritan soldier', 'that preaching, praying, psalm-singing man', a latter-day Cromwell or Hampden. At sixty-three Havelock had come into his own.

He never lived to enjoy his glory. For nearly two months Havelock and Outram held on in Lucknow. In November Sir Colin Campbell arrived with a strong force to relieve them. The garrison broke out to join him, and while the battle was still raging the three generals met on the outskirts. Havelock, although already ill, had run twenty-five yards under fire to greet Campbell. A week later, worn out by his efforts and struck down by dysentery, he died, 'happy and contented', in a common soldier's tent, not knowing that the news of his death would throw

Britain into national mourning, and greatly advance many of the religious and reforming causes he had pioneered.

In Lucknow, the night before he died, he lay in his one faded uniform. He scarcely slept though suffering little, and his mind was clear. When the thirst was bad he would call and Harry would bring him water, his father smiling weakly, abundantly happy that they were one in heart and spirit. Daylight came. Havelock called faintly, 'Harry, Harry.' As Harry answered, Havelock looked up, smiling. 'Harry,' he said, 'see how a Christian can die!'

10. Sir Herbert Edwardes, 1819–1868
HE TAMED THE TRIBES

Early in 1847 a young British subaltern of the Bengal Infantry set out on a task to quell the stoutest. Lieutenant Herbert Edwardes had been ordered from Peshawar, the dust-ridden frontier town of the Punjab at the foot of the wild Khyber Pass, to bring peace and government to the Bannu Valley.

Bannu was a paradise of nature, but its people were lawless, 'robbers and murderers from their cradles'. They butchered one another and had refused to pay taxes to their overlords, the Sikhs, whom the British had lately conquered. As Edwardes said, they 'wear arms as we wear clothes, and use them as we use knives and forks', while the Sikh soldiers with him would be looking for nothing but loot.

Edwardes, a vivacious young man with laughing eyes, who could as easily turn from soldiering to writing essays and verses, and who had a remarkable capacity for friendship, was not afraid. He had fought in the recent war with distinction, but courage of a different kind was needed now. His fearlessness sprang from his faith. He believed that it was God who was sending him to heal a tortured land. And he knew that his Saviour was beside him as the column toiled upwards, beneath forbidding rocks and over turbulent streams, with the hot Indian sun above.

When Edwardes reached the Valley, some of the Bannus fled to the hills, other stayed in sullen fear. Soon they were astonished by this lone Englishman whose strange power belied his youthful face. They saw looting suppressed by instant punishment. When, suspicious and diffident, they brought complaints and arguments, Edwardes heard them with patience, good humour, and kindness. When they tried to deceive him, he knew it instinctively and would punish them as he punished the Sikhs. Warring chiefs were soon sitting together beside him; four hundred forts were destroyed at his word; even the taxes were paid. 'In my little sphere,' he wrote, 'I gave my whole soul for the establishment of that vast and priceless blessing, peace.' And early each morning, in the quiet of his tent, Edwardes would lay all his problems, dangers, and hopes before his Lord.

The pacification of Bannu was the first of many achievements which brought Edwardes resounding fame – crushing rebellion at Multan, bringing peace and prosperity to the intractable tribes of Jalandhar, and negotiating in the face of official opposition and disbelief a treaty of alliance with the powerful Amir of Afghanistan. But good administration was not enough. Edwardes' greatest desire was to see the fanatical Muslims of the hills and the Hindus and Sikhs of the plains united at the foot of the Cross. As agent of the government he was forbidden to preach, but when a fellow officer, Colonel Martin, approached him as Commissioner of Peshawar for leave to found a mission, Edwardes gave wholehearted support, and in 1855 was able to introduce the first two missionaries of the Border Mission and see the first native Christian baptized.

Edwardes was one of that remarkable band of unashamed Christians who transformed the tyrannized, blood-drenched Sikh kingdom into the prosperous and contented British Punjab. The gay Henry Lawrence, 'father' and master of them all, who was killed in the siege of Lucknow; his wife Honoria, who rode with them, worked, prayed, and endured with them; his brother John, afterwards Viceroy, dour and severe but earnest in his faith; young Nicholson, who died a hero's death at Delhi – the basis of their life was faith in Christ. 'This morning he read a chapter of the Bible to George and me,' wrote Edwardes of Henry Lawrence at Lucknow during a visit a bare month before the Mutiny, 'and then he prayed with great earnestness.... The whole prayer was for peace and forbearance and good-will and the help of Christ himself in our whole lives.'

By their Christian characters such administrations did much to prove to Eastern races the love and power of Christ. They would have done more. 'The greatest and oldest and saddest of India's wants', said Edwardes, 'is religious truth, a revelation of the real nature of the God whom for ages she has been ignorantly worshipping.' Edwardes and his friends recognized that the government itself could not attempt to convert, but they believed the accepted policy of absolute religious neutrality to be harmful. Had the Bible been taught in the native schools, false views of Christianity would not have spread, the Mutiny might never have occurred, and India would steadily have yielded to Christ. 'An open Bible,' pleaded Edwardes, 'put it in your schools, stand avowedly as a Christian government.' Only then would India be truly fitted for freedom, 'leavened with Christianity'.

When the storm came in 1857, the Punjab stood firm. The Afghans abided by Edwardes' treaty and took no advantage of British troubles. At Peshawar Edwardes and Nicholson boldly disarmed the mutinous regiments. 'If Peshawar goes,' a loyal Sikh sirdar had said, 'the whole Punjab will be rolled up in rebellion.' And had the Punjab revolted, all Bengal might have fallen.

Yet it is not the statesmanship of Sir Herbert Edwardes that is relevant today so much as his witness to a layman's influence for Christ in the ordinary course of his calling. 'I never knew anyone so bold in confessing Christ as Edwardes was', said a brother officer on the Frontier. 'Many of us felt as he did but we had not the courage to avow it.'

'This great country India,' Edwardes would say, 'has been put into our hands that we may give it light.' Edwardes' words are still a challenge: 'Other dependent races in other parts of the world are equally in heathen darkness. If we are looking for the coming of our Lord again upon the earth, we surely should bestir ourselves to gather in as much of his inheritance as we can while time is left.'

Edwardes was barely forty-nine when he died, on sick leave in Scotland in 1869. 'Jesus only.... Triumphant Jesus,' were his last words, 'I am quite happy. I trust entirely to Jesus and I couldn't do more if I lived a thousand years!'

The news was telegraphed to India and carried into the hills. An old, bent Muslim heard it and found his way to a missionary. 'I lived with Sir Herbert all the years he has been in India,' said the old servant, 'and I followed him everywhere. My sahib was *such* a good man. He can't have made a mistake in his religion. Will you teach me his religion? for I should like to believe what he believed.'

11. Thomas 'Stonewall' Jackson, 1824-1863
STONEWALL

One Saturday evening late in April 1861 Major Thomas Jackson, thirty-seven-year-old professor at the Virginia Military Institute, Lexington, was with his wife preparing the next day's Sunday School lesson.

All at Lexington knew that the brilliant artillery professor, quiet, strong-willed, rather reserved with a hint of smouldering fires within, was a firm and thoroughgoing Christian. As a hotheaded young lieutenant in the Mexican War of 1847-8, he had found himself serving with a commander who held Bible readings for officers and men. Ever since, Jackson's faith had been as obvious as his military skill, and his hour's Bible study as regular as the daily cold bath.

Every Sunday for years he had held a Sunday School for local blacks. But this Sunday in 1861 would be different; Virginia, with the other seceded States, was on the verge of invasion by President Lincoln's Army. To Jackson, as to all Virginians of 1861, the issue of the American Civil War was not slavery, which he detested and believed would die a natural death, but the right of his native State to decide its own future, in or out of the Union. He hated war: 'I have seen enough of it,' he had said a few days earlier, 'to make me look upon it as the sum of all evils,' and in the local churches he had organised prayer meetings for peace. But once war was declared, 'All I am and I have is at the service of my country – Virginia.'

On the Sunday morning at dawn the Jacksons were knocked up by a telegraph man who delivered a message ordering Jackson to bring the cadet battalion of the Institute at once to Richmond, the Confederate capital. The morning was a bustle of preparation and parades; at

Jackson's request divine service was held and at one o'clock the battalion marched away in enthusiasm to the war. A few days later Jackson was made a Colonel and received an independent command at Harper's Ferry on the Virginian frontier. 'Little one,' he wrote to his wife, 'you must not expect to hear from me very often; but don't be concerned about your husband, for our kind Heavenly Father will give every needful aid.'

In July 1861 the first great battle of the war took place at Bull Run. So confident were the Federals that ladies had come out from Washington, not far away, to see the Southerners whipped. Jackson, now a Brigadier-General, was ordered in haste from Harper's Ferry and by forced marches arrived on the field just before the action. His brigade was placed in reserve. The battle developed hot and furious, the wide plain shrouded with smoke and dust, and the warm summer air filled with the whine of shells and the screams of wounded horses and men. Slowly the dark blue masses of the Federals edged on into the crumbling first line of the grey-jacketed Confederate army. Jackson, as ordered, waited behind a low hill, the brigade enduring a heavy fire from the Federal guns. Suddenly a dusty and sweat-covered general came galloping up from the front crying to Jackson, 'General, they are beating us back.' 'Then, sir, we will give them the bayonet,' replied Jackson coolly, and led his men to the brow of the hill. The other general rode down again into the smoke and noise, and the medley of broken regiments retreating under the hail of Federal bullets and shells. 'Look!' he shouted encouragingly, 'there is Jackson standing like a stone wall! Rally behind the Virginians!' Jackson's brigade advanced invincibly; the day was saved and the Federals retreated in disorder, to cause panic among their light-hearted ladies.

Their nickname stuck; henceforth Jackson was Stonewall Jackson. Yet his secret was simple. Three days after the battle an officer asked, 'How is it you can keep so cool and appear so utterly insensible to danger in such a storm of shell and bullets?' Jackson 'instantly became grave and reverential in his manner,' related the officer, 'and answered in a low tone of great earnestness, 'Captain, my religious belief teaches me to feel as safe in battle as in bed. God has fixed the time for my death. I do not concern myself about that, but to be always ready, no matter when it may overtake me ... That is the way all men should live, and then all would be equally brave.'

To Jackson the battle of Bull Run was just an incident in his daily duty and witness. When the anxious inhabitants of Lexington were crowding round the post office waiting for news, an envelope in Jackson's writing was handed to the pastor, who exclaimed, 'Ah, now we shall know the facts.' He opened the letter. It was dated the day after the battle. All it said was, 'My dear Pastor – in my tent last night, after a fatiguing day's service, I remembered that I had failed to send you my contribution to our Sunday School. Enclosed you will find my cheque for that object ...'

In the grim two years that followed, as North America became deeply scarred by the bloodiest and most grievous conflict that the world had ever seen, Stonewall Jackson rose to be the hero of the South, second only in leadership to General Robert E. Lee, a man of equally deep and humble Christian faith. Jackson proved a master of war, a supreme strategist and tactician. In the Shenandoah Valley he operated with great effect, his flanking marches surprising his enemies by their speed and vigour. In the greater battlefields of the East, later in the war, he caused Lincoln and his generals more fears and alarms than any other Southern commander.

'He is tall, handsome and powerfully built but thin,'

said an English visitor who reached his camp one pouring wet evening; 'The general, who is indescribably simple and unaffected in all his ways, took off my wet overcoat with his own hands, made up the fire, brought wood for me to put my feet on to keep them warm while my boots were drying. At the dinner hour we went out and joined the members of his staff. At this meal the general said grace in a fervent, quiet manner which struck me very much ...'

Jackson was a rigid disciplinarian, knowing that discipline was the key both to victory and the happiness of his troops, many of whom were wild volunteers from frontier homesteads. He expected instant obedience, and could flare up in anger if a subordinate was slack or refractory; he would give his orders in abrupt, laconic phrases, sucking a lemon (he hated to be without a lemon) and throwing up his left hand in a characteristic gesture to emphasise his points.

He drove men hard, but his unfailing courtesy to the most junior private or rawest recruit, and his care for both officers and rankers earned him their devotion and worship. Nor did he care only for their bodies: years after the war a New York banker was tramping the wilds of the Shenandoah Valley with a former Confederate general; they were obliged to put up for supper and the night in a small isolated railway shanty. When their host came in and took his seat at the head of the table, 'a bear out of the woods could hardly have been rougher, with his unshaven hair and unkempt beard. He answered to the dark type of border ruffian, and his appearance suggested the dark deeds that might be done here in secret in the forest gloom.

'Imagine the astonishment of the travellers,' related the banker, 'when this rough backwoodsman rapped on the table and bowed his head. And such a prayer! Never did I hear a petition that more evidently came from the heart. It was so simple, so reverent, so tender, so full of humility and penitence as well as thankfulness.' The banker whispered in awe to the general, 'Who can he be?' 'He must be one of Stonewall Jackson's old soldiers,' replied the general. 'Were you in the war?' they asked the backwoodsman. 'Oh yes,' he said with a smile, 'I was out with old Stonewall.'

Stonewall Jackson looked on all life as a spiritual responsibility. His work lay among the horrors of war but this made a quiet but uncompromising witness all the more important; those committed to him were living in the shadow of death. Whenever he and his staff were not actually in action he held morning and evening prayers at headquarters. In his haversack in battle were always three books: the Bible, Napoleon's *Maxims of War* and Webster's Dictionary (his spelling was shaky). And all that he did or planned was prayed over. 'The General is a great man for prayin',' said his faithful black servant, Jim. 'He pray night and mornin' – all times. But when I see him git up several times in the night an' go off and pray, *den I know there is goin' to be somethin' to pay*, an' I go right away and pack his haversack!'

'He certainly has had adulation enough to spoil him,' wrote a great friend in the winter of 1862 after a year and a half of war, 'but it seems not to affect or harm him at all. He is the same humble, dependent Christian, desiring to give God all the glory, looking to Him alone for a blessing and not thinking of himself at all.' 'I am so thankful to our ever-kind Heavenly Father,' Jackson wrote to his wife at this time, 'He continually showers blessings on me ... My desire is to live entirely and unreservedly to God's glory. Pray, my darling, that I may so live.'

In the early months of 1863 the opposing armies were

in winter quarters on either side of the Rappahannock river. The Stonewall Brigade (which was now part of Jackson's wider command) had built a large log church in the Confederate camp and during the long winter evenings the army listened earnestly to the foremost preachers of the South, expounding in simplicity the gospel of peace, while the pinewood torches flared in the wall-brackets. 'And,' said one of the chaplains as he described the scene, 'perhaps the most supremely happy of the gathered thousands is Stonewall Jackson.'

On April 29th 1863 the Federals crossed the river and on May 1st the battle of Chancellorsville began. Nearly two hundred thousand men were locked in conflict for five days, the Confederates outnumbered by over two to one. After nightfall at the close of the second day, when the scales were already tipping in the Confederates' favour, Stonewall Jackson with his staff and some regimental officers rode forward in the darkness to reconnoitre during a lull in the battle. 'General, you should not expose yourself so much,' said one of the officers. 'There is no danger, sir,' said Jackson, 'the enemy is routed.' He had reached a hollow, which happened to be some eighty yards in front of one of his detachments. A shot rang out in the forest and was followed by a staccato of renewed firing. Some of the regimental officers turned bridle and galloped back to rejoin their units. The Confederate detachment, alarmed at seeing strange horsemen riding towards them and unable in the dark to distinguish the uniform, fired a volley; several of the officers fell dead – and three of the bullets hit Jackson beyond.

His horse plunged in terror into the forest, but Jackson brought it under control and turned back to his lines. An officer caught the reins and Jackson fell off the saddle into his arms. 'General, are you much hurt?' 'I think

I am, and all my wounds are from my own men.' The battle was now fully joined again. 'The air seemed to be alive with the shriek of shells and the whistling of bullets,' recalled one of the officers standing with him, 'horses riderless and mad with fright dashed in every direction; hundreds left the ranks and hurried to the rear, and the groans of the wounded and dying mingled with the wild shouts of others to be led again to the assault. Almost fainting as he was from loss of blood, desperately wounded, and in the midst of this awful uproar, Jackson's heart was unshaken,' and he was able to prevent retreat.

When at last they got him to a dressing station his condition was grievous, and amputation of his shattered arm did little to help. The next morning when the first stage of the battle had ended in Confederate success, Lee sent a message telling the wounded Jackson that the victory was due solely to him. 'General Lee is very kind,' murmured Jackson when they read the message, 'but he should give the praise to God.' He lingered on for four more days; modern surgery would have saved him. Two months later, at Gettysburg, the tide turned against the South. 'If I had had Jackson at Gettysburg,' said Lee afterwards, 'I should have won, and a complete victory would have established Southern independence.'

After the Civil War the re-united nation claimed Jackson as part of the heroic heritage of the whole USA. But Jackson saw himself as no more than a man doing his duty to the country he loved, secure in his trust in the Saviour. His life was a stirring call to those whose Christian faith must be witnessed, not from pulpit or rostrum but in the hard paths of a profession. If such will direct their lives by God's word, steeping even the most secular actions in prayer as Stonewall Jackson did on the fields of war, they will, like him, point many to Christ.

ASSIST ME
TO PROCLAIM

12. Brownlow North, 1810-1874
RAKE'S PROGRESS

The fashionable mothers of Cheltenham were in despair. The Earl of Guilford's heir had proposed to no less than nineteen young ladies and was accepted by them all. Brownlow North, in this winter of 1827, was only seventeen but his skill at dancing, brilliant horsemanship and zest for life – to say nothing of his prospect of a peerage – made him irresistible. Fortunately his mother had a strong sense of humour and by the end of the season had disentangled her son, leaving him free to fall in love properly with an Irish girl the following summer and marry her before he was twenty.

Brownlow North was well up to the mark as a George IV buck. At twelve he was a constant smoker. At sixteen, sent on the Grand Tour, he won at écarté from his tutor all the money allowed for expenses, and thereafter did what he liked. He grew up a heavy drinker and constant gambler. Immensely strong, he was a hard rider with the hounds, a tireless walker, a crack short – and hopelessly extravagant. His uncle the Earl, a parson, considered his nephew a disgrace and when the childless countess died he promptly announced that he would marry again, in the hopes of cutting him out of the succession. He chose a woman twenty-five years his junior and soon had three sons.

Brownlow, no longer rich, dumped his young family at Boulogne and tried his luck with the Spanish Pretender in the Carlist Wars, and then settled in Scotland where living was cheap. He became a local legend for his daring rides and heavy wagers, his jolly nature and generosity to his friends, and his addiction to the bottle.

But Brownlow North's mother knew how to pray. She had taught him as a child the truth of Christ; nothing could dissuade her from praying for him. And when he was nearly thirty-three it seemed as if prayer would be answered. He was staying near Huntly in Aberdeenshire for the shooting, and received an invitation to dine with the Duchess of Gordon, a woman of courageous faith. North was placed beside his hostess. The ducal servants were handing the dishes and the large party of ladies and gentlemen were in animated conversation. Suddenly North said quietly, with 'much gravity', 'Duchess, what should a man do who has often prayed to God and never been answered?' The Duchess was silent a moment. 'I lifted up my heart to God,' she recalled, 'to teach me what to say. I looked him quietly in the face and said, so as not to be overheard by others, "Ye ask, and receive not, because ye ask amiss, that ye may consume it upon your lusts." His countenance changed, he became very greatly moved, and was very quiet during the evening, and thanked me ere he left.'

Shortly afterwards the near-death of one of his sons, and a tract sent by the Duchess, impressed him further. With a vigour which surprised his friends he suddenly determined to go to Oxford and read for Holy Orders. Brownlow North became a changed man, conscious of his sins and striving manfully to combat them and to behave as an ordinand should. 'The house,' he said years afterwards, 'was swept and garnished – but *empty*.'

After two years at Magdalen, Oxford, and the promise of a curacy in Buckinghamshire he received a sudden summons from his prospective Bishop. He found the Bishop with a letter in front of him, packed with unsavoury and accurate details of North's past life. 'Mr. North,' said the Bishop, 'if I were in your position and you in mine, would you ordain me?' North thought for a moment of his past, and of the weary struggle of the present, and replied, 'My Lord, I would not.'

The disappointment was too much. By the following autumn, 1845, Brownlow North was back in Scotland making up for lost time at the card table and on the moors, thoroughly ashamed of his absurd tinkering with religion. As if to emphasise his outlook he would often, on a Sunday morning, make a point of driving past the kirk-going crowds with fishing rods and luncheon basket prominently displayed, off for a day on the river.

When friends of his mother tried to warn him he would courteously but firmly reject them. 'To die the death of the righteous,' he wrote in reply to extracts from a worthy sermon, 'we must live the life of the righteous, dear Auntie, and I am not prepared for that yet.'

For nine years more his mother, now of great age, continued to pray for his conversion.

The grouse season of 1854 began like any other. Brownlow North had again taken the Dallas moors in Aberdeenshire, and at forty-four was still a crack shot. The weeks passed, and as the last leaves were falling from the trees Mrs. North noticed that her husband was sometimes strangely silent. One of his mother's friends, with whom he dined, heard him murmur 'Sometimes I think I shall give it all up.' But these depressions soon blew away and life continued as before.

One evening in the second week of November Brownlow North was sitting in the billiard room after dinner playing cards and smoking a cigar. Violent pains suddenly struck him. Dropping his cigar he gasped to his son, 'I am a dead man, take me upstairs.' They helped him to his room and he threw himself on his bed. 'My first thought then was, "Now, what will my forty-four years of following the devices of my own heart profit me? In a few minutes I shall be in hell." At that moment I felt constrained to pray, but it was merely the prayer of a coward, a cry for mercy. I was not sorry for what I had done, but I was afraid of the punishment of my sin.'

The housemaid hurried in to light the fire, while her master lay groaning on the bed. Unwittingly, she had a part to play in that night's work. 'Though I did not believe at that time,' continues North's account, 'that I had ten minutes to live, and knew that there was no possible hope for me but in the mercy of God, and that if I did not seek that mercy I could not expect to have it, yet such was the nature of my heart that it was a balance with me, a thing to turn this way or that, I could not tell how, whether I should wait till that woman left the room or whether I should fall on my knees and cry for mercy in her presence.'

The girl struck a match, and the fire blazed up. At that moment she heard a movement behind her and turned round. To her astonishment her pagan master was on his knees – and praying aloud. 'I believe it was a turning point with me,' said North in after years. 'I believe that if I had at that time resisted the Holy Ghost it would have been once too often.'

The next day he told his guests that he had given his heart to Christ. 'He seemed as if just risen from a long illness, and very gentle and subdued in manner.' Family prayers were instituted forthwith, and his dissolute friends informed that 'I am, I trust by the grace of God, a changed man'. His aged mother, when he went to see her, said, 'Brownlow, God is not only able to save you but to make you more conspicuous for good than ever you were for evil.'

The past now caught up with him. Weary weeks and months of spiritual conflict assailed him. Temptations, doubts as to his salvation, the suspicion of those who might have helped but doubted his sincerity, cravings for the alcohol which he had abjured, all this put him through the fire. He read nothing but the Bible. His wife

113

would hear him groaning aloud and find him rolling on the carpet, agonising in prayer. He would listen greedily to the exposition of Scripture in kirk. 'I had scarcely reached the pulpit,' said one visiting preacher, 'when I was arrested by his appearance. There was the exhibition of such force of character, such a strength of will, the lines of a life for self and evil, an air of unrest, and a hungry look of soul, as with lowering brows he looked into the speaker and listened to every utterance. When I came down from the pulpit I asked, "Who is that remarkable person? He looks as if he had been a servant of evil and yet he looks as if yielding wholly to God."'

At last, after six months of stress North realised, late one night when he could not sleep and had turned back to his Bible and was studying Romans, that Christ had done all that was needed, that a simple trust in him was sufficient for life and death.

With peace in his heart Brownlow North was happy again, with a contentment deeper than he had dreamed. The days passed pleasantly in reading and praying. He sometimes felt that he should not keep in his good news yet to do anything seemed impossible. He began to wonder whether he ought to give away a few tracts but feared ridicule, until at length he disappeared into the most distant part of Elgin, where he was living, and offered a tract to the first person he saw, an old woman, who to his astonishment accepted it without laughing at him. Next he tried visiting sick cottagers to read them the Bible, screwing himself up to stomach the 'nasty smells in poor people's houses'. As he put it, 'God took Brownlow North from his comfortable seat beside the fire, where he was reading some religious book, and crucified him at the bedside of some poor, bed-ridden woman.'

Not long after, a dying girl besought him to speak to

114

her father about his soul, 'for father is a bad man.' North had never tried to speak his own words before, but the result was so startling that soon the cottage sickrooms crowded with neighbours whenever he was seen approaching, and he found himself holding informal meetings every night of the week.

More was to come. On a visit to London he was asked by a young Scotsman to come and hear him street-preaching in the grimy slums behind King's Cross. The young man was virtuous but dull. The roughs cheerfully expressed their boredom in blasphemy so choice that it staggered even Brownlow North. Then one of them called out, 'We'll hear that stout man with the dark eyes.' Unwilling enough, in such company, North began to speak. To his amazement his words seemed to grip them. When at last he stopped, exhausted and short of breath, they cried out, 'Go on, sir! We want to hear more.' 'Sir,' said an old man, as they finally turned away, 'your words should be written in letters of gold.'

From that small beginning Brownlow North rose in a few months to be Scotland's most popular lay preacher, filling churches, making the most unlikely men and women concerned about their souls and bringing them to Christ. The public astonishment was great. Newspapers suggested it was done for a wager. One acquaintance, thanking him for a sermon, said, 'The last time I saw you you were lying on your back in the hunting field, your horse rolling over you.' A minister who had known him since youth caught his name in a religious paper: 'Brownlow North preaching the gospel! Did my eyes deceive me? What could be the meaning of his preaching? Was it some mad or impious jest?'

One night, as North was about to enter the pulpit in a highland town, a man handed him a letter, asking him to read it before he preached. The letter reminded him in no uncertain terms of some of the more repulsive excesses of his past and ended, 'How dare you pray and speak to the people this evening when you are such a vile sinner?' North mounted the pulpit and the service began. At sermon time he announced his text, looked down at the sea of expectant faces – and read out the letter. The hush was intense. He spoke again: 'All that is here said is true. It is a correct picture of the degraded sinner I once was. And oh – how wonderful must the grace be that could raise me up from such a death in trespasses and sins and make me what I appear before you tonight, a vessel of mercy, one who knows that all his past sins have been cleansed away through the atoning blood of the Lamb of God. It is of his redeeming love that I now have to tell you ...'

'I'll tell you what I am,' he would say, 'I am a man who had been at the brink of the bottomless pit and has looked in, and as I see many of you going down to that pit I am here to "hollo" you back, and warn you of your danger. I am here as the chief of sinners, saved by grace, to tell you that the grace which has saved me can surely save you.'

'He is as destitute of pulpit airs as when he was a leader of fashion and a keen hand at the turf,' reported an Edinburgh paper, 'but in spite of his short shooting-coat, and the negligent tie and the gold eye-glass dangling on the breast of his tightly buttoned coat, there is tremendous energy and force in his preaching.' The more staid of the Kirk elders were somewhat shocked, but the hungry crowds pressed in to hear. He would begin 'with a low, faltering voice; but before he has got half way through the opening prayer his breast begins to heave with a convulsive sobbing, and the tears stream over his cheeks ... Edinburgh is flocking in its thousands to see the strange sight of a godless man of sport and fashion transformed into a fiery, weeping messenger of the Cross.' It was emotional, but it met the need of the hour.

And so he went on, year after year, an evangelist to all classes in Scotland and to many parts of England and Ireland, a key figure in the Revival of 1859 and a precursor of the greater Moody to come.

Twenty years almost to the day he was given, dying in November 1874. 'He preached the gospel with singular power,' they inscribed on his tomb, 'and was greatly honoured in winning souls to Jesus.'

But in the fly-leaf of his Bible was his own estimate: 'B. North, a man whose sins crucified the Son of God.'

13. D. L. Moody, 1837-1899;
Ira D. Sankey, 1840-1908
MEN OF GOD, MAN OF SONG

In the summer of 1873 two Americans landed at Liverpool for an evangelistic campaign. Moody and Sankey landed utterly obscure. They found no arrangements and no funds. Yet when they left Britain two years later they had Scotland and England at the feet of Christ.

D. L. Moody and Ira D. Sankey emerged from very different backgrounds and came to Christian service in different ways.

Moody was a countryman from New England. As a young man he emigrated to Chicago, having 'gone West to grow up with the country'. By 1860 he was a successful travelling salesman in a shoe business, his lack of education being outweighed by the force of his personality and almost incredible energy. He was on the way to becoming a millionaire. However, much of his time was absorbed by Christian work in the roughest part of the city. He would drum up the boys and girls and tell them stories of Jesus, his powerful voice conquering the wildest whoops of the slum lads. Soon he had the largest and most lively Sunday School in the slums, with many faithful teachers.

It was one of these, 'a pale, delicate young man,' who staggered into Moody's office on a hot June day, and threw himself down on a box.

This teacher was tubercular, and Moody was sorry to learn that he was now leaving Chicago to go home and die. The man looked so upset that Moody asked the trouble: 'You are not afraid of death? And you are ready to go?'

'I am anxious for my class,' he replied. 'I have failed. Not one of my girls has been led to Jesus.'

Moody recalled those frivolous girls. He offered to hire a cab and take the man to their homes.

They drove into the slums. At the first tenement a girl listened wide-eyed as her teacher told her he was dying and begged her to put her trust in Christ. Then 'he prayed as I never heard before,' and the girl promised to 'settle the question then and there'. They called on three others, until the man's energy gave out.

Ten days later the teacher again climbed Moody's stairs. This time he was radiant. 'The last one of my class has yielded herself to Christ. The great vital question of their lives is settled. They have accepted my Saviour. My work is done and I am going home.'

That night Moody gave a tea for all the girls to say farewell. After a last hymn had been sung and the two men had prayed, Moody 'was just rising from my knees, when one of the class began to pray for her dying teacher'. Moody listened astonished at the faltering extempore prayer of a girl who had been a scoffer. Others followed. As Moody listened to these fervent, artless prayers his business ambitions died. He must spend his years as the teacher had spent the days – if courage and faith could make the break.

The struggle lasted three months. 'It was a terrible battle. But oh,' he would say in after years, 'how many times I thanked God's will.'

Then came the American Civil War. It turned Moody into both a homespun preacher and a skilled personal worker. Beyond all else he became an evangelist. Tending the wounded and dying after the terrible battles, he could not let things drift. He must make Christ plain then and there as shattered boys begged: 'Chaplain, help me to die.'

D. L. Moody was led step by step towards his life work, learning all the time. He never attended college (though later he brought education to hundreds), yet he had great instructors, such as an ex-pickpocket, little Harry Moorhouse from Lancashire who taught him to preach the *love* of God. And a converted butcher, Henry Varley, who on Moody's first visit to Britain in 1867, let slip the immortal words: 'Moody, the world has yet to see what God will do with a man fully consecrated to him.' Moody resolved, after turning the remark over and over in his mind: 'By the Holy Spirit in me *I'll* be that man.'

By 1870, happily married with a small family, Moody was becoming known in the Middle West as an evangelist and organiser, with his own church, which had grown up haphazardly round his Sunday School. But he lacked a singer. That year he went to a YMCA convention at Indianapolis. Unknown to him, another delegate was there, called Ira D. Sankey.

Sankey, three years younger than Moody, was the son of a bank president and State Senator in Pennsylvania, and always had about him a faint air of colonnaded bank and senate plush. His baritone voice was untrained but had a natural beauty. He gave much of his spare time to singing solos at Christian functions. During the Civil War, when on sentry duty at night in the front line, a Confederate soldier had him in his sights and was about to shoot. Sankey, unaware how close to death he was, began to sing the man's favourite hymn. The Confederate put down his rifle.

At the Indianapolis convention in 1870 which Sankey attended, Moody was announced to lead an early prayer meeting one morning at seven. Sankey, a fastidious dresser, arrived late, every hair of his handsome muttonchop whiskers in place. A windy delegate was praying. Sankey's neighbour, a Presbyterian minister from his own county, whispered, 'The singing here has been abominable. I wish you would start up something when that man stops praying, if he ever does.'

Sankey began *There is a fountain filled with blood*. The congregation joined. The meeting moved with pace.

The Presbyterian introduced Sankey to Moody. Moody sized him up in a second.

'Where are you from? Are you married? What is your business?'

'New Castle, Pennsylvania. I am married, two children. In Government service, Revenue.'

'You will have to give that up.'

Sankey was amazed. 'What for?' he exclaimed.

'To come to Chicago to help me in my work.'

To Sankey's protest that he could not abandon his business Moody retorted: 'You must. I have been looking for you for the last eight years.'

Sankey was aware that the singing of another delegate had been 'a revelation to me of the marvellous power there was in a simple gospel hymn when the singer put his whole heart and soul into it. I shall never forget how the great gathering was thrilled by the wonderful pathos of the singer's voice. It was an entirely different style of singing from that which I had so often heard in many churches where I attended. Every word could be distinctly heard in the remotest part of the building.' There had arisen 'a great desire in my own heart that I might some day be able to use my voice in like manner.'

Sankey left Indianapolis undecided: 'I presume I prayed one way and Mr. Moody prayed another. However, it took him only six months to pray me out of business.'

When Moody and Sankey landed in Liverpool in 1873 to find no arrangements, organization, or funds (partly through Moody's fault) they took up a half-answered invitation from a chemist in York, where their unprepared mission in a most unlikely city met such success that they were invited to Newcastle. The real breakthrough came at Edinburgh at the turn of the year. Moody's unconventional preaching and Sankey's singing reached right to the rather frozen heart of a strongly religious nation.

All Scotland was stirred by Moody and Sankey during 1874, and out of their Scottish campaign came Sankey's best known song, *There were Ninety and Nine*. Sankey saw the poem, then unknown, in a newspaper in the train between Glasgow and Edinburgh, and cut it out. Two days later, in Edinburgh, they had been preaching on The Good Shepherd. Moody asked Sankey to sing an appropriate solo. He thought of the poem, but it had no tune. He felt an urge to use it, took it out and laid it on the organ. 'I lifted my heart in prayer, asking God to help me so to sing that people might hear and understand. I struck the chord of A flat, and began to sing. Note by note the tune was given, which has not been changed from that day to this. As the singing ceased a great sigh seemed to go up from the meeting, and I knew that the song had reached the hearts of my Scottish audience.'

It became a powerful weapon. The well known writer A. C. Benson (author of *Land of Hope and Glory*) recalled a Moody and Sankey meeting which he had attended at Cambridge when he was an undergraduate. He described Sankey as 'an immense bilious man, with black hair, and eyes surrounded by flaccid, pendent, baggy wrinkles – who came forward with an unctuous gesture and took his place at a small harmonium, placed so near the front of the platform that it looked as if both player and instrument must inevitably topple over; it was inexpressibly ludicrous to behold.

'Rolling his eyes in an affected manner, he touched a few simple chords, and then a marvellous transformation came over the room. In a sweet powerful voice, with an exquisite simplicity combined with irresistible emotion, he sang *There were Ninety and Nine*. The man was transfigured. A deathly hush came over the room, and I felt my eyes fill with tears; his physical repulsiveness slipped from him and left a sincere impulsive Christian, whose simple music spoke straight to the soul.'

Moody and Sankey were the men for the hour. By the second half of the nineteenth century steamships had brought the continents nearer. Railways had spread across America and Britain. Horse tramways eased access within cities, which were growing vast through increased mobility, high birthrate and multiplying industries.

Population movement and industrialisation had tended to weaken the churches, especially in the big cities, where people from the countryside or small towns often lost close touch with religion, though almost all were Christians in name and background. There was a need as well as an opening for a man like Moody who could proclaim the name of Christ to many thousands together, working closely with the churches, which reaped the great benefit of his campaigns.

Scotland made Moody and Sankey famous, and when they came at last to London in 1875 they had already taken England by storm as well. The London campaign of 1875, reaching rich and poor, dockers and duchesses, is one of the peaks of English religious history.

Moody and Sankey, more than any others, revived the faith of Victorian England and Scotland. If Moody brought men and women face to face with their sin and with the love of Christ, it was Sankey who prepared their hearts for the message. The meetings were often in exhibition halls or theatres, but Sankey's singing could transform the atmosphere and concentrate the thoughts of the most hardened on the God who sought them.

Sankey diffused England with song. His hymns were sung in churches and mission halls, in drawing rooms, round the piano in workmen's kitchens. Barrel organs ground them out. Errand boys whistled them. 'I heard a boy whistling one of Moody and Sankey's hymns down the street; which made one really feel that one was in England again,' wrote a young lady in the 1870s on returning from abroad. The music halls would parody them or crack jokes ('I am feeling rather Moody today, how are you?' 'Oh, I'm a bit Sankeymonious, I'm afraid') but more often than not the gallery would retaliate by roaring out their favourite hymns until the comedians were driven from the stage.

Sankey without Moody would have been nowhere. Moody without Sankey was great in his own right although he was the first to acknowledge an enormous debt to his handsome and faintly absurd singer. But Sankey fossilised at a certain growth. Moody was learning and climbing to the day of his death.

He grew in vision: a city for Christ, two nations for Christ, the whole wide world for Christ. Although Moody's attempts to reach the Orient were thwarted, his heart enlarged until it encompassed every race, every land.

He was not a polished orator. Moody's English was ungrammatical and his diction Yankee (he said the word Jerusalem in two syllables) but he made the Bible come alive, and by the force of his absorption in Christ made men and women long to know him and feel they must decide for him without delay.

Moody had a great chest, and a short neck behind his big black beard. Gladstone, one of the finest intellects of the age, and a great orator, said to him: 'I wish I had your chest, Mr. Moody.' And Moody shot back: 'I wish I had your head on top of it!' Moody's powerful chest enabled him to reach great crowds before the days of amplifiers. He seemed to be chatting to someone in the eighth row yet could be heard clearly right at the back of a hall holding twelve or fifteen thousand.

'The sermon,' said Sankey, 'that would hold the rapt attention of the most intelligent of his congregation would also be listened to with the same eagerness by the children present. Anyone – everyone – understood what he said. His meaning was clear to every child. It was also convincing to the old. No other preacher ever mastered this art – if anything connected with Mr. Moody may be called an art – of reaching the understanding of the old and young at the same time. His simplicity of language was remarkable. The strong individuality of the man spoke out in every sentence. The beauty of his powerful nature shone in his works.'

Moody had a delightful character. He had a practical, no nonsense air but a marvellous charm and kindness, and a great sense of humour. He was bitterly attacked, and he felt it, but never harboured resentment. 'I made up my mind to keep sweet,' he would say. 'You cannot do any good unless you keep sweet.' If there had been a dispute or misunderstanding, his advice was always: 'Finish it up sweet.'

Moody's sweetness arose not just from his wonderfully happy marriage and family life, but because he soaked himself in the Bible, and was, above all, a man of prayer, and therefore of humility. An elderly evangelist once said to him: 'How glad I am to see the man that God has used to win so many souls to Christ.' Moody replied, 'You say rightly, Uncle John, the man whom God has *used*.' Moody stooped down and picked up a handful of earth and poured it through his fingers. He said: 'There is nothing more than *that* to D. L. Moody, except as God uses him!'

Moody's fame never dimmed, and when he died (it was in the papers the day the news broke of Winston Churchill's escape from the Boers) *The Times* ran a long leader assessing his contribution to British religion.

Moody the evangelist, Moody the founder of institutions, Moody the arch-begger for Christ's sake, who milked the millionaires: through it all he remained unspoiled, a New England farmer at heart, never happier than in his buggy careering across rough pasture, passenger holding on for dear life, smart little 'Nellie Gray' spanking ahead as if life depended on getting D. L. Moody to his destination a couple of minutes quicker.

Yet of all that Moody and Sankey achieved, no episode stirred the hearts of men and women more than the first British campaign of 1873-5. 'Across all the years,' wrote a youthful convert as he looked back in his old age, 'my heart still kindles at the glory of that time. I feel like crying out to the dwindling survivors of that generation; crying out to remind ourselves of that mighty rush and sweep, when all over the land the souls of men were bound before the Lord, like the standing corn in a harvest wind!'

14. Reuben Archer Torrey, 1856-1928
FAILED SUICIDE

In the small hours of a winter's night in the early 1870s a student at Yale lay sleepless and tossing. His mouth was dry from constant smoking, the brandy glass stood empty at the bedside (though he was not drunk that night) and his mind was whirling. He tried to doze, and at once seemed to be back in the ballroom, brighter and more noisy than any, proving once more his skill as a dancer; yet inwardly loathing his very existence. Wide awake again, he cursed himself for his losses at the card table, and then tried to reckon the chance of a heavy win next time he played.

The college clock tolled the quarter: the student began to look to the future. And the future was black. His indulgent father who had poured money into his young pocket and never asked how it went, had suffered severely in the recent New York financial crash. But that was not the trouble. Despite intellectual brilliance and athletic ability the boy – he was only seventeen – felt caught in a cleft of selfishness, aimlessness and self-contempt, with 'life fairly burned out'. Physically, young Americans in the 'seventies matured quickly; he had already been down to the red-light district despite his Christian home. Each time he went he had felt more guilty and now, in the stillness of the night, the burden of guilt seemed crushing.

He could bear it no longer. Wild with despair he threw back the bed clothes and groped his way in the dark toward the washstand. In the washstand was his pistol, 'the weapon that would end the whole miserable business.' A bare few seconds stood between him and an ignominious death. He fumbled around for the pistol. 'For some reason or other I could not find it. I still think it was there.' And then the thought of his mother flashed through his mind – a woman of faith and prayer. A woman who, as he discovered later, was praying for him at that very moment. 'In my awful despair I dropped upon my knees and lifted my heart to God, and I told God that if he would take the burden off my heart I would preach the gospel.'

The student kept his word. Reuben Archer Torrey became the great evangelist of the early 1900s.

Torrey never looked back from the night of his conversion and was soon reading theology, but he felt too scared to be of use. At last he plucked up courage to accost a former dancing partner and ask her if she would become a Christian. After two hours' talk they knelt down and she gave herself to Christ. 'Mr. Sankey has talked to me,' she said as they got up. 'Mr. Williams has talked to me. Dr. Dodd too, but you have helped me more than all of them.' Torrey felt proud. 'Yes,' she went on, 'I thought if Christ could save you after what I knew you used to be, he could save anybody!'

Then came the first test of public speaking. He determined to start at a small prayer meeting. He composed a short address, learnt it by heart, delivered it clinging to a chair-back with sweat pouring down his face, and sat down. At the close of the meeting an old lady came up and sat down. 'It was so touching, your voice trembled so.' And though most speakers start that way Torrey continued in it even when ordained, to a country church in Ohio in 1878. 'It was agony to preach. I was obliged to hold on to something to brace myself up. How happy I used to be every Sunday night. I would say it is over for another week! But one day I learned the lesson that God does not look to me to do the preaching; that it was my privilege to stand up and let him do it. I have had no more dread of the pulpit since then.'

Torrey had much to learn and God taught him in an unexpected but effective way. As a young minister with a wide-awake mind and a voracious appetite for books he was soon engrossed in the exciting new theologians from Germany whom men were calling Higher Critics. Before long he became, as he once put it, 'so wise that I believed so much of the Bible as was wise enough to agree with me.' What is more, he determined to cross the Atlantic and sit at the feet of the great. For a year, in 1882-3, he studied at the universities of Leipzig and Erlangen. Germany, however, had an unusual effect. Torrey abandoned speculations and returned to firm belief 'in the Bible, the whole Bible, as the Word of God: an altogether reliable revelation from God himself of his own character, his will, his purposes; and of man, his nature, his possibilities, his duty, his destiny.' This knowledge of liberalism and its answer, gained when the movement was young, did much to make him, years later, a sure guide and strength when Higher Criticism seemed to be carrying all before it.

Back in America, after hard years as superintendent of a city missionary society in Minneapolis, which tested and deepened his faith, Torrey was called to what seemed would be his life work. D. L. Moody had founded a Bible Institute at Chicago. In September 1889 he invited Torrey to be first Principal. 'The Lord said "Come" and I came,' wrote Torrey the following June, 'I have had many difficulties since I came, some of which seemed insuperable, but the Lord in answer to prayer has overcome them all.'

For over ten years Torrey taught and preached at Chicago. It was work for which he was pre-eminently fitted. 'He was a thinker,' wrote one of his colleagues, 'who probed into the great mysteries of spiritual truth. Combined with his thinking power there was an insatiate desire for truth. He was a man of cool demeanour, who thought and acted with much mathematical precision.' Logical, unemotional, outwardly severe, he imparted to term after term of students an unrivalled knowledge of the Word of God and a determination to win men and women to Christ.

And so it went on (except for a somewhat unpredictable disappearance into the dust and grime of the Spanish-American War of '98, where he acted as chaplain in Cuba). But one summer evening in 1900 Torrey went as usual to a large prayer meeting held each week expressly to pray for world-wide revival. At the close he and a small group remained and prayed on into the night. In the small hours, at about the same hour as he had been saved from suicide nearly thirty years before, Torrey felt an overwhelming urge to pray 'a prayer that I had not dreamed on offering when we entered. The prayer was this, that God would send me round the world preaching the gospel; and when I had ceased praying I knew that I was going round the world to preach the gospel. How, I did not know ...'

A few days later two Australians approached him. They had been commissioned to find a man who could be used to bring a revival in Australia; for Moody, who had originally been invited, had died the previous winter. They had not found their man in England. They had now heard Torrey teach, and had heard him preach. They asked him to come. But despite his prayer he could not see how present responsibilities could be left, and it was not until December 1901 that Torrey, with his wife and the singer Charles M. Alexander, sailed from New York harbour for Melbourne.

Australia, Tasmania, New Zealand, and so at last to Britain, in January 1903. There were no doubts that Torrey and Alexander were the men of the hour. For two years they toured the British Isles, their work culminating with the opening, early in 1905, of a seven weeks' campaign at the Royal Albert Hall, to be followed by three months in other parts of London.

But if the Torrey-Alexander Mission was a fore-shadowing of Harringay, Wembley and Earls Court, some features were quite different. One was the weekly service for drunkards and prostitutes. The problem of intemperance was unsolved, where every night crowds of men and women, not all in rags and poverty, would stagger from public houses at a late hour. Saturday nights were the worst. And on that night, in whatever city they were, at the close of the ordinary evangelistic service Torrey and Alexander would send out groups of skilled assistants who would shepherd as many drunks as they could towards the hall.

'Arriving at the auditorium,' wrote young Robert Harkness, the missioners' Australian accompanist, 'one beheld a veritable pandemonium. Men and women in all stages of intoxication voiced their views upon many subjects in general and religion in particular. It seemed as if chaos must reign supreme. The great choir of twelve hundred voices sings an old time song. Strangely enough it becomes a prime favourite with the howling mob. In full fortissimo the refrain rings out: "Where is my wandering boy tonight?" Gradually the tone is lessened until it becomes a whisper. And, as the singing softens, the raucous laughter of the brain-befuddled revellers decreases, some fall asleep, others sober up. Over and over again comes the strain of the song. It is doing its appointed work admirably.

'Dr. Torrey sits with folded arms quietly waiting his time. Now, as an almost imperceptible echo of the refrain seems to haunt the assembly, seven thousand drink addicts are hushed. The preacher rises to proclaim the only message of hope that can meet the need of such a motley aggregation of broken earthenware ...'

Whether preaching to drunks, or in the great services at the Albert Hall, or at the temporary hall at Aldwych, on vacant land where slums had been pulled down and Kingsway not yet built, or addressing City business-men at his lunch-hour Question Box, Torrey made his mark. With his white hair and beard, his blue eyes and erect stance, 'the whole figure is striking,' wrote a contemporary journalist. 'You can tell at once that here is a man who knows where he stands. There is no wavering, no compromise, no middle course. He speaks, and the ring of certainty is in every note ... a man who believes every word he says, who speaks what he knows and testifies of what he has seen and experienced, a man who stands upon a rock and who knows its strength and his own ... But it is the eyes that haunt. From them there is no escape. They are upon you from the first to the last ... You will never again be the same after hearing the truth as the preacher puts it.'

Uncompromising conviction of truth seemed Torrey's outstanding characteristic. 'Dr. Torrey's conviction was the catapult with which he battered the citadel of sin,' wrote one of his team. 'He could indulge in no meaningless revelries. He must ever be alert to sound the warning of impending judgment. Men without faith in Christ were lost. He was convinced of the fact, therefore he must preach Christ and him crucified.'

Yet Torrey never lost his humility, nor sense of humour. Once in America a campaign committee had failed him badly. Torrey did his best. But after a while the penitent Committee felt that he was referring publicly to their sins too often. They sought out Robert Harkness and poured out their complaint, and Harkness agreed to try to put matters right. Back at the hotel he found Torrey studying his Bible. When Harkness, not knowing how to deliver his message suggested prayer, Torrey agreed at once. 'You pray first,' said Torrey. 'The prayer was commenced,' recalled Harkness, 'and in it I gave the Lord my private opinion of the evangelist. The prayer had not proceeded far when I was conscious of a dig in the ribs. "You don't need to tell the Lord that, he knows it already. Pray for the campaign." Dr. Torrey was always direct. Later he poured out his soul to God. It was a prayer of thanksgiving for the privilege of service, followed by confession of the sin of criticism, and closing with an appeal for forgiveness, with a note of praise for the victory which was sure to come.'

When Torrey left Great Britain in 1905 the sponsors said, 'We know that tens of thousands have opened their hearts to Jesus Christ ... and there have been blessings that cannot be counted, a spiritual force and influence and awakening which is immeasurable.' Yet despite the thousands who stayed faithful for the rest of their lives; despite Torrey's return in 1911, where similar results were seen, especially at Cambridge University, no lasting national revival took place. The Churches failed to follow up their advantages, and they were soon engrossed again in theological and ritualistic controversies. The drift from religion continued, and the Great War snuffed out the last hope of a true evangelical awakening in that generation.

Torrey was a rock who stood unbroken against the rising tide of unbelief. He lived until 1928, at Chicago and then at Los Angeles, renowned and honoured as an evangelist, and writing books – *How to Pray, How to Work for Christ, The Power of Prayer* and many others – which helped a great many to serve Christ as faithfully and effectively as he did.

15. Bramwell Booth, 1856-1929
CHIEF OF STAFF

The scum and filth of Cardiff's underworld were crowded in a circus arena listening to a fiery preacher. Back among the audience sat a small boy, hoping that all were fully aware that the man on the platform was his own father – William Booth, as yet unknown to the world, but a source of intense pride to Bramwell, his eldest son.

Bramwell Booth, born in Halifax seven years before, on March 8th, 1856, had heard often enough the message his father was preaching. His home – if constant changes of furnished lodgings could be called a home – centred round it. But tonight it sounded different. The call to repentance and faith in Christ seemed a personal call to himself. And Bramwell ('I was a regular little rascal! Wilful and proud') determined to have none of it. He could be proud of his father but his father's message was not for him. His life was his own, young as he was, and no Christ should steal it.

The meeting ended. An after-meeting began. Bramwell's mother saw him sitting on his chair, defiant and yet miserable. She came across and sat beside him. 'You are very unhappy,' said Catherine Booth. 'Yes,' replied the boy. 'You know the reason?' 'Yes.' Mrs. Booth 'urged him very earnestly to decide for Christ. For a long time,' she recalled, 'he could not speak, but I insisted on his giving a definite answer as to whether he would accept the offer of salvation or not.' There was another pause, and Bramwell Booth 'deliberately looked me in the face and answered "No!"' Catherine burst into tears. 'I knew what those tears represented,' Bramwell would say years later, 'but still I said "No!"'

Three months passed, outwardly happy but inwardly with an increasing sense of guilt. Bramwell sought to be more religious, but in his heart 'I could not bring myself to say "Yes" where I had already said "No."'

The family were now at Walsall, near Birmingham, for yet another mission. A children's service was taken by Mrs. Booth, 'the most timid and bashful disciple,' as she once called herself, 'the Lord Jesus ever saved.' Among the grimy mill-children sat Bramwell. He could never remember what his mother said that afternoon, but at the close of the meeting, 'ashamed and broken up', and all resistance gone, he was kneeling 'at the Communion rail among a crowd of little penitents'. A young man 'made me confess my wickedness, made me realise what a fearful thing it was to want my own way – it was going against the One who died for us. I saw that it was. And that pride was the sin that sank Satan into hell. He said, "It will send you there too," and I felt it would.'

As the man led him deeper into a sense of sin, young Bramwell began to cry. The man left him. Mrs. Booth knelt beside him, and prayed, and 'led me to cast myself with faith in his promise upon my Saviour. Gradually light came to me, and the accusing sense of guilt was taken away, and then my Lord gave the assurance that I was forgiven and made one of his own.'

Ten years later, in the early '70s, Bramwell Booth was perhaps the busiest young man in the East End of London. The 'Christian Mission' which his father had founded in 1865 in Whitechapel was expanding rapidly, and Bramwell, not yet twenty, was his right hand. He managed the 'Food-for-the-Million' shops, where dinners could be bought cheap by the poorest; organised a 'Garrett and Gutter Brigade,' spoke in the open air on Mile End Waste, and acted as the Mission's accountant, secretary and editor. He was tall, with brown eyes and an attempt at a beard, which in due course became luxurious. Though high spirited, with engaging manners and a strong sense of fun, he was delicate, for the boys at his school had once caught him, 'head and legs, and bashed him against a tree to bang salvation out of him,' and a serious illness had followed, which left him slightly deaf.

There was only one activity which Bramwell Booth declined: formal preaching at a service. He could say his bit in the open air. But he was convinced that he had no gift as a preacher. His parents disagreed. '*You* go doing the coachman and lackey,' wrote his mother, 'while such tweedledums as some I know lord it over God's heritage. I hope the Lord will make you so miserable everywhere and at everything that you will be compelled to preach.' But Bramwell, sensitive and highly-strung, could not for years bring himself to start.

He tried a little preaching at Whitechapel, but believed it was a failure. He was sent on a tour of the Mission 'outstations' in the North, and wrote back in distress. William Booth would have none of it. 'Think of the perishing multitudes and then say whether you *dare* "wind up" ... P.S. Mrs. Shepherd is here cleaning. She asks, "How is Mr. Bramwell, bless him?" and goes off into ecstasies about the blessings she gets when he speaks, etc., etc. She does not know that he is in the dumps because he cannot do the grandiloquent.'

Bramwell Booth's fears were at last overcome, and his quiet, matter-of-fact sermons, a contrast to his father's eloquence but equally effective in their place, soon began to be known in the slums and kennels where the Booths were doing great things for God. In 1878 William Booth could write to Bramwell, 'I told the people last night that the old cry of what would become of the Army when the General was gone was answered now, for never father had a son as wholly devoted to the same great purpose. They roared out, "Ah, God bless him." I was quite taken by surprise.'

The Christian Mission had become the Salvation Army. Bramwell had been mainly responsible for the change, and it had occurred almost by accident.

The Mission's Annual Appeal was in preparation, and Booth, Bramwell and George Scott Railton, their lieutenant, were in Booth's bedroom early one morning. Booth was walking up and down in his dressing-gown. Railton was reading the draft aloud. 'We are a volunteer army,' he read. 'Volunteer?' cried Bramwell, with thoughts of the ridicule then poured on the Volunteers, the amateurish ancestors of the Territorials, 'Here! I'm not a Volunteer! I'm a regular or nothing!' Booth stopped in his tracks, looked up, walked across to Railton and took the pen from his hand. Stooping over Railton's shoulder he crossed out 'volunteer' and wrote 'salvation'.

Young Bramwell, with all the enthusiasm of twenty-two, followed up the 'Salvation Army' idea. Overcoming his father's hesitation he encouraged military terms and began calling mission officers by military titles. Flags had already been designed for each 'citadel', and soon the Christian Mission's name was changed officially. Then came the thought of uniform. Bramwell realised what *esprit de corps* a uniform could give the converted drunks and tramps whom the Army were leading into Christian service. 'I do not think it will look like the madmen,' he wrote to his sister, 'you see, the people who wear it will have such a different appearance.' The women were to have bonnets. Bramwell sent for one of the leading women officers. 'He came into the little office,' wrote Mrs Evans, 'with the bonnet in his hand, and asked me what I thought of it. "I think it's queer, Mr. Bramwell. I hope you don't expect me to wear it." "Yes, I do," he said, "At the meeting tonight." I said, "No, never me." At which he opened his black frockcoat, and showed me a red jersey thing with Salvation Army on it in yellow, and he said in his quiet way, "I am sure if I can wear this for Jesus you can wear the bonnet." And I did. I was the first to wear it.'

As the Army expanded, William and Bramwell Booth proved a well proportioned pair, the father providing the drive and the vision, the son the organisation and codifying without which the Army could never have stood the test of time. But in 1885 Bramwell's intervention was again to prove decisive.

He had married, and his young wife Florence had agreed to look after a Rescue Home for prostitutes, mere girls, who were constantly being brought to the Army's attention in the East End. In the course of her work Florence discovered that in civilised England, with its culture and wealth and imperial power, young girls were actually bought and sold. Bramwell was incredulous; but he agreed to go out '*incog*. and wander about some neighbourhood and see things for myself.'

Three weeks later a striking scene took place in Bramwell's office. He had been 'wading through a sea of sin and defilement, my heart sickened and appalled,' and now he had turned for help to W. T. Stead, the great editor of the powerful *Pall Mall Gazette*. Stead listened as the City Chamberlain, a lawyer friendly to the Army, explained the legal position of the 'White Slave Traffic', with all its ramifications on the Continent. A converted brothel-keeper and three or four girls, only one over sixteen, were brought in and put through their stories. 'When the girls had withdrawn,' recalled Bramwell, 'there was a pause, and I looked at Stead. He was evidently deeply moved. Raising his fist, he brought it down on my table with a mighty bang, so that the very inkpots shivered, and he uttered one word, 'Damn!' This explosion over, I said, 'Yes that is all very well, but it will not help us.' Then they prayed together for an hour and a half, the important editor and the humble Salvationist, and Stead went out to get the facts 'in such a form that we can publish them'.

The revelations which followed shook England to the depths and brought violent persecution to the Army, but led to a change in the law. It also led Stead and Bramwell to the dock of the Old Bailey. To prove their allegations they had actually bought a girl – 'a child of fourteen,' wrote Stead, 'beautiful and innocent as the day, brought to you to be ruined – willingly – yes, for she wants money for her mother who is lying ill ... It made my heart bleed. £10 for the price of her shame.' But the law, not caring to follow up the scores of criminals who had bought and sold children, prosecuted the reformers.

After a trial of twelve days, Stead was sentenced to three months in gaol. Bramwell was acquitted on lack of evidence. ''Ere, old cove,' shouted a cockney loafer to a Salvationist in another part of London, 'I'll tell yer what'll cheer yer 'eart. Bramwell ain't guilty!'

In all the long years that followed, as the Army grew worldwide, neither Bramwell nor William Booth forgot their primary aim, 'to subdue a rebellious world to God'. In 1912, on his father's death, Bramwell succeeded as General, serving for nearly seventeen years. His work will never be remembered as vividly as that of his father, yet it is a challenge to those who have been born in the precinct of great Christian service, that they should be worthy of their forbears; and a reminder to parents that every child must make a personal decision for Christ.

Bramwell Booth died in 1929. His last months were clouded by misunderstanding and sorrow. But nothing could damp his passion for souls, nor the intensity of his praying, nor the fervour and humility with which he strove, despite the fears and worries of an over-sensitive nature, to be a loyal soldier in the army of the Lord.

16: Lord Radstock, 1833–1913
LORD APOSTOL

Colonel Paschkov, wealthy darling of St Petersburg society, lolled back in his sumptuous, elegant carriage as it took him swiftly from the palace of his Sovereign and personal friend, Alexander II, Tsar of all the Russias, to a soiree given by a Grand Duchess, a member of the Imperial Family. He thought with satisfaction of his popularity, of his vast estates in the Urals, where his thousands of toiling peasants provided him the wherewithal to live in the extravagant luxury to which he had been bred.

At the Grand Duchess's, gilded doors swung noiselessly open and footmen bowed as the Colonel, resplendent in his Guards' uniform, walked with nonchalent hauteur towards the red-carpeted staircase. The major-domo at the entrance to the great ballroom did not announce him, but respectfully murmured that the guests of her Imperial Highness were already seated. Surprised, Paschkov looked across the long room with its Chinese silks and priceless works of art, and saw a circle of fashionably dressed men and women, most of whom he knew, sitting listening to a plainly dressed gentleman with an English face who stood close to the vast fireplace, talking quietly but earnestly in French, the normal language of the Russian nobility.

Intrigued, Paschkov took a seat and listened. 'This same Jesus,' the Englishman was saying, and the words seemed strangely out of place in such surroundings, 'who sought the fallen woman of Samaria, and Saul of Tarsus, is alive still, the Son of Man, "who came to seek and to save that which was lost".' Soon the theme changed, and without raising his voice the speaker was castigating the selfish luxury and idleness of his hearers; and his bluntness shook Colonel Paschkov, who had never realised before how empty and self-centred life had been. Then the theme changed again, passing from the certainty of judgement to the wonder of a Saviour who died on the cross. Despite himself, Paschkov was stirred to the depths. This was so different from the contemporary Orthodox Church, with the 'insipidity of its traditional bakemeats served by the official clergy in their heavy plates of gold'; it was personal and alive.

As the address closed Paschkov urgently asked his neighbour, a Prince (the highest rank below the Imperial Family) who the man was. 'An English milord,' the Prince whispered back. 'Lord Radstock. The Grand Duchess met him in Paris. She's been a different woman since.' That night, kneeling beside Lord Radstock, a Bible open between them, Paschkov gave his life to Christ....

It was a few months later in this season of 1873-4. The Minister of the Interior, the clever and cynical Count Brobinsky, was annoyed. His wife had got herself mixed up with this ridiculous 'drawing-room revival' and had just told him that the cause of all the trouble was coming to dinner. Brobinsky, who had been reading the latest novel, a brilliant skit called *Lord Apostol* which neatly took off the English milord and his absurd converts, had no wish to meet him, but to be absent would be insulting. At dinner, as course after course was handed round on gold plate, Brobinsky listened with half-amused tolerance as Radstock, who appeared to have no idea as to what subjects were taboo at table, discoursed on the Epistle to the Romans. The Count was frankly agnostic, though to satisfy a vow he had once made when he had believed himself dying he used to say a prayer each day to the Unknown God.

Brobinsky was certain he could refute all Radstock's

statements – the fact of Christ, his resurrection and the possibility of personal faith. When the dessert came, he excused himself, went into his study, and wrote a long refutation which so pleased him that he sent it to be printed. But the eyes and the quiet conviction of the 'Lord Apostol', and his sense of the reality of Christ, haunted Brobinsky. When the manuscript returned and he began to read it, something snapped. As with a flash of light, 'I found that Jesus was the key, the beginning and the end of all.' He fell on his knees, Cabinet Minister though he was; the Unknown God had revealed himself....

Young Princess Catherine Galitzine one day that same year went round in her sleigh through the winter streets to see a newly married friend, Princess Lieven. Both were devout, their emotional natures drinking in the ritual and stately ceremonial of the Russian Orthodox Church. The quarterly reception of the Communion had just taken place, and religion filled Princess Catherine's heart. Her one distress was that the glorious feelings would so soon evaporate, and she must labour on until grace could once more be received at the next Communion.

As she ran lightly up the wide staircase of the palace, the boudoir door opened and Princess Lieven, in her rich brocaded day dress, hurried down to meet her. Lord Radstock had come to call. The two girls began to tell him breathlessly of the happiness the Communion had brought.

'Would you like to possess it for ever?' he asked.

'Impossible,' they said.

'And thereupon,' Princess Catherine recalled in her old age, 'commenced the Message of Grace offered us, without the least pressure on our most precious feelings. Henceforth all the addresses, the meetings to which we hastened, became as seeds which the Lord brought to life. At length, one day, in the American chapel, after a most blessed address when the never-to-be-forgotten hymn, 'I do believe, I will believe that Jesus died *for me*,' was sung, I remained for a special conversation – and there we were both on our knees before *my own Saviour for ever*....'

'Who is Lord Radstock?' – the question was heard continually as he visited and revisited St Petersburg and Moscow. Wealthy guardsmen such as Paschkov threw open their palaces to reach the poorest with the Gospel; Brobinsky set himself to win the great novelist Tolstoy; counts and princes began to treat their peasants as human beings; and great estates became centres of evangelism.

He had been born in 1833, the son of an Admiral who after his retirement had spent many years in Christian work. By the time he inherited the title in 1857 Lord Radstock had become a Christian through the influence of his mother, and in intervals of soldiering with the newly raised Volunteers, and absorption in music and literature, he and his young wife, a famous beauty, had given select Bible Readings in their house in Bryanston Square.

Revival was moving across England in 1859, and for Lord and Lady Radstock it brought a call to deliberate service among their own class. Screwing up his courage, Radstock began to give out tracts, with a polite lifting of his top hat, at the daily parades of wealth and fashion in Hyde Park, when all the world sauntered or rode or sat in gleaming carriages, to exchange the gossip of Mayfair and Belgravia. Radstock's tracts, and his invitations to gospel addresses in the Bryanstone Square drawing room and his Hampshire seat, disgusted his rich titled contemporaries, secure in their regular churchgoing and the respectability which too often camouflaged a carefully hidden immorality.

Despite a life transformed here and there, it seemed, as so often before, that a man could not reach his own sort, and Radstock turned to the poor who were never far from the streets of fashion in Victorian England. He built them mission halls and refuge centres, and could often be found preaching in the East End of London. As the revival spread in the sixties he became an evangelist who filled halls in watering places and inland towns, moving from mission to mission. In 1867 he was invited to a conference of the Evangelical Alliance in Holland; and the severe, sober, rigidly correct Dutch Calvinist nobility discovered that God could use him to bring them to warm personal faith.

After Holland Lord Radstock went to Paris, brilliant capital of the Second Empire, where the ladies of the court in their huge crinolines danced and flirted, oblivious of coming disaster. All the aristocracy of Europe flocked to Paris, and it was among visiting Russians that Radstock found himself most used. His energy was inexhaustible, and he was forever thinking up fresh schemes of evangelization. His impetuousness and bluntness would attract some and alienate others, but those who knew him well were shamed by an unwavering devotion and constancy, by his prayer life, and by his tact in personal dealings, abrupt though he might be in his addresses.

Above all Lord Radstock had that indefinable touch of a man who has learned the secret of steady abiding in Christ. He seemed never to lose contact, however busy the day, and thus had an uncanny knack of being in the right place at the right time, even when a minute or two made all the difference. What others might call coincidences were continually occurring, and it was in this way that he met the Grand Duchess, who had previously refused categorically to be introduced to such a man. But she happened to arrive, uninvited, to spend an evening with a Princess; by a series of 'chances' Lord Radstock was unexpectedly with the Princess when the Grand Duchess was announced. And after her conversion she invited him to Russia.

The great writer Dostoievsky heard Radstock preach in 1873. 'I found nothing startling,' he wrote in his *Diary of a Writer* (1876). 'He spoke neither particularly cleverly nor in a particularly dull manner. But yet he performs miracles over human hearts; people are flocking around him, many of them are astounded; they are looking for the poor, in order as quickly as possible to bestow benefits upon them; they are almost ready to give away their fortunes.... He does produce extraordinary transformations and inspires in the hearts of his followers magnanimous sentiments.'

Brobinsky's palace and his country estates, like those of Paschkov and other converts, became centres of the new evangelical movement and models of agricultural and humane reform. The Revival went from strength to strength. Lord Radstock, whose Russian was not fluent enough for preaching, worked in the drawing rooms and his converts went out among the poorer classes. New Testaments, almost unknown to the ordinary Russian, were distributed in tens of thousands from the Neva and the Vistula to prison camps in Siberia. Prayer meetings began in place after place.

The Radstock revival had incalculable possibilities for Russia. Many of the educated classes were intensely religious yet unsatisfied by the detached formalism which encrusted the Orthodox Church; they were intensely patriotic yet disturbed by Russia's monolithic, repressive political system and by 'the segregation', as Dostoievsky called it, 'of the educated strata of society, our detachment from our own soil, from the nation'. The evangelical revival could have done much to end this fatal detachment, for nobles and *muzhiks* met as brothers. Here was a better road than that of Nihilist revolutionaries.

But the wrath of the Russian Orthodox Church was aroused. What might have been a reformation within the Church was forced to be a sect outside it; the informal groups of all classes which gathered round Paschkov, Brobinsky and other friends of Lord Radstock in St Petersburg and in their country estates, became known as 'Evangelical Christians'. Leadership lay with nobles and gentry, and at first they were protected by their position. 'Leave my widows alone!' the Tsar replied when church authorities wished to proceed against Princess Lieven, in whose palace the St Petersburg Evangelical Christians held their services.

In 1881 Alexander II was blown to pieces by a Nihilist bomb. He had been on the verge of granting a further measure of political freedom and religious toleration. His son Alexander III answered his father's murder by stark reaction.

In 1884 Colonel Paschkov convened a united evangelical conference, and some four hundred converged on St Petersburg. He hired a hotel and gave them hospitality, having already paid their fares. They met in a hall in Princess Lieven's palace where every servant was a convert except the surly old *dvornik* or doorkeeper, and represented the three major strands of Russian evangelicalism, the Baptists, the Evangelical Christians, and the Stundists. These were a sect which had arisen when Russian peasants had attended (illegally) the *stunden* or Bible hours conducted by evangelical German farmers in the Ukraine, who had been given liberty of worship when invited to settle but were forbidden to proselytize.

Each strand was of different origin, but a classic example of the spontaneous expansion of the Church: Christians from another nation had touched off a movement which propagated itself, thoroughly indigenous in leadership and character. The three movements, unrelated yet emerging almost simultaneously, affected North and South, the illiterate peasants, the merchants, the nobility. This evangelical revival, widespread, gathering momentum, might have changed the course of Russian history.

The conference of 1884 continued happily for three or four days. On the next, no provincial delegate appeared. Princess Lieven, Colonel Paschkov and their aristocratic allies were puzzled by the disappearance of these men from their homes. The hotel was empty. Two days later a scared *muzhik* delegate slipped into the palace. He told how they had been arrested shortly after leaving the conference. In the fortress of St Peter and St Paul they had been searched and questioned. Some of them were told that revolutionary literature had been seized from the others, at which they laughed. 'The only revolutionary document possessed or used by any of us is the Bible! We aim at no revolution other than that which the Cross of our Lord Jesus Christ effects.'

Police had escorted them railway stations for despatch home at government expense; the *muzhik* who gave the news to Paschkov had cannily asked for a ticket to a place near St Petersburg and had doubled back at risk of arrest and punishment.

The collapse of the conference was a prelude to an intense and violent persecution in which Church and State vied to suppress the evangelicals. Princess Lieven had to retire to her estates. Paschkov was banished. When, on petition to the Tsar, he was allowed a brief return to settle his affairs, Alexander III soon peremptorily ordered him to private audience.

'I hear you have resumed your old practices!'

'My friends have certainly called to greet me, and we have prayed and read the Word of God together....'

'Which you know perfectly well I will not permit. I will not have you defy me. If I had thought you would repeat your offences I should not have allowed you to return. Get out. And never set foot in Russia again.'

No such mild fate awaited the majority of the evangelical leaders. They were harried, persecuted, imprisoned, exiled to Siberia, Transcaucasia or other barren confines of the Empire. Not being men of rank, they were treated as any criminals – beards and hair half-shaved, wrists and ankles shackled by heavy chains – they were driven across mountains and deserts beside bandits, swindlers and rapists. They suffered worse than Lenin and most revolutionaries whose exile was unmarred by flogging, hard labour or the treadmill. Their wives would have been destitute without the charity of their fellow believers; when a man's sentence was served he would be kept in exile by administrative order and his family could sometimes join him – travelling under such inhumane conditions that women and children often died on the road.

Faith was bent and tested. That of a few broke. That of most proved gloriously resilient. 'How good the Lord is,' exclaimed Paschkov's Inspector of Forest at the start of the march to Siberia. 'I have been praying to work among the prisoners and this is how my prayer is answered.'

'Radstockism', as its detractors called the movement, was sent underground. But if in England the Methodist Revival prevented revolution in 1789, the Evangelical

Revival of the eighteen seventies, had it been allowed to take its course, might have so purified Russian life and government that the revolution of 1917, with all the misery that Communism brought the world, would never have occurred. God gave Russia her opportunity, and his Wesley was Lord Radstock.

Excluded from Russia, Radstock's work was not done. In Sweden, Denmark, Finland, and often in Paris, now republican and bitter in defeat, he moved quietly among both upper classes and the poor. Seven times he went to India, and in 1897 he organized a scheme by which every native official received a New Testament on Queen Victoria's Jubilee.

At home, news of his work in Russia opened doors hitherto closed among the aristocracy of England; his ambition to reach his own class was rewarded, though without spectacular results. And scarcely an evangelical work or mission was untouched by him. For over thirty years, almost to the Great War, his name crosses and recrosses the story of England's religious movements. The Cambridge Seven were influenced by him; he helped Moody and Sankey, and Torrey and Alexander; man after man on the mission field or in home service could point to some moment when an address or a personal word from Radstock changed the course of their lives.

The missionary to Imperial Russia died in December 1913, little more than three years before the Russian Revolution.

His movement, however, did not die.

When Lenin separated the Orthodox Church from the state, and all sects were briefly allowed freedom to worship and evangelize, the three evangelical strands, united as 'The Evangelical Christians/Baptists', experienced great growth. Then the Soviet Union attempted to extinguish religion and promote militant atheism. A violent persecution swept across the land. Thousands of Christians of all churches were killed, or suffered hardship, torture and hunger in labour camps, until Stalin at length restored a small measure of religious freedom during the Second World War, followed by further restriction under Khrushchev.

The Orthodox Church had been purged as by fire, and now saw the evangelicals as brothers in Christ. As one archbishop said to me, deep in Soviet Central Asia at the height of the Khrushchev repression: 'Once we chased them with a pitchfork; now we draw them to us with a kiss of peace.'

Through all the slander and persecution the Christians loved their enemies and prayed for those who despitefully used them. When restrictions were again eased, while the spiritual bankruptcy of atheism, and of Communism, became yearly more obvious, the evangelists were already showing a better way by the purity of their motives and the beauty of their lives. Thus they were a strong component of the Russian religious revival of the later twentieth century.

The Soviet state at last admitted, in 1989, that the attempt to abolish religion had been wrong. The church bells rang again; Christian services and preachers were seen and heard on state television; evangelists were allowed to use stadiums. When Communism fell two years later and the Soviet era ended, the Evangelical Christians/Baptists were helping the nation into paths of righteousness because the Lord was indeed their Shepherd. Thus Lord Radstock's greatest harvest began to be reaped three-quarters of a century after his death. He had sowed in love and faith. As Mary Slessor had said, 'God and one is a majority.'

INTO ALL THE WORLD

17. William Carey 1761–1834
ALL MY FRIENDS ARE BUT ONE

Outside a tumbledown shed on the edge of a steamy swamp a few miles north of Calcutta sat a dejected Englishman. His name was William Carey. The year was 1794. He was thirty-two years old.

In the shed lay his eldest son, desperately ill of dysentery. Beside the boy lay his mother, not only ill but wandering in mind and bitterly reproaching Carey for having dragged them all from a placid English pastorate across dangerous seas to a land of disappointment and destitution. The three other boys (there was a baby too) could not be allowed out of Carey's sight for fear of dacoits – the thieves and brigands who infested the countryside. Although they would disdain to molest a destitute sahib, since fat Indian moneylenders were easy to find, they could get a good price for a kidnapped white child in native states up-country.

The Careys had been in India less than two months and everything had gone wrong. As Carey wiped the sweat off his spectacles, picked up his Bible, and turned pages already spoiled by mildew, he wondered whether he had mistaken God's call. It had all begun more than ten years earlier. Carey, then twenty-one and a mere village shoemaker in the Midlands of England, a man of no account in an aristocratic age but already a fervent Christian, had been reading a borrowed copy of *Captain Cook's Voyages*, an especially topical book because the news of the great explorer's murder by South Sea islanders had only recently reached Europe. Captain Cook was not particularly known as a Christian, yet the book brought the young shoemaker Christ's orders to serve as his missionary in the South Seas, where none had so much as heard his name.

Missionaries in the 1780s were an almost extinct race. When Carey attempted to enthuse his fellow Baptists with the project, he was rebuffed with the crushing retort: 'When God pleases to convert the heathen, he'll do it without consulting you!' Carey became a full-time pastor, and still the Christless millions overseas dominated his prayers, and even turned him into a pamphlet writer.

In 1792 he persuaded his brethren to found the Baptist Missionary Society. They began collecting a little money, in the form of pledges thrust into a snuffbox, and designated Carey their first missionary, to sail to Tahiti as soon as their funds allowed.

'Expect great things from God. Attempt great things for God,' Carey had proclaimed. And here he was, little more than a year later, sitting on the edge of an Indian marsh, almost a castaway.

His plan to evangelize the South Seas had been changed through the influence of a surgeon on leave from the British East India Company in Bengal. John Thomas painted a vivid picture of the Hindu civilization of India. His soul was eaten up by compassion for Indian sufferings, and zeal for the conversion of Indians to Christ, and he believed the time was ripe.

Carey agreed to go to India, with the Baptist missionary committee's approval but at the cost of separation from his timid, stay-at-home wife until the mission should be established.

Carey, his eldest son Felix, and John Thomas set sail in 1793, only to be put ashore again. The East India Company was implacably opposed to missions, which might endanger commercial profits by angering the Hindus. A friendly captain had smuggled the three aboard. But creditors pursued Thomas, who, though a sincere missionary, was totally irresponsible regarding money.

'All I can say,' wrote Carey, watching the sails of the convoy of East Indiamen disappear over the horizon, 'is that however mysterious the leadings of Providence, I have no doubt but that they are superintended by an infinitely wise God.'

Ten days later, his lips filled with praise, Carey was embarking on a Danish ship whose crew cared nothing for the anti-missionary growls of the British company. What is more, Thomas had not only squared his London creditors but Dorothy Carey had rejoined her husband with their whole family, including baby.

When the ship reached the mouth of the Ganges, Thomas insisted that they all disembark secretly downstream from Calcutta, partly for fear of more creditors, partly to avoid arrest and expulsion by British officials.

Within two months William Carey, despite the thrill at his first steps in Bengali, of hearing Thomas preach in the crowded Bengal villages, and of all the sights and sounds of India, was on the edge of despair. The sheer weight of Hinduism seemed to crush hopes that a Christian church would arise quickly. Dorothy and Felix fell ill, and Dorothy's mind began to unhinge. Then John Thomas announced that he had misjudged their finances and they were nearly destitute. Carey was reduced to accepting the loan of a native moneylender's garden house in a neighbourhood abounding in snakes, tigers, and cut-throat dacoits.

As Carey sat in the steamy heat outside that shed, his wife moaning in the shadows behind, it would have been hard to believe that here was the 'father of modern missionaries' whose translations of the Scriptures would pioneer missionary work in India, whose name, when he died, would be known and honoured from Cape Cormorin to the Himalayas.

The would-be missionary to India might have cut his

losses at that moment. The spirit within him was too hot to abandon the ministry – he had heard the call and must follow. But he might have concluded that the door to India was closing, that he had mistaken God's guidance when he had agreed to go to India, and that he had best change back to Tahiti where there was no entrenched Hinduism, where no 'Christian' company officials would frustrate his designs.

Carey decided to seek advice from David Brown, a well-known evangelical chaplain to the East India Company's Europeans in Calcutta. He walked through the heat of the city to see Brown, but Brown received him frigidly because of distrust of John Thomas. In later years Brown and Carey would be close friends, but on this January day of 1794 the chaplain sent his ex-cobbler away without even offering him refreshment after his long walk.

'All my friends are but One,' thought Carey as he trudged home again, 'but he is all sufficient.' In his diary he wrote: 'Towards evening felt the all-sufficiency of God, and the stability of his promises, which much relieved my mind. As I walked home in the night, was enabled to roll all my cares on him.'

Soon he was allowed to occupy and clear a small area of jungle in another, more healthy district. He intended to support his family by small farming, like the Indians around him, while learning the language and beginning to preach. Then Thomas secured for him the post of manager of an indigo plantation at Malda several hundred miles away, and the whole situation was transformed.

Carey became a well-paid planter with a pleasant home and unrivalled opportunity for getting to know the language, the people, and their customs as he travelled far and wide, buying the indigo crop and supervising the processes which turned it into the blue vegetable dye much prized in eighteenth-century Europe. In slack periods he could preach and teach. He had a friendly employer, George Udny, a vigorous Christian who as a magistrate could protect Carey from government attempts to forbid his preaching.

The road ahead was not easy. Carey survived a serious attack of malaria, but his little boy Peter did not. Mrs Carey fell ill again and began to rail against her husband. For weeks he endured her violence against himself and all he held dear, and because so little was then known about the influence of body upon mind, it was a long time before he realized that her ravings and bitterness were part of her illness. To Carey it seemed that his much-loved Dorothy had become his enemy.

In the midst of these troubles he received a letter from the mission committee in England deploring his being a planter. Had he not, they asked, left England to be a missionary?

A missionary he was. William Carey, planter of Malda in Bengal in the closing year of the eighteenth century, is a sort of patron saint of the many hundreds of men and women today who are not listed as 'missionaries', yet are full-time missionaries at heart. They may be in commerce or industry, United Nations or diplomatic service, or in any of the hundred and one positions open to Western Christians in lands where Christianity is a minority religion, but their vocation and intention is to be witnesses and ambassadors for Christ.

Whereas Carey's employer, George Udny, a devout evangelical, put his secular concerns first (he loved the Bible and encouraged missionaries but never preached to Indians himself), Carey put business concerns last. He lived simply and devoted the bulk of his income to the translation of the Scriptures. 'I am indeed poor, and always shall be,' he told the home committee, 'until the Bible is published in Bengali and Hindustani and the people need no further instruction.' His considerable spare time went to translating, or to preaching under the tamarind tree of each teeming village of the district.

The preaching made no impact on the entrenched hold of Hinduism. All around were the miseries imposed by the caste system, yet its iron grip held the hearts of the people to idolatry. As John Thomas, managing a nearby plantation, wrote to the home committee: 'Do not send men of compassion here, for you will break their hearts. Do send men *full* of compassion, for many perish with cold, many for lack of bread, and millions for lack of knowledge.'

All but two of Carey's handful of converts proved to be frauds or became backsliders. 'I am almost grown callous,' he wrote in 1799, 'and tempted to preach as if their hearts are invulnerable. But this dishonours the grace and power of God.' Meanwhile, he and Thomas had completed the translation of the New Testament into Bengali, and Udny had bought them a printing press.

The future again grew obscure. Several bad seasons and a calamitous flood followed by drought and epidemics made Udny determined to abandon his plantations. Carey would be without a home or a job, and four English missionaries with their families were on the outward voyage to join him. He therefore invested all his savings in buying an indigo plantation to form their base.

One of the new missionaries, William Ward, fresh from landing, reached him with the news that they had been offered land and sanctuary. In the tiny Danish enclave of Serampore, British orders of expulsion could not affect them. And Serampore, only fourteen miles upriver from Calcutta, was a strategic centre, whereas Malda lay remote.

'Carey has made up his mind to leave all and follow our Saviour to Serampore,' wrote Ward. 'Indeed, whilst he has opened a door there to us, he has shut all others.'

Ward was a printer, his ambition 'to *print* among the Gentiles the unsearchable riches of Christ'. The other leader of the party, Joshua Marshman, was a self-taught schoolmaster, brilliant but cross-grained, with a wife of inexhaustible good humour. Carey joined them, and for over thirty years the Serampore trio of Carey, Marshman and Ward was the spearhead of Christian work in India.

How Carey translated the whole Bible into five Indian languages, and parts of it into nearly thirty more; how Ward printed the versions and, as converts came, spread them the length and breadth of India; how the Marshmans founded schools to support the community, and Carey taught in the East India Company's college in Calcutta; and how they launched the first mission to Burma which Judson was to join at their suggestion – all this is part of the imperishable saga of the growth of the Church of God.

Yet it would have come to naught had the destitute Carey of January 1794 abandoned his Indian designs and attempted to reach Tahiti. The discouraged recruit became the foremost missionary of his day.

18. Adonirum Judson, 1788-1850
JUDSON'S DARKEST HOUR

The American couple sat down to their meal nervously.

On this June day of 1824 in the Burmese capital of Ava, four hundred miles from the sea, Adoniram and Ann Judson, both in their thirties, lived by sufferance of the Burmese king in a little house he had allowed them to build. The home was of teak, which could not keep out the heat of the day, but it was within sight and sound of the royal palace.

The king was contemptuous of their message as Christian missionaries, and suspicious of their motive. But richly dressed nobles and even the king himself would condescend to listen to their words occasionally when they visited the royal audience rooms. Yellow-robed Buddhist monks filed past their rough veranda, begging bowls in hand, on the way to the bazaar. Sometimes a priest accepted an invitation to listen to the American teacher's earnest declaration that the Truth could be *known*, and that the Way was not a path of merit leading to ultimate Nothingness but a living Person who brought Life.

For twelve years the Judsons had struggled, first in Rangoon, and for the past months at Ava, the capital. Their work had at last begun to show the small beginnings of a Christian church in a Buddhist land. Now all was at hazard again because war had broken out between the Burmese and the British, who had sent an invasion force from India. The three or four British residents of Ava had already been thrown into prison. This is why the Judsons were nervous as they toyed with their food. The Burmese knew no distinction between the subjects of King George IV and the fellow citizens of President James Monroe.

The Judson dinner had barely begun when a Burmese officer rushed in, accompanied by a knot of men. They were led by a brute whose spotted face and depraved features proclaimed him a jailer – a murderer reprieved on condition that he torture and kill as required.

Despite Ann's protests and her hurried offers of money, Adoniram Judson was thrown to the ground. A cord was deftly wound round his upper arms and chest and tightened until it cut. Then they hurried him away. When Ann sent their Burmese assistant, a convert and true friend, to follow the party and again offer money, the words were barely out of his mouth before the jailer tripped Judson on the pathway and tightened the cords until he could barely breathe.

At the jail he was stripped of most of his clothes, manacled, and placed alongside the other white captives already in the death prison. The tiny compartment was packed with local criminals and crawling with vermin. He was soon joined by his sole American missionary colleague, the bachelor Dr. Price.

June heat and the small size of the windows made misery enough. But at night time an atrocious contraption, a long bamboo pole attached to a pulley, was thrust between the fettered legs of each prisoner and jacked up until the weight of his body and the irons had to rest, all night long, on his shoulders and hands.

In the months that followed, Judson survived only through Ann's indomitable courage. Though expecting a baby she daily spent weary hours walking through Ava to petition officials and nobles. She brought him his only food. She smuggled in his New Testament, and she kept up his courage by brief visits, made at the risk of being arrested herself and sent into slavery.

Years earlier, on his first voyage from America Judson had been imprisoned in the hold of an English ship after its capture by a French privateer. He had been tempted then to regret his refusal of the assistant minister's post at the largest church in Boston in preference for the hazards of missionary life.

Such temptation had long lost its force. At Ava he was proving in appalling conditions the accuracy of some gallant words which he had penned in a comfortable New England home when facing the prospect of being the first American preacher in Asia. 'O the pleasure which a lively Christian must enjoy in communion with God!' Judson had written. 'It is all one whether he is in a city or a desert, among relations or among savage foes, in the heat of the Indies or in the ice of Greenland; his infinite Friend is always at hand. He need not fear want or sickness or pain, for his best Friend does all things well. He need not fear death, though it come in the most shocking form, for death is only a withdrawing of the veil which conceals his dearest Friend.'

In those first days in the death house, as his cramped limbs, chilled with loss of circulation, were lowered to the ground in the morning, Judson knew that his dearest Friend was beside him. When the bell began tolling the afternoon hour at which victims would be let out to be beaten or mutilated or crucified, and a ghastly stillness settled on criminals and prisoners of war alike, waiting to know who should be chosen next, Judson proved the peace that passes understanding.

Days lengthened into months. Conditions became slightly better, thanks to Ann's persistence, but a tide of frustration began to mount in Judson's mind.

His beloved converts were scattered. He could no longer go out under the shadow of a golden pagoda to engage passers-by in religious conversation. He could do no work on the Burmese dictionary which would enable American reinforcements to learn the language. Nor could he continue the Burmese translation of the Bible which he knew was an essential preliminary to the growth of a strong church.

What was worse, his imprisonment, unlike the apostle Paul's, did not seem to be furthering the gospel. It was a mere accident of war. It meant little to anyone in Ava.

Had Judson been called upon to suffer publicly for his faith, or to withstand attempted brainwashing like Geoffrey Bull in China a century and a quarter later, or even to perform hard manual labour in slavery, he could have borne it. To be condemned to lie everlastingly doing nothing in a fetid jail day after day made him depressed and irritable. His faith remained, but his joy was gone.

It returned when the white prisoners were flung back into the inner prison. Their feet were again made fast in the stocks, like Paul's and Silas's at Philippi, and a rumour was strong that they were to be executed at three in the morning. As the hour approached Judson grew calm. When he led the others in prayer his joy at the prospect of the immediate presence of Christ was muted only by sorrow for his wife.

The rumour was false. Then came a period of fever which prostrated his body and spirits. Again he was saved by his wife's intercession. He was allowed to move into a little bamboo hut – until an awful day when the weakened Judson and the others were taken away.

They were to be burned alive as a sacrifice to the spirits who should then give the Burmese victory over the English. No announcement was made, however, of their intended fate.

Judson's fetters were removed, together with the shoes and socks with which Ann had kept her husband supplied. The men were roped together two by two and driven like animals down the sandy, flinty road which was baking in the midday sun. On feet which for nearly a year had been allowed no exercise but a brief fettered hobble round the yard, and which were now unwontedly bare, blisters grew fast and soon burst. Every step was torture, and the jailers moved their prisoners fast.

Judson's morale collapsed. As they passed high over a watercourse he contemplated throwing himself and his companion to death. 'The parapet is low,' he gasped. 'There can be no sin in our availing ourselves of the opportunity.'

A modern biographer of Judson doubts this story, which he had read in the reminiscences of a fellow prisoner writing thirty years after the event. He considers it 'difficult to conceive' that even in temporary desperation such a man as Judson could have contemplated both the sin of suicide and the treachery of leaving his wife alone in a hostile land. But Ann Judson confirms the story herself as it was told to her the next day by her husband: 'So great was his agony, he ardently longed to throw himself into the water to be free from misery. But the sin attached to such an act alone prevented.'

The Lord's words, 'I will keep thee in all thy ways,' proved true even when Judson was physically past controlling himself. His Lord was at his side; he was intervening in other ways too. The Bengali servant of one of the prisoners caught up with the column and saw their distress. He pulled off his turban, tore it in two and handed half to his master and half to Judson, who tied it around his feet. The servant supported and half-carried Judson the rest of the way.

The prisoners were by now in such poor shape that the eight-mile journey planned by their jailers had to be broken by a night's rest. A kindhearted Burmese woman risked official wrath to refresh them with fruit. But next day, when they had reached the ruined bamboo dwelling which was to be set on fire as soon as they were chained to stakes inside, the situation had changed. The high government leader who had plotted their execution had fallen from favour and been summarily executed.

Judson's darkest hour passed. The place of intended immolation became a prison where captivity was less rigorous than at Ava. But Ann, who had followed him into the countryside with their baby daughter, fell seriously ill.

Judson was able, however, to look forward with hope, for the British forces advanced slowly up the Irrawaddy. 'Here I have been for ten years preaching the gospel,' he remarked to a fellow prisoner, 'to timid listeners who wish to embrace the truth but dare not – beseeching the emperor to grant liberty of conscience to his people, but without success. And now, when all human means seem at an end, God opens the way by leading a Christian nation to subdue the country. It is possible that my life will be spared. If so, with what ardour and gratitude shall I pursue my work. And if not, his will be done: the door will be opened for others who will do the work better.'

His life was spared. The door was opened, and in a way he could not have foreseen. The Burmese territory newly annexed by the British (who permitted missionary work unreservedly) contained a race, the Karens, of whom Judson had known nothing at the time of his imprisonment. The Karens were mostly animist, not Buddhist, and listened to the gospel with open ears. The Karen church became the principal base and spearhead of Christianity throughout Burma.

Adoniram Judson bore marks of the iron fetters for the rest of his life. The long imprisonment had marked him in another way too. He could not bear to be idle.

When the American mission grew large, and missionaries developed a tendency to concentrate in the larger centres, Judson pushed out into the wilds. He travelled endlessly among the Karens and Burmese whenever his health permitted. He grudged the time which administrative duties, and even the translation work and scholarship which he loved, forced him to spend at his base.

Wherever he went he preached and baptized. He was in a hurry, as if seeking to recover the years lost in prison. Judson would not wait until a convert had grown old and wise. When any man he met on tour sought baptism, having heard the gospel from a native evangelist, Judson would question him and his neighbours closely. He believed that if the man had been born again the fact would be evident in his transformed life and baptism need not be delayed. Judson was seldom deceived, and the Karen church grew fast.

Before the prison years, evangelization had depended almost entirely on his own labours. When Judson's feet were bound in the stocks, the Word of God had seemed shackled. He sought therefore to extend himself by urging his converts to go out two by two through the jungle paths to distant villages. He was among the first missionaries to teach that a church must be self-propagating. Thus the Karen church grew and became strong. Its members were outward looking, willing to suffer hardship, danger and long absences from home to enable others to know Christ as the One who delivers from fear and despair.

Judson's twenty months of stench and frustration in Ava's jails had not been futile after all.

19. Hudson Taylor, 1832–1905
YOUNG MAN WITH A PIGTAIL

Old carpenter Wang wandered down the street towards the river, the mighty Yangtze, so broad that the farther shore looked like a mere smudge on the horizon.

All around were the familiar sights and sounds of a small Chinese town of the 1850s: loose-trousered peasants carrying their baskets on long bamboo poles across their shoulders, vendors shouting their wares, women hobbling on tightly bound little feet; a teacher, in the robe of his class, trod delicately to avoid the offal; scavenger dogs snarled and fought. Wang knew no other world. He had heard of Outer Barbarians beyond the Middle Kingdom, and pitied them that they could never taste civilization, though he had been told that a few of the more adventurous traded with the Celestial Empire.

His eye caught sight of a knot of excited townsfolk, and as he drew near he saw an extraordinary sight – a 'foreign devil'. No wonder the crowd was amused: the young man had sandy hair and large grey-blue eyes, a most odd combination for a human being. And even odder were his clothes – black trousers like a coolie's only narrower, black coat complete with pleats and buttons back and front reaching to his knees, leather boots. And no pigtail.

The foreign devil answered questions patiently and began to preach ... about one Jesus who came into the world and died on a cross, like the poor criminals, Wang supposed, whom sometimes you saw suffer the 'death of a thousand pieces'. Wang caught snatches. But he could not pay close attention. He was absorbed in study of the foreign devil's amazing clothes, and edged closer to get a better view until almost next to the man, who evidently spotted this rapt interest and directed his talk right at him.

The foreigner paused.

Wang spoke up. 'Yes, yes,' he said. 'What you say is doubtless very true. But, honourable Foreign Teacher, may I ask you a question?'

The young foreigner looked delighted.

'Foreign Teacher, I have been pondering all the while you have been preaching. But the subject is no clearer to my mind. The honourable garment you are wearing has upon one edge of it a number of circular objects that might do duty as buttons, and on the opposite edge, certain slits in the material probably intended for button-holes?'

The Foreign Teacher seemed disappointed. 'Yes, that is so,' he murmured.

'The purpose of that strange device I can understand,' Wang continued. 'It must be to attach the honourable garment in cold or windy weather. But, Foreign Teacher, this is what I cannot understand. What can be the meaning of those buttons in *the middle of the honourable back*?'

'Why, yes,' chorused Wang's neighbours, 'in the middle of the back!'

The poor deflated preacher (who had no idea why a Victorian frock coat always had three buttons in the small of the back) soon wandered sadly away, for after Wang's question he was quite unable to draw the crowd back to the great subject of the Good News he had risked his life to bring to inland China, where no foreigner might lawfully go.

James Hudson Taylor, the Foreign Teacher as Wang had called him, was only twenty-three. He came from Yorkshire, England, and had been in China two years. He was small and of sickly physique, which today probably would never have passed the doctors. He was impulsive, warm-hearted and merry, though with a streak of introspective melancholy. His consuming passion was to win Chinese to Christ. He felt thoroughly impatient with the little band of missionaries then in China, who clung to the coast attempting to reproduce for the Chinese the church life and church buildings of England and America.

Hudson Taylor had gone inland. Yet his attempts were failing because he was a foreigner.... 'In the middle of the honourable back' – the words flung themselves at him, summing up the absurdity of wearing Western dress in the China of those days, where everything foreign was utterly despised.

To put on Chinese dress, pigtail and all, would scandalize brother missionaries and infuriate Western merchants, who would consider that he betrayed the British Empire by demeaning himself in the eyes of the natives. Hudson Taylor, however, had already seen what would not be generally accepted by missionaries for another two generations. As he wrote some years later: 'Why should a foreign aspect be given to Christianity? We wish to see churches of such believers presided over by pastors and officers of their countrymen, worshipping God in their own tongue, in edifices of a thoroughly native style.'

Such words were revolutionary. Their spirit remains pertinent, for if differences of dress are no longer a wall between Westerners and Orientals, other barriers remain, or are thrown up. Western confidence that we know best still bedevils some missionary situations, and Hudson Taylor points to the way out – the way of identification. And to the cost: when he adopted Chinese dress, pigtail and all, he lost the respect of his Western contemporaries. But he won the love of the Chinese, could travel widely, be heard quietly, free from urchins who jeered 'Foreign Devil!' and earnest inquirers who ruined openair sermons by awkward questions about buttons.

Furthermore, Hudson Taylor is proof that youth is no bar to being God's recipient of new insights. He is a lasting example of the lead that young men (or women) may sometimes give the church of Christ if they are walking close to him and will let him grant them imagination, courage, and persistence, even when, like Hudson Taylor, they are obscure in name and background, without wealth or influence or particularly good health.

The long life of Hudson Taylor, founder of the China Inland Mission (now the Overseas Missionary Fellowship) and one of the greatest of all missionaries, teaches many other lessons, such as the Principle of Faith immortalized by his words, 'Depend upon it, God's work done in God's way will never lack for supplies.' And the realization that the way to get men and means for the mission field is to deepen the churches until, imbued with the Holy Spirit, their priorities come right and they put the spread of the gospel before the solace of themselves.

Before he could teach such lessons or find his lifework, the opening of all inland China to the Word of God, the young Hudson Taylor had to learn that courage, initiative, and passion for souls are not enough.

In 1856, about a year after the incident of the Buttons-in-the-Honourable-Back, Hudson Taylor in his pigtail, rock-crystal spectacles, and teacher's robe, returned to Shanghai from Swatow[1], a notoriously wicked tropical

---

1. In this book Chinese names are spelt in the traditional way, in use at the time of the incidents and more familiar than the new pin yin spelling)

port nearly a thousand miles to the south, where with an elderly Scottish missionary he had laboured happily, if haphazardly and without apparent effect, for five months. Unable to secure a preaching hall Taylor, who was a physician though not yet qualified, knew what he would do – sail back up the coast to Shanghai, collect medicines and his surgical instruments, and return to labour on in Swatow.

He reached Shanghai to find the building where he had left his entire stock of medical supplies burned to cinders. Except for a few instruments all was gone. 'My disappointment and trial were very great,' he wrote. Vexed and puzzled he determined to go down the network of canals to Ningpo, the next Treaty Port, where he might buy some replacements from a missionary friend; afterwards he would sail to Swatow.

In the intense summer heat he travelled at a leisurely pace, preaching and distributing tracts, until the low level of the Grand Canal made further progress by boat impossible. Taylor set out before sunrise through a district disturbed by civil strife, intending to reach a seaport whence he could take a junk to Ningpo.

Everything went wrong. Leaving his servant (whom he had only recently engaged) to bring on the baggage coolies, Taylor hobbled off in his tight Chinese shoes. At the first stage he had a tedious wait in a tea-shop before the coolies straggled in exhausted. They were opium smokers. He dismissed them, and made the servant engage others, and stupidly walked ahead.

He never saw servant, coolies, or baggage again. At the second stage he waited hours. 'I felt somewhat annoyed, and but that my feet were blistered and the afternoon very hot, I should have gone back to meet them and urge them on.' At dusk there was no sign except a rumour that they had passed through towards the sea.

Taylor spent a miserable flea-ridden night in the public dormitory of a tumbledown inn, and awoke feeling sick. Next day he pushed towards the coast, and though at a half-way house during a short shower of rain he managed to preach a little, he reached the seaport upset and unhappy.

Inquiries were fruitless. He was questioned by the police, who saw that he was a foreigner. At dusk he was refused by two inns because the police were shadowing him, and turned out of another which at first had accepted him. Still searching for a bed he was led around, desperately tired and sore, by a young man who pretended to be friendly but deserted him at one in the morning, so that he had to sleep in the open on the rough steps of a temple where he was in danger of murder by three thieves. He kept himself awake by singing hymns and repeating portions of Scripture and praying aloud in English until the ruffians disappeared in disgust. At last he slept.

He was awakened rudely at sunrise by the young man, who demanded payment for his time the previous night. This was the last straw. When the fellow laid hands on him Hudson Taylor lost his temper. He grasped the man's arm and shouted at him to shut up.

Everything, everyone was against Hudson. The baggage containing almost all he possessed had been stolen by his faithless servant. Any hope of getting to Ningpo was lost, and somehow, almost penniless, entirely friendless, he must return to Shanghai. He dragged blistered feet eight miles of physical misery, in anger and spiritual rebellion, to the place where he had spent the night in the inn. He managed to bathe his feet, eat, and have four hours' refreshing sleep in the early afternoon.

He walked on, a little less upset, still puzzled. Surely God had intended him to reach Ningpo; it was the obvious course. Why this abandonment? Had he not surrendered home and comfort and safety on God's behalf?

Before the first milestone it dawned on him that he had *denied his Lord*. Tension suddenly slacked. Anger and pain dissolved in repentance as the truth broke through that he had not asked for guidance or provision before sleeping in the temple steps.

He had lost his temper, thoroughly un-Christlike. He had fussed, worried, forgotten the souls around. He had resented disasters, had expected God to order his affairs as he, Hudson, thought best. 'I came as a sinner and pleaded the blood of Jesus, realizing that I was accepted in him, pardoned, cleansed, sanctified – and oh the love of Jesus, how great I felt it to be.'

Hudson Taylor's troubles were not over, but the glorious sense of the love of his Lord swallowed up the miles.

The initiative, the control had passed to Christ – and that was what God had been waiting for.

When at length Taylor reached Shanghai, he received a letter posted in England months earlier which contained a cheque for exactly the amount of his loss. And before long he discovered that had he got through to Ningpo when he had intended, he would have reached Swatow in time to have been imprisoned, perhaps executed.

Words Hudson Taylor wrote at this time come shining through the mist of nearly a hundred and fifty years. 'At home you can never know what it is to be alone – absolutely alone, amidst thousands, without one friend, one companion, everyone looking on you with curiosity, with contempt, with suspicion or with dislike. Thus to learn what it is to be despised and rejected of man – of those you wish to benefit, your motives not understood but suspected – thus to learn what it is to have nowhere to lay your head; and then to have the love of Jesus applied to your heart by the Holy Spirit – his holy, self-denying love, which led him to suffer this and more than this – for *me this is precious*, this is *worth* coming for.'

20. James Chalmers, 1841–1901
CANNIBAL EASTER

A mob of howling, naked, war-painted savages swarmed around a native house above the sandy foreshore of a river mouth in unexplored New Guinea on an afternoon in December 1877. Inside the house a white woman sat sewing. The movement of her fingers gave no indication of her fervent but not quite agitated inward praying. Near her crouched three Polynesian teachers and their wives. Strong Christians from distant South Sea islands, they were struggling now with the uncomfortable conviction that their missionary service was about to end summarily in a cooking pot.

Down on the shore the white woman's husband had been signalling to his lugger for some stores when he heard the commotion behind. James Chalmers, a strongly built Scotsman of thirty-six, with bushy black beard, ran up to the native house, pushed his way through a ring of cannibals, and climbed the platform.

'One evil-looking fellow wearing a human jawbone and carrying a heavy stone club rushed towards me as if to strike,' Chalmers wrote later. 'Looking him steadily in the face our eyes met, and I demanded in loud, angry tones what he wanted.' By signs and unintelligible noises the cannibal demanded tomahawks, knives, iron and beads, adding 'that if they were not given they were going to kill us'.

'You may kill us,' shouted the white man, 'but never a thing will you get from us.' His tones conveyed the intensity of his displeasure to men whose language he had not yet had time to learn.

A Polynesian teacher approached. 'Tamate,' he implored the white man, using Chalmers' South Seas name and speaking in the language of Rarotonga, the island which they had all left to evangelize New Guinea, 'please give him a little something or we will all be murdered!'

'No,' Tamate replied. 'Can't you see that if I give them something because they threaten us, every group in the district will try the same trick. When there's nothing left they will murder us. Let them murder us now and be done with it!'

One of the cannibals, a friendly man from the house where the missionaries had lived since their landing three days earlier, told Tamate by signs that the violent savages came from across the river. He had better give them something to get rid of them.

Tamate, ignoring the angry roars and brandished clubs, smiled at him but shook his head. He would not give anything to armed men. 'We have never carried arms and have lived among you as friends.' The friendly cannibal harangued the crowd – which then retired to consider the situation. Thus the immediate danger was past. A deputation came forward to repeat the request, and again met refusal. Then they dispersed.

Next day their chief came, unarmed and unpainted, to say 'Sorry!' Tamate grinned happily at him, took him into the house and gave him a present. Jeanie Chalmers, still sewing, prayed that the cannibal would soon receive the Best Gift of all.

James and Jeanie Chalmers had served some ten years in the settled island of Rarotonga before pioneering in New Guinea. James Chalmers, 'Tamate', was the son of a stonemason in the western Highlands of Scotland, where he had been thoroughly grounded in the deep if stern religious convictions of an unbending Calvinism. He had even determined as a boy to be a missionary to cannibals, but subsequently decided that he was not among God's elect. Missionary ambition faded in favour of allowing full play to an irrepressible sense of fun. His practical jokes and youthful escapades sent shudders through the staid little fishing port of Inveraray, nestling beside the great castle of the Duke of Argyll.

When Chalmers was eighteen, during the revival of 1859, two evangelists were invited to Inveraray. Chalmers attended a meeting in a loft during a heavy rainstorm, and there became aware of the truth of Christ, through the verse from Revelation, 'Let him that is athirst come. And whosoever will, let him take the water of life freely.'

During training in England he showed himself more than ever a leader – in student pranks as well as in evangelism. A young man of strength, high spirits, humour and intense dedication, he 'used to pray for help as if he were at his mother's knee, and to preach as though he were sure of the message he had then to deliver.'

His arrival on the mission field was, characteristically though unintentionally, unconventional. The ship was wrecked on a reef in Samoa, and James and Jeanie chartered the brig of a local white pirate whom Chalmers temporarily tamed!

'Tamate', as he was named by the South Sea islanders, had hoped to pioneer at once, but the leaders of the London Missionary Society kept him nearly ten years in an island already evangelized. At last, with a group of his own Rarotongans, he was allowed to adventure into New Guinea. Only six years earlier a small group of missionaries had become the earliest white settlers in a land where strangers lived in hourly expectation of being clubbed, cooked, and eaten. (A friendly native tried to present Jeanie with a portion of oven-fresh human breast.)

After that first landing, which had so nearly ended in death, Chalmers placed a chain of Polynesian teacher-evangelists along the southern coast of Papua New Guinea. In each place he made the first, dangerous contact and stayed until the Papuans were reasonably friendly. He was a man whom they immediately respected and soon loved – tall, strong, impulsive, generous, quick-tempered but quick to laugh. He had no trace of a white man's pomposity, yet his character conveyed such authority that no native liked to cross him. He was fearless, again and again taking his life in his hands. And he brimmed over with a genuine, utterly unsentimental love, knowing that even the most depraved and cruel could be transformed by the love and Spirit of Christ.

Tamate's methods were always unconventional. He had no horror of using tobacco or tomahawks as currency. Once he caused merriment in the City of London by cabling: 'Send one gross tomahawks, one gross butcher knives. Going east try make friends between tribes.' He was a great explorer, but always as a means of spreading the gospel. He found a people sunk in degradation, violence and fear. Chalmers knew that his hard and dangerous labour was worthwhile because in time 'all these evils would yield to the gospel. God is Love, seen in Christ: this was the life word we brought them. The gospel was working its way in bush-clearing, fencing, planting, housebuilding; through fun, play, feasting, travelling, joking, laughing, and along the ordinary experience of everyday life.'

Tamate lived Christ. He preached Christ as the one who could save to the uttermost those who came to him. And he rejoiced at last to hear a young Papuan, so recently a cannibal, say to his fellow tribesmen, 'The time has come to be up and doing. Foreigners have brought us the gospel; many have died of fever, several have been speared and tomahawked. Now let us carry the gospel to other districts and if we die, it is well: we die in Christ. If we are murdered, it is well: it is in carrying his name and love, and will be for him. Let us do it!'

For twenty-three years Tamate and his Polynesians and Papuans evangelized, pacified, and civilized great stretches of the New Guinea coastland, and up into the nearer mountains as far as they could go. While her husband pioneered, Jeanie stayed bravely in their first cannibal village in order to show the trust that always breeds trust, but eventually the climate drove her to Australia where she died. After nine lonely years Tamate married again. It was soon after this that Robert Louis Stevenson, then living in Polynesia, described him in letters home as 'a man nobody can see and not love.... A big, stout, wildish-looking man, iron grey, with big bold eyes and a deep furrow down each cheek.... With no humbug, plenty of courage, and the love of adventure.... He has plenty of faults like the rest of us but he's as big as a church.'

All this time Tamate had no permanent white helper. 'We need help,' he wrote home, 'missionaries willing to live among the savages, men and women who will joyfully endure the hardship of the climate for Christ's sake.' When at length he heard that someone was appointed he commented, 'I hope he is a good all-round man without namby-pambyism, ready for all sorts of roughing it.' And in Oliver Tomkins he found a man after his own heart.

Within weeks of Tomkins' arrival Chalmers' second wife fell ill. In the long period of nursing her before she died, the young recruit became as a dear son to the veteran. After the burial they spent months touring the settled stations which Tomkins would supervise. Then they set off for the notorious Aird River delta where Tamate planned to pioneer, along coasts which no missionary had penetrated, where Christ had 'not been named'. He had reconnoitred the area, knew 'the savages there are splendid fellows. If only I can get hold of them they will make splendid missionaries.'

As Tamate and Tomkins, with their party consisting of a Polynesian teacher, a Papuan Christian chief and ten embryo Papuan missionaries, approached Goaribari Island, it happened that the inhabitants of a village named Dopina had just completed a new *dubu* or communal house for fighting men. Built of sago-palm timber, a *dubu* was not ready for use without human sacrifice. The next strangers to the island would serve for the consecration and the feast.

When the mission lugger rounded the headland, the men of the village at once paddled out and swarmed aboard. Tamate was used to such invasions, the normal prelude to his entry into a new village.

It was Easter Sunday evening, 7th April 1901. As the sun dropped swiftly to the brief tropical dusk, Tamate promised to visit the village in peace. He tried in vain to persuade the armed men to leave the vessel. To draw them off he said he would go ashore at once in the whale boat for half an hour and be back for supper. Tomkins said he would go too. They set off, crewed by the ten mission boys and the chief.

Tamate knew nothing about the new *dubu*, but he was ready as always 'to die for the name of the Lord Jesus'. Young Tomkins had no fear of death either.

The boat reached shore. While the chief and most of the mission boys stayed on guard, the two missionaries accepted the villagers' pressing invitation to enter the *dubu* for refreshment. They sat down on the floor, Tamate cracking jokes with his new neighbours and, as always, praying in his heart to the Companion whose Easter message he brought. All around him in the fading light were piles of human skulls at the feet of coarse wooden images.

Two swift blows from behind by stone clubs. Two cassowary-bone daggers swiftly plunged into the gullets of the white men. While the mission boys were set upon and murdered, the heads of Tamate and Tomkins were severed from their bodies. They were stripped, deftly cut into joints and passed to the women to be cooked, mixed with sago.

To the Western world, when the news came, the Easter massacre seemed a foul and obscene ending to two lives of goodwill – one famous and honoured, one young and promising. To the people of the village the cannibal feast was the prelude to their eventual discovery of Christ.

To Tamate and Tomkins it was a painless transition from the Easter Faith to the Easter Presence.

21. Mary Slessor, 1848-1915
LASSIE QUEEN OF CALABAR

The chattering stopped. Wives, their black bodies fattened according to custom, and widows, emaciated according to custom, moved closer together as a little white woman strode into the centre of the palaver where the chiefs of the tribe were seated in judgement on two young wives. The people of the village watched in wonder as the chiefs, who scorned women as mere chattels of men, rose in respect for Mary Slessor, already widely known up the creeks of Calabar as 'Ma'.

She wore a shapeless, sleeveless garment, not the formal long-sleeved dress which was normal for white women in the tropics in 1882; and her head was uncovered except for her shock of close cropped red hair, for she refused to wear the sun helmet which the doctors insisted was vital for Europeans. And since she always ate African food, and slept on the floor among the wives, all the village of Ibaka loved their guest, for her laughter and jokes, and her medicine chest, and because she taught about God.

Today she was grave. Two of a chief's wives had crept out of the wives' compound and had been caught in the hut of a young man, thus breaking tribal law. Two others were held as accomplices; and a palaver of chiefs had sentenced all four to a hundred lashes each with the crocodile whip – a virtual sentence of death. Mary had heard at once and gone to the head of the tribe, Chief Okon, the man who had invited her to visit their village from her base upriver at Old Town.

She urged him not to have the girls flogged. He was amazed. She persisted. At length he said, 'Ma, it be a proper big palaver but if you say we must not flog we must listen to you as our mother and our guest. But they will say that God's word be no good if it destroy the law's power to punish evildoers.' He had agreed to delay the sentence and reconvene the palaver. Thus Mary Slessor could now address the tribal court.

First she turned to the girls and address them in fluent Efik. Among Europeans she spoke broad Scots, but she had absorbed the local language so fully that every inflection and grunt made her sound almost like a native.

She scolded the girls for abusing their master's trust. 'Though God's word teaches men to be merciful it does not pass over sin. I cannot shield you from punishment. Ask God to keep you in future so that your behaviour is not a reproach to yourselves or to the word of God which you have learned.'

The village elders looked pleased; but now she turned on them. 'It is *you* who are to blame!' she cried. 'It is your custom of many wives to a man which is a disgrace!' Her blue eyes flashing, she lashed the men with her tongue. 'It is a disgrace to you and a cruel injustice to these helpless girls. Only sixteen years old, full of fun and frolic, yet you shut them up in a hut. It is a blot on your manhood! Obedience to your sort of laws is not worth having!'

She sat down. The palaver debated the case until at last the sentence of each was reduced to ten strokes of the whip, and no salt to be rubbed in the wounds, and no mutilation to follow.

Mary went into the hut to prepare bandages and ointments. Soon she heard the whistle and thud of the whip, the screams of the first victim and the laughter of those who watched. A naked, bleeding girl ran in, shivering in her agony. Mary washed and dressed the wounds and gave her a dose of laudanum to send her into an uneasy sleep. Soon came the next, screaming in shock and pain.

Some days later Mary Slessor boarded the royal

canoe for the homeward journey through the forest. She knew that her visit had only thrown into sharper relief the cruelties and miseries, and the spiritual hunger, of a land scarcely touched as yet by the gospel and kindness of Christ.

Mary was then thirty-four. She had been in Calabar for only six years, including a furlough to recover her health, for she was frequently down with the fevers which caused the death of numerous missionaries in 'the White Man's Grave' of West Africa. Mary Slessor always survived.

She had been brought up to hardship and poverty in the slums of Dundee, one of the many children of an alcoholic father and a devout mother who had a special interest in the Free Church of Scotland's Calabar mission. This had been founded in 1849 by Scottish missionaries from Jamaica, at the urging of elderly ex-slaves who had been abducted from the region before the abolition of the slave trade, and who well knew that Calabar was a land of violence and sorrow.

Mary had worked for fifteen years as a weaver in a Dundee factory. At first she was wild, until converted to Christ through the words of an old woman who terrified her with fear of hell fire – a method which Mary herself, though grateful, would never use on a soul. She became a skilled Sunday school teacher among the roughest boys and girls in the slums, until the inward call to Calabar became too insistent to resist.

The Foreign Mission committee sent her to Edinburgh for three months to improve her education and increase her experience, until at last, in 1876, she reached Calabar at the age of twenty-eight.

She found swamps and forests and broad rivers; a land of great natural beauty, with kingfishers and cranes and parrots; with elephants and leopards in great numbers which, with poisonous snakes on land and crocodiles in the rivers, made travel a hazard. And always the myriads of insects, especially mosquitoes, which had not yet been identified as the carriers of the malaria which was so often fatal.

Except for small settlements on the estuaries, where white traders bought and exported palm oil, Calabar was unpacified by any colonial power. Britain claimed it as a 'sphere of influence' but had not attempted to annex or control; inter-tribal warfare and the legacy of the Atlantic slave trade, abolished only seventy years earlier, had made the people of Calabar a byword for savagery and degradation. Brutal and arbitrary justice was administered by a secret council called Egbo; and if a chief died, his funeral required human sacrifices of many of his slaves and some of his wives.

Brought up to hardship and life among the poor, Mary Slessor soon felt at home. She quickly grew impatient with the formal European ways of the Scottish missionaries who had survived the climate. She recognized their sincerity and courage but was determined to understand the African's outlook. She soon realized that the men and women of the forest and river banks were instinctively religious, gripped by witchcraft and spirit worship; and that many of the cruellest customs were imposed by religion, a religion which knew nothing of the love of God.

Twins must be strangled or thrown alive into the forest, because one of them was begotten by the devil in a secret mating. Missionaries had done their best to teach otherwise, but Mary was willing to hurry at once on news of twins to save them from death, even if it meant walking a forest path at night, with the terrifying sounds of animals and night birds, and the vampire bats flying. She rescued twins and orphan babies – who would have been thrown out too – and always seemed to have a family of them around her: two of those whom she adopted, Jean and David, grew up to be her devoted companions and fellow workers for God.

The senior missionaries patiently put up with Mary being late for meals, and running races with the blacks, and even climbing trees with the boys if she thought it would help to open their hearts to Christ. At last the mission allowed her to live on her own in a poor part of the town. She could now eat as the Africans did (except that she liked a nice cup of tea whenever she could get it), and soon had an extraordinary influence, especially among the slaves.

It was while living in Old Town, by herself, except for her rescued babies, that she had visited Okon's village and saved the lives of the young wives who had been sentenced to a hundred lashes. On her way back in Okon's canoe she had nearly been lost in a violent storm in the estuary. She huddled terrified beside one of Okon's large wives, but when the crew panicked, the drummer stopped beating, the crew stopped paddling and the canoe tossed aimlessly, Mary lost her temper and yelled at the drummer to start again. The paddlers recovered their rhythm and brought the canoe to an island, where they all clung to an overhanging mangrove tree until the storm died down.

Mary's great desire, however, was to settle up-country among a tribe of powerful physique named the Okoyong. Two senior Scotsmen of the mission had visited them and seen the violence of their ways, and were not disposed to allow Mary to venture there. But in 1884 the British declared a Protectorate. Just four years later the mission leaders allowed Mary Slessor to visit the Okoyong to see whether they would accept her.

'Like all isolated peoples,' she wrote, 'they are

conservative and independent. They are brave, almost fierce, war-loving, and as reckless of their own lives as they are of others.' She made three preliminary visits to their biggest village, Ekenge, and its neighbourhood.

At last the Okoyong allowed her to settle. When she arrived the tribe had gone off for a week of riot around a funeral. Only a few weeks earlier, she learned from the head chief's sister, Eme Eta, they had celebrated a funeral by strangling the dead man's four wives, together with the eight slave men, eight slave women, five girls and five boys.

Mary began to hold services every day, attended mostly at first by women, children and slaves. Almost every other minute was spent in treating patients in a village which had never known modern medicine. In the evenings the tribe would give itself up to drink. '*Everybody* drinks,' she wrote. 'I have lain down at night knowing that not a sober man and hardly a sober woman was within miles of me.'

Then she saved the life of a chief's wife by walking with her medicines eight hours through pitiless rain in response to an urgent call; and by saving the woman she saved those who would have been human sacrifices at her death. The tribe began to recognize that their visitor's God had power. Mary herself experienced, over and over again, the power of God through prayer. She started a little garden so that she could pray as she hoed, for it was difficult to pray in the noise of her hut, crowded with visitors, village cats, cockroaches and wandering chickens. And her adopted son, Daniel Slessor, once an abandoned orphan, remembered how she would stand in 'forest clearings looking up, her blue eyes fixed steadfastly above, her lips moving.... She was praying to God for help, strength, courage and resource.'

One day a valuable and beautiful slave girl, bought

from another tribe, went to the hut of a young male slave, with whom she had fallen in love, and tried to persuade him to run away with her; but he knew that they were sure to be caught and die a terrible death. He refused. She went into the forest and hanged herself.

The young man was summarily tried by the village council and sentenced to be flogged and then executed. Mary at once protested that this was unfair: he had refused the girl. The chiefs retorted that he was being punished for bewitching her. 'What evidence have you?' demanded Mary. They replied that evidence was not needed: since the girl had entered his hut, he must have bewitched her.

Mary would have none of it. A court of law must not convict without evidence, she insisted.

At that the village council erupted with rage. The chiefs and the watching freemen leaped and yelled at Mary. They waved knives and guns, and threw dust, and glared at her. Mary was frightened. To show fear might cause her own death, and if she gave in and allowed the man to die she would lose all her growing influence. She glared back, and soon her quick Scots temper took hold of her; she was so angry that all fear went, and she stood there, blue eyes blazing under her red hair, until suddenly the storm subsided. The chiefs sat down, certain that this was no mere woman. As she once wrote in her Bible, 'God and one is a majority.'

They agreed to let her argue the slave's case and at last they compromised: he should be flogged but not killed. Knowing she could go no further she thanked them for their clemency, to save them face.

But they carried out the flogging, once a day for three days, close to her hut, so that she heard the whip and his screams. They gave him no food or water, and set guards so that she could not reach him. After three days they released him from chains and she nursed him back to health.

A few nights later the yard near her house was the scene of a drunken orgy to entertain visiting guests, with the men noisily taking their pleasure on slave girls, willing or not. Mary wrote: 'If I did not know that my Saviour is near me, I would go out of my mind.'

In 1891 the British set up a system of vice-consular justice in Calabar. Mary Slessor had established such an influence over the Okoyong that Sir Claude Macdonald, the counsul-general, made her a vice-consul, the first woman to be so appointed in the British Empire. Justice emphatically was done, though her court could be a little eccentric. One British official found her in a rocking chair with a baby in her lap, listening to litigants and witnesses, all treating her with great respect. 'Suddenly she jumped up with an angry growl.' The baby was transferred and she hurried to the door, 'where a hulking, overdressed native stood. In a moment she seized him by the scruff of the neck, boxed his ears and hustled him out into the yard.' The man 'a local monarch of sorts', had disobeyed her and been forbidden her court until he apologized.

Yet on her infrequent furloughs to Scotland, when Mary Slessor was expected to speak at missionary meetings, she was overcome. 'I am suffering tortures of fear,' she wrote before one meeting, 'and yet why is it I cannot rest in Him? He sends me work, surely He will help me to deliver His message, and to do it for His glory. He has never failed me before.' Nor did He fail her: on that occasion, as often, she gave an extempore address which enthralled and moved her audience.

After fifteen years among the Okoyong she could rejoice in a small church of strong Christian believers but a widened acceptance of Christian values, helped by the law and order brought by the British Empire. Human sacrifice had stopped at funerals; floggings were no longer at the whim of a master or husband; the dreaded ordeal by poison bean – by which guilt or innocence, death or life, were determined by chance or by the manipulation of a witch doctor – was stopped, though slavery still continued.

For years the Scottish mission did not find any one to replace Mary. Those Scotswomen who came to help her were inclined to give up, through illness or despair of the conditions. Once she became engaged to marry another missionary, much younger than she was, but when his health prevented his return to Calabar the engagement quietly lapsed.

At last arrangements were made which would free Mary Slessor to go farther inland, to the sorrow of all the Okoyong. She set her sights on the Aro, a tribe which was the terror of Calabar. She had met several of their chiefs when they visited Ekenge. Deep in their territory was a famous shrine which attracted many pilgrims from other tribes. Few returned home: the Aro took their offerings, killed them or sold them into slavery. The shrine's fame ensured a steady supply of victims until the British authorities determined on a military expedition to pacify the country and end the murders.

Just then, Mary had planned to visit the Aro. By a mischance which she saw as a providence, she missed the launch; when she hailed the next, on the following day, she found the British commander on board. He treated her with great respect and when they landed at the Aro's principal town, she bareheaded in her shapeless dress and he in his immaculate uniform and sun helmet, he was most impressed that her Aro friends crowded round to greet her.

It was the Aro who gave her the title by which she became known throughout the West Coast of Africa: *Eka kpukpro Owo*, 'Mother of All The Peoples'. As the British built roads and opened up the country, little Mary Slessor, with her laughter and her prayers and her hot temper, had more influence than any government officer. Once she spent an entire furlough, with the reluctant permission of her home committee, in travelling deeper inland on her own responsibility, teaching and using her medicine chest, and opening the way for the less adventurous to follow.

As the High Commissioner of Nigeria said in 1909: 'Miss Slessor can go where no white man can go. She can sway the people when we cannot sway them.' She grew old and weak but no less of a legend on the Coast, and was still at work. 'My life is one daily, hourly record of answered prayer ... for guidance given marvellously, for errors and dangers averted, for enmity to the gospel subdued, for food provided at the exact hour needed, for everything that goes to make up my life and my poor service. I can testify with a full and often wonder-stricken awe that I believe God answers prayer, I know God answers prayer.'

She died, aged sixty-six, in January 1915, among the Africans she loved. The strong church of Nigeria honours her memory and so does Scotland: when Queen Elizabeth II first visited Calabar, she laid a wreath, at her own express wish, on Mary Slessor's grave.

22. Rosalie Harvey, 1854-1932
THE LAME COW'S FRIEND

On 26th March 1884, a dark-haired, frail looking young English woman stepped down from the Down-Mail at Nasik Road station, a pet dog in her arms. Rosalie Harvey was one of the numerous children of the Vicar of Seaford in Sussex. She had offered for missionary work in 1874 at twenty, but the doctors were sceptical and not until 1882 did she reach India. Her father thought she would stand three years. She stayed fifty with one brief break.

After two years in Poona she came to Nasik. And for the first time drove in a *tonga* along the road from the railway, under massive banyan trees, roots draping from their branches, and the clumps of golden mohurs, their flowers bright red in the sun, to the Mission compound, former summer palace of the Mahratta Peishwas, but now 'with no shadow of the claim to the title of palace'. Yet the inner hall, separated from the verandas by cane screens on which flickered the light of a lamp suspended from the high ceiling, 'rivalled in quaintness anything I had yet seen'.

Nasik, the sacred city of Western India, close to the source of the sacred Godavari, which flows across the Deccan down to the Bay of Bengal, had a fine climate and natural beauty, offset by the bigotry of its priests and Brahmins; even the railway, which at Benares runs in sight of the bathing *ghats*, had been kept six miles off.

Rosalie's mission worked among women, who by both Hindu and Muslim custom were segregated in zenanas.[1] Her gay spirit was undeterred by difficulties,

---

1. The Zenana Bible and Medical Mission became later the Bible and Medical Missionary Fellowship, working among both sexes, and is now Interserve, operating in several countries.

and she was soon immersed in the normal work of a zenana missionary.

A girls' school had been started – in a haunted house, the only one extracted from reluctant landlords – and Rosalie and her colleague opened others, to which small boys also were admitted. She visited zenanas, and the jail. She wished she could open a pauper widows' home: 'how many poor old people are left to die of neglect and distress just because they are old and useless. If someone would leave me a fortune how gladly I would open such a Refuge!' She began a school for high-caste married girls, for *purdah* was not much observed among Hindus in Western India and they could go to and from their zenanas with little restraint. 'Think what the result would be,' she wrote, 'if a hundred Brahmin girls of Nasik, wives in name but children in reality, were brought daily into contact with the influence of Christian ladies, whose sole aim would be to promote their temporal and spiritual welfare.'

She visited in the villages, where the gospel was more readily accepted than in the proud homes of the city, and whenever she found a girl or a child-wife suffering, the offending males would be astonished at the vigour with which this shy and retiring Miss Sahib would berate them with her tongue. 'You dare to admit it to me openly?' she retorted to a husband whose maltreatment of his childwife had caused injury to her spine. 'Get out of this room at once!'

'Will this city ever become Christian?' she wrote one evening, after walking back through the dimly lit streets and glancing in at the dark interiors where vegetable-oil lamps feebly flickered. 'The people seem so to be locked up in Hinduism, so content – so hopelessly content to let things go on as they have ever gone.'

Early in January 1887 Rosalie was walking to her

latest school. 'On the way, met a drove of cattle and a woman beating a cow whose leg was broken. I stopped her, and took the cow away and took it to our bungalow.... This is only one of the many instances which one comes across in this country of lame or maimed cattle being driven into the jungle when they ought to be at home.'

Rosalie knew well that a Hindu would never kill a cow, since it is sacred, but cheerfully leave it to die in agony, and could be callous to animals and work them to death.

She decided then and there that this had gone on long enough. In the absence of the Collector (the principal civil officer), the Civil Surgeon was the leading English resident. 'So I thought, "I will go at once to him while the feeling is hot upon me", and off I started. It was nearly ten o'clock, and the sun was getting hot, but I could not stop to get a *tonga*, and to bring one from the town would take so long. Taking the gardener with me, I started across the plain and arrived at the doctor's bungalow with a red, hot face, my sun topi turned down, and I fear, a slightly crazy appearance, but all this would help to make an impression....

'Before I got to the door the doctor was out on the veranda to see who was come, flying in with a native flying after. He said, "This is an unexpected pleasure." I replied, "Please don't think I'm mad – don't think I'm mad!" and then related the circumstances. As I did so, the recollection of the poor animal's pain made the tears come into my eyes, and I could scarcely speak for crying. The doctor said, "We can do nothing. There is no Royal Humane Society here." Then I said, "Can't we get one?" He did not seem to think that it was either practicable or possible, and I felt chafed at this restraint. "We ought, we English ought to do something," I said.

"We ought not to stand by and see these things go on." '

The lame cow became a permanent inmate of the mission compound. In September it was joined by an ox, whom Rosalie had found yoked to a heavy quarry cart, despite a gaping wound in its neck; she sent for the Deputy Collector, 'who was disgusted at the men's cruelty'.

A month later a donkey came, a large wound in its chest and side. The donkey's owner asked for it back. 'I told the young man that he could stop in the compound day and night if he liked and see that his animal was safe, but that if he took it away now I should summons him for cruelty. The watchman told the people about the cow and the ox that have been rescued, and after loitering about a bit they went away.' A little later 'a man came here with a cow with a broken leg for me to mend. Was obliged to tell him this is not a "Cow Hospital", tho' I wish it were.' The next day 'Donkey's owner came bothering about the donkey; got into a rage with him; at which he was somewhat subdued. He says, "I am a poor man – give me back my donkey!" I say, "You are a poor man, therefore I will feed and doctor your donkey for you, and when it is well I will give it back to you." He says again, "I am a poor man, give me back my donkey. I will give it better food than you do." Then I turned on him and told him to "*chup* and go". He wants to make me buy it.'

Before the end of 1887 Rosalie had badgered the local Indian and English notables to found a branch of the Bombay Society for the Prevention of Cruelty to Animals, which took financial responsibility for the growing array of maimed, tired and diseased cattle in the compound yard, and built 'a kind of hospital', a collection of sheds close by.

For two years Rosalie bore the brunt of the Animal

Hospital management in addition to her other work, until a veterinary officer was appointed. From her scanty personal allowance she was already supporting two three-legged calves, Sonya and Bapu, old Tommy the horse, and the big buffalo Ahjiba, to say nothing of two human babies. As Rosalie wrote in her diary, 'It *is* difficult to work things properly in Nasik.... There is money – money for bribes – money for unjust stewards who keep back money meant for Government purposes – money for useless feasts and vices – but for the poor and needy how hard it is to get money – like drawing a heavy bucket from a deep well!

'If they won't give of their abundance – oh, that God would entrust some of that abundance to me, and with it wisdom to dispense it wisely!... I long to build a new Hospital for Animals, schools for the Mission and a new Z.M. House, with such rooms for the agents and servants, as we now also much feel the need of. Lord Jesus, hear my prayer. Indulge my long-cherished and ardent wish.'

In 1892 she paid a visit to the famous Animal Hospital near Bombay. On the drive back to the city her companion, Mr Hills, promised to try to get money from old Sir Dinshaw Petit, a Parsi millionaire baronet and cotton millowner, the real founder of Bombay's industrial power and a great philanthropist.

Reports were sent, including photographs of Sonya and Bapu hopping on their three legs, and a note describing the amputations. On 1st November Rosalie was taken by a mutual Parsi friend to Sir Dinshaw's magnificent house on Malabar Hill, close to the sea. As they entered the large hall, 'out of a side room an old gentleman came, wearing a cashmere dressing gown and a cap on his head. He was a nice looking man.... In shaking hands I bowed to him. He looked a little surprised and then returned the bow.' He promised Rs. 5,000 provided the hospital was called after him, and to endow it later. As Rosalie discovered, 'it was the calves with three legs that did it.'

Lord Harris, Governor of Bombay, laid the foundation stone of the Sir Dinshaw Petit Hospital for Animals in January 1895. To Rosalie's delight, one of her dogs, Tippoo Sultan, went and 'sat under the Governor's chair before he came. When I pointed this out to the Secretary with an air of great satisfaction he said solemnly, "I think he had better be removed." Darling Tippoo! He was there to receive the Governor on behalf of all the animal world – and he was to "be removed" – led off on his chain!'

Rosalie's dogs were one of the features of missionary life at Nasik. 'They were by no means always of high degree,' wrote a colleague; 'if some were handsome some were the reverse.' Butterfly was a prince, but even Rosalie admitted that Spot was a 'cross between a Pig and a Bear.' Sometimes they fought, or bit the Collector's dog. One October there was desolation when Rosalie's favourite, Piggy, disappeared. All Nasik was set looking for him, from the magistrate to schoolchildren. 'No news of Piggy', Rosalie wrote in her diary on 14th October. 'Does "if any of thine be driven out unto the uttermost part of heaven" refer to dogs? If it does, then there is hope in the promise, "From thence will I bring them back" ...' 'Piggy! Piggy!' she wrote three days later, 'all day long I am thinking of him. Will he come back again?' On the evening of 1st November some small boys said they had found Piggy. 'Ran with the small boys and Bhaskar Rao to the Chandolkar's Ali – but the dog tied up there was a dog like Tippoo. It was not Piggy. Rao sahib's tonga came racing to meet us, and all the household was in expectation – and all faces fell when I said, "It is not he"…. Piggy! Piggy!' He never came back.

During the closing years of the nineteenth century and the first of the twentieth India experienced a succession of famines and plagues. In Nasik these terrible years not only gave Rosalie more work than she had ever had, but brought forward two causes close to her heart – the cause of the lepers, and the cause of the babies.

Lepers had long come for alms to the Mission bungalow. 'Those who are not too lame,' wrote Rosalie in May 1893, 'crawl to our bungalow on Sunday to receive alms and to listen to the service, which I really think they enjoy.'

The lepers of Nasik, about thirty in number, 'haunted the river-side by day and slept on the verandas of the temples at night, their chief haunt being the Bell Temple called also Naro Shankar's temple. The front of this sacred place is rented by sweetmeat sellers, and in front of these shops the lepers used to sit exposing their sores, and black with flies. People shuddered as they passed them, and one day a man stopped me as I was crossing the river and exclaimed, "You have built a hospital for animals. Why can't you build a home for these poor people?" '

'Asked the lepers if we should build them an asylum,' Rosalie wrote in December 1893. 'They said, "Oh do, Sahib – but let it be in the temple neighbourhood, and make provision for our food." It was obvious that mere shelter was not enough, yet there was no money to build a fully equipped asylum. A few weeks later, "a poor cripple leper cried out to me, 'Sahib, I cannot walk, I cannot come to your bungalow now.' " I saw that he couldn't, poor fellow. Near the lepers' refuge there is a tree where we might go on Sundays and preach to them and give them alms.' This they did, especially as the contemporary medical view of leprosy frowned on encouraging them to come through the city to reach the

197

Mission House, now moved from the Peishwa's palace to a better site.

Early in 1897 Rosalie was asked by the Collector to join the Famine Relief Committee. The monsoon had failed and distress was grievous, but funds were pouring into India from Britain and abroad, and relief work – railway and road building, bridging and quarrying – for the able bodied, and Free Kitchens for the weak were organized by the Government. Every day Rosalie and her colleagues were at the kitchens helping the Collector and his committee or distributing blankets and grain, rescuing the helpless and weeding out able-bodied shirkers. She did not forget the lepers. 'Went down to tell the lepers they would get food from the kitchen.... The poor lepers were very grateful.'

The monsoon, late, broke the famine. Then came bubonic plague, from China or, as some said, brought by pilgrims from Mecca, sweeping up-country along the railway lines. In October the administration ordered evacuation of the plague-infected parts of the city, threatening to send in British troops to clear out those who remained. '*18th October, 1897*. Monday.... We are closing one school after the other.... Wherever one went, one met people going out of Nasik with their bundles on their heads. They all wore a look of great amusement. No one seemed to mind.' To the lepers, the evacuation was disaster. 'When the people were gone,' wrote Rosalie, 'who was there of whom the lepers could beg? Not only were they starving but their miserable shelter also was gone. They with the rest of the people had to leave the city, and had literally no place to flee into. The nights were bitterly cold, they had very little bedding and they lay shivering on the hillside in the vicinity of Indra Kund. Here there had been created a small plague shed, but it had caught fire and all that remained to shelter the lepers from the cold night winds were the bare posts and rafters blackened by smoke. In this miserable apology for a shelter I found them awaiting death.' At Rosalie's behest the Collector supplied sacking, and a daily dole of flour, dal and rice.

Her days were now spent in the Plague Hospital and Segregation Camps, nursing, changing clothes and bedding, cheering the friendless and comforting the dying. The Mission House was compulsorily evacuated after dead rats – the worst plague-carriers – had been found. Rosalie lived in a tent at the hospital, and then at the Church Missionary Society (CMS) bungalow nearby.

To the lepers, thanks to Rosalie, instead of starvation the plague had brought food and shelter. 'They look so well,' she wrote, 'having been fed regularly for six months. They beg us to continue the dole – always. If the Mission could only build and endow an Asylum down near the river, they would all no doubt come into it. How I would love to build one for them!...'

When the plague receded the Relief Committee gave notice that the dole would cease and the temporary shelter be taken back. 'If I cannot raise money for them,' Rosalie wrote, 'then they will have to leave their present refuge just as the rains break, and wander about the river banks without food and shelter. They will have to beg, as they did before. No one seems inclined to realize how hard their lot is – and they trust me to stave off all this that is coming upon them. How to meet so huge a demand I do not know – to feed thirty-two lepers daily, and to build them a home!... Poor people! They feel so sure I will do something for them. O good Lord, let them not lack and suffer hunger. Open up a way of escape, as Thou didst for the lepers of old.'

The Zenana Mission had no funds to help. The Mission to Lepers was sympathetic but could not offer ready support. The Collector nobly continued official aid for a further month (and gave from his own pocket), and Rosalie went to Bombay to raise money. She wrote to *The Times of India* and called on Sir Dinshaw Petit, 'who was very jovial and gave me Rs. 100', which provided a corrugated iron roof. 'Even strangers could not withstand an appeal from her,' wrote a colleague, 'for it would be couched in such racy and clever terms as to be quite irresistible.'

Money came slowly, for times were hard. Hindus feared that her proposal to build an asylum was mere cover for proselytizing, while 'Christians grumble because so few of the lepers become Christians.... The course is to relieve pain unconditionally, and to tell the lepers what we believe to be the remedy for future suffering. Only the Holy Spirit can bring home to their hearts the truths which fall upon their ears.' In January 1900 Rosalie made a sketch plan of the proposed asylum, but before sufficient had been raised plague struck again, 'like the waves of a hungry sea'.

'A postman at the city P.O. says every fifteen minutes a corpse is carried by', she noted in June 1900; the burning ground was 'white with the ashes of the newly burned dead'. In September, as famine once more stalked the burnt-up land, the Government sanctioned the new site for the Leper Asylum.

Rosalie's lepers adored her. 'A man of the carpenter caste – not a bad leper – came. I allotted him a place in the shed with the old lepers, whereupon they began to abuse him. As remonstrances did no good I went into the room, gave the ringleader two cuts with my umbrella, kicked their cooking vessels over, and told them to clear out into Naru Shankar's temple.' Another time, after a Hindu had made them a present of old sepoy blue coats and red caps, 'when I next went to issue the food I found them all lined up in military order, and was greeted with a sepoy salaam. The lamest of the lot said that nothing more was needed but my word of command for them all to go off to chase the dacoit who was terrifying the neighbourhood!'

The lepers called her *Aayi* (Marathi for Mother). 'They used to beg for themselves,' she said, 'but now their "Mother" begs for them. I have a very helpless family.'

The famine of 1900 raised her number from thirty-two to over a hundred. The first permanent building on the asylum site was opened in 1901 – a home for untainted children. The Mission to Lepers had assumed responsibility, with Miss Harvey as superintendent so long as she wished, and the Leper Asylum at last opened, with wards for men and women, a dispensary and a school room, in 1903. 'I am aiming at things beyond my power,' she had written ten years before, 'but not beyond the power of God.'

When Rosalie was a young missionary, fresh from England, she was taken round the wards of the Civil Hospital. Seeing a mere skeleton of a baby tossing in its cot she asked why it was restless. 'The baby does not want a doctor, but a mother,' replied the English Civil Surgeon; 'you take it home and care for it.' Her senior missionary refused permission; when Rosalie told the doctor, he looked her in the face and said, 'If missionaries won't do this work, then who will?'

At Nasik in January 1889 the Indian Matron of the maternity hospital asked Rosalie to take a little girl, the child of Brahmin parents. The parents had no use for this baby, Sita, and she would have been left, like so many babies in India at that time, to die in the fields, or to be thrown into a well or a ditch. Rosalie found an *amma* for Sita ('It is not difficult to get a foster mother in India,' she wrote, 'because so many babies die'), and brought them to live in the mission compound. On 2nd March the baby was baptized but three weeks later she died. 'If an adopted child can take such a hold on one, what must it be to own a real child? And when I see her, she will know me and love me as she could not know me and love me here. The empty cot – her clothes are lying about – I can't put them away, her nurse has gone home – sorrowing relinquishing her place.'

Six months later Rosalie adopted another, Venu, a week old. 'Venubai's mother wanted to know when I would take her away!', and announced that she would leave the hospital in four days, regardless of the fate of the child. But her callousness had already been fatal, for Venu died in the hospital. In 1890, prison visiting, Rosalie found a young Gujeratir girl-widow with a three-months-old baby which she had tried to kill. 'She said she had wandered all over Bombay asking people to take it, but no one would. She had not gone to the "white people". I told her I would take it.' In 1891 a man of good caste who had lost his wife carried their baby girl, dosed with opium, the six miles into Nasik and dumped it at Rosalie's feet. 'He bluntly informed me that if I did not take it he was to make it over to the dancing-girls. Though a healthy child of about six weeks old, it was reduced to a skeleton.'

And so the list grew; a baby Brahmin boy, who grew up to be the delight of Rosalie's later years, was adopted in 1894. Rescue work was not easy, for until the famine the 'natives would rather see their children die than become Christians'.

The famine turned Rosalie's personal adopted family into an official Babies' Home, authorized by the Mission at Christmas 1896, the Government undertaking to make a grant for each child. As it happened, though other districts were swamped with orphans, her seven babies were not at first joined by others, even when she put an advertisement in the Press. 'It is sad to think,' she commented, 'that in one locality children are starving to death, in others we have to hunt for them.'

Seeing her advertisement a Hindu official asked if conversion was intended. Rosalie replied unequivocally: 'My offer as a missionary to receive girls of three to ten years of age, who through the famine have lost all their natural guardians, necessarily includes the placing of them in a Mission School, where they will be brought up in the Christian religion.'

Rosalie at once planned a proper building for the foundlings, and before long they were arriving: 'A baby was brought in a basket with a blanket erected over it by means of bent reeds. A man carried the basket on his head, a police sepoy walked by the side with a large official letter, and a coolie followed with a tin pot containing milk. Despite all these arrangements the infant was wailing, and only stopped when it got into its natural element – a mother's arms.' In 1900, with the famine at its height, the Babies' Home was opened in the Mission compound.

The babies, often coming in two at a time whenever the missionaries visited the relief camps, would be put in groups with foster mothers, 'responsible women who have lost their babies. They live in little rooms in the compound.' The babies would grow up not knowing they were orphans. A Parsi convert was chief assistant, and in 1901 Rosalie was joined by a young Englishwoman who was to be with her for the rest of her life and succeed to her work at the Babies' Home.

As the famine and plague receded the Babies' Home remained. 'In our Mission,' Rosalie wrote in 1902, 'we all meet morning and evening for prayers. All the babies come, however small, and sometimes a dog or two. All the heathen servants come. Sometimes the babies crow, and make a joyful noise or walk about the church.'

Rosalie had yet another dream: that Nasik's women should have their own efficient hospital. She even said, 'If I were younger I would come home and study medicine myself.'

A Hindu widow had founded a hospital for women, but few entered because only a cactus hedge separated it from the men's hospital and no woman surgeon or physician served on the staff. It was about to close.

Rosalie harried its trustees to sell and the Mission to buy and equip and send out a lady doctor. She had no direct responsibility for the medical mission, once the new hospital had opened in 1903, but regarded it as the 'crowning happiness' of her life's work.

She refused to return to Europe for a furlough, and took only one holiday in the hills to recover her health after the plague years, until in 1906 she at last agreed to an eleven-month rest in New Zealand, where her brother lived. She returned to Nasik on the evening of 21st November 1907. Everyone was at the station to meet her. 'The old groom was overwhelmed with joy and flinging himself on her neck and kissing her, he cried, "Oh, Mother! Mother!" while her poor hat was sent rolling in the dust.' At the bungalow the children let off fireworks. The lepers held a thanksgiving service and recited poems in her honour. Next day she went once again to the Animals' Home.

She worked on, for another sixteen years, seeing a better hospital built in a healthy suburb, and the Babies' Home run by her devoted assistant.

Her concern for animals never wavered. Pained by

the condition of the bullocks who drew the town's water carts, she formed a relief corps to give the regulars occasional rests. She instituted periodic inspections of *tonga* ponies. 'Would you,' runs a typical letter to the Collector, 'be able to attend a meeting of the Nasik SPCA at the Sir D.M. Petit Animal Hospital some time this month or next? We wish to protest against the condition of the Nasik tram ponies and horses. They are miserably thin now, and as the weather gets hotter and traffic increases their condition will grow worse and worse.' Once she was badly bitten by a monkey, and for some months was seriously ill. She refused to have an operation, and when convalescent went about with a chain and weight round the leg to counteract the contraction, with success.

In 1924, on reaching the age of seventy, Rosalie Harvey was officially retired. She went to live at the Lepers' Home, where she continued as Superintendent, occupying the bungalow across the road with its gay bougainvillea and pleasant garden, where with her dogs, books, photographs and memories she remained the human inspiration and the delight of all Christian workers in Nasik.

Every day after her retirement 'Aayi' would walk round the Lepers' Home, a loved figure in her deaconess dress and veil, with a shiny stick to lean on, attending service in the chapel (where grain and water were always left in case birds flying about during service should be trapped when the doors were locked), seeing that all the lepers were happy, encouraging those in pain, having a word with the Biblewoman or the blind Christian minstrel, and then passing on to the children's home.

In the last months, before her death in 1932, her jubilee year of missionary service, the lepers ruled their Superintendent, but no one could suggest separating Aayi from her family.

23. THE CAMBRIDGE SEVEN

Stanley Smith, 1861-1931

On a bluff day in 1882 the river banks of the Thames were crowded once again from Putney to Mortlake as people watched the annual Oxford-Cambridge boat race. Cambridge had the inside station and was away to a good start. But on the umpire's launch, chugging slowly behind with a swarming trail of little boats, it was soon seen that the Cambridge Eight were not together. By Hammersmith, the Oxford Eight were level, and excitement was intense. In a few moments they were ahead, and as Stanley Smith the Cambridge stroke ruefully remarked, 'We were treated to their wash, after which we went awfully; and finally Oxford won by seven lengths!'

Though Oxford had won, the critics were loud in their praise of the Cambridge stroke, who had given a splendid exhibition of oarsmanship. Three years later this popular young stroke oar with his 'handsome address and winning manners' was a humble missionary in China. And the manner of his going made a stir across the world and lit fires still burning. The 'Cambridge Seven' will never be forgotten.

The event which put S.P. Smith on the road to China was the visit of the American evangelist D.L. Moody to Cambridge University in November 1882. The mission began in derision and ended with 'the most remarkable meeting ever seen in Cambridge', a University transformed, and proud undergraduates humbled at the foot of the Cross.

Smith had already finished Cambridge and was working as a schoolmaster in South London. But as a former member of the Cambridge Inter-Collegiate Christian Union (CICCU), he took leave for the weekend, and was stirred to the depths by what he saw. 'Marvellous,' he wrote, 'verily God's measure is *running over*.' Smith had been a Christian since he was twelve. From a fluctuating introspective faith he had passed to settled determination to serve Christ. But it had been on his own terms, with 'insincerity, sham and "men service".' Never before had he seen God's unfettered power, nor realized his own insignificance.

Though humbled, Stanley Smith had more to learn before God could show him his life's work. The scene changes to a little seaside village on the east coast – Pakefield, Norfolk, on a raw January day two months later. The previous summer Smith had been holiday tutor to the young brother of a Cambridge friend, and had thoroughly enjoyed himself with this Christian family, the Burroughes at Normanstone, near Lowestoft. He had eagerly accepted an invitation to a fortnight's winter visit. The first ten days were much as in the summer – driving and walking, battledore and shuttlecock, or word games in the evening; and Bible readings, hymn singing and evangelistic work among the poor and the navvies. On 18th January Mrs Burroughes and George were to go on ahead to Burlingham Hall, George's grandfather's place some fifteen miles inland, but Harry had wired that he would not be returning that night, and the three unmarried daughters would be left alone except for the servants. Victorian convention demanded that the young bachelor guest must sleep under another roof. Stanley was to lunch with old Mr Price at Pakefield, and he walked over with a small handbag to stay the night as well.

In this trivial manner Smith was led to the second most decisive experience of his life. Price was a man of generosity and spirit – an old people's dinner was proceeding when Stanley arrived, and an evangelistic meeting followed; but he had discovered also a secret too little known among Christians in the 1880s: 'the secret of liberty and delight in the service of the Lord'. He had proved that on a definite consecration of the whole self to God – not in intent but in simple deed – the Holy Spirit would shed abroad the love of God in the heart, producing a realistic sanctity beyond any previous imagining, and providing a lasting sense of the presence of the Lord, 'turning your life of duty into a life of liberty and love.'

That night of 18th January, 1883, Price and Stanley Smith sat up late. As they talked Smith saw something of the self-will that was hindering him. Because he enjoyed Christian activities he did them, but the direction remained in his hands. There were blemishes in his character; and no 'hourly abiding', in the presence of Christ, which could only occur, said Price, when Stanley denied himself and took up the Cross, when he handed himself a willing slave unreservedly dedicated to his Master's service, to the Christ who had died to redeem him.

It was after midnight when they went up to their rooms. Stanley Smith had never before seen so vividly the meaning of God's holiness and of his own sin, nor the demands and the possibilities of faith in Christ. Before he got into bed he sat down and wrote in his diary, 'I must *fully* consecrate myself.'

The next morning they talked again and read Bible passages. Christ was calling, and Smith was in no mind for refusal. Before morning was out he knelt down with Price in the little room in the east coast village, and prayed that the Lord would take his whole life to use it as he wished.

At midday he left Price and walked back to Lowestoft for his navvies' meeting. As he went, 'very happy', he found himself singing, 'My all is on the altar.' At the meeting he experienced a new freedom in speaking. The navvies filled the cramped hall, late-comers content to remain outside in the raw January inshore wind. 'His word was with power not mine,' wrote Smith. 'These dear men with their grasp of the hand and "God bless you, sir!" repay anything.'

'Bless the dear Lord,' he could write a few days later. 'He is in me and *fills* me. How good he is. Oh that all Christians knew this full surrender.' Thenceforth his work, his athletics, his friendships became one unhesitant happy witness to Christ, and time was spent preaching, and bringing others to know Christ as Saviour or, knowing him, to yield to him as Lord.

But if Smith thought he was now ready he was wrong. Clear command for the future was not given for ten months, until the last day of November 1883.

At a country vicarage in Surrey, close to Leith Hill, Smith was a speaker at a weekend convention. During that weekend a verse of Scripture was so burned into his consciousness that he saw it as a call from his Lord demanding instant response: 'I will give thee for a light to the Gentiles, that thou mayst be my salvation unto the end of the earth.' Stanley Smith was in no doubt. It was a call to foreign service. God was sending him 'far hence to the Gentiles.'

Smith's prayers and interest had long followed the China Inland Mission. Its uncompromising spirituality and its tolerance attracted him as they attracted Hoste, and it carried the gospel 'not where Christ was named'. Before the end of the year Stanley Smith had written to the CIM and on 4th January 1884 he went down in the morning to Mildmay, though suffering from gastric trouble, 'to call on Mr Hudson Taylor of the China Inland Mission. Stayed till 8 p.m. Had tea there and a nice long talk about *China*; I hope to labour for God there soon.'

In due course he was accepted. Nor was that all. Smith felt an urge to awaken others to their responsibilities to the Christless millions overseas. Before long, after talks and prayer together, a Cambridge friend joined him – Willie Cassels, a London curate. Independently a gunner subaltern, D.E. Hoste, was being led along the same road. Two brothers, Arthur and Cecil Polhill-Turner, sons of a wealthy Member of Parliament and country squire, were also sensing the call. Both were former members of the Eton cricket eleven. Arthur was a Cambridge undergraduate, converted through Moody, Cecil a cavalry officer won by his brother.

Smith met them and encouraged them. One of his greatest Cambridge friends Monty Beauchamp, also joined. The climax came with C.T. Studd, the most brilliant all-round cricketer of the day, an Eton, Cambridge, and England player, who in November 1884, after going with Smith to a CIM meeting, determined to leave all and follow Christ to the ends of the earth....

C.T. Studd, 1860-1931: Test Cricketer

C.T. Studd was born in luxury. His father, Edward Studd, had returned from jute planting at Tirhoor in North India to spend his fortune. At Hallerton in Leicestershire and later at Tedworth House near Andover, the young Studds grew up in a spacious world dedicated to hunting, cricket and their father's fine string of racehorses.

In 1875, when Charlie and his two elder brothers, Kynaston and George, were at Eton, their father's sudden conversion through Moody and Sankey made a startling difference to their lives. Edward Studd now thought only of bringing his friends and family to Christ; as his coachman remarked, 'though there's the same skin, there's a new man inside.'

The boys had been brought up in the arid formality

of conventional religion, 'a Sunday thing', so C.T. said later, 'like one's Sunday clothes, to be put away on Monday morning'. But now his father was 'a real live play-the-game Christian'. 'But it did make one's hair stand on end,' was C.T.'s memory, telling the story long afterwards to young people, in the merry way he loved to use. 'Everyone in the house had a dog's life of it until they were converted. I was not altogether pleased with him. He used to come into my room at night and ask if I was converted. After a time I used to sham sleep when I saw the door open, and in the day I crept round the other side of the house when I saw him coming.'

The following year Edward Studd's prayers were answered. One by one on a single summer's day at Tedworth Hall, each of his three elder sons, J.E.K., G.B., and C.T., all in the Eton eleven, were won for Christ by a guest, a young man called Weatherby, who had earned their respect by his reaction to a cruel practical joke. 'Right then and there joy and peace came into my soul,' recalled C.T., 'I knew then what it is to be "born again", and the Bible, which had been so dry to me before, became everything.'

None of the brothers had the courage to tell each other what had happened; it was only disclosed by a joint letter from their father early in the following half at Eton. Edward Studd died shortly afterwards, but Kynaston maintained his tradition, organizing a college Bible Reading. Of C.T., when he left in 1879, his housemaster wrote, 'he has done no little good to all who come under his influence.' Sport, however, increasingly absorbed his attention. By determination and hard training rather than by native genius he made himself an outstanding all-rounder and was 'incomparably the best cricketer' in the Eton and Harrow of 1879, when Captain. He was in the racquets pair, and won the House Fives.

Going up to Trinity in 1879, a freshman with Smith, Beauchamp and William Hoste, Studd won his blue and thus played for Cambridge for four consecutive years, following his brother G.B. as Captain in 1883, to be followed by J.E.K. in 1884. His national fame dated from his great century in 1882 when Cambridge University, against all expectation, defeated the unbeaten Australians. That August, still an undergraduate, twenty-one years old, he played at the Oval in the famous Test Match which England seemed about to win, yet lost to the Australians by eight runs, and the term 'The Ashes' was coined. By his Captain's error of judgement in changing the batting order, Studd went in last and never received a ball. The match was so exciting that one spectator gnawed right through the handle of his umbrella.

That year of 1882 C.T. Studd had the highest batting average, and in bowling, though only fifteenth in the averages, had the second highest score of wickets taken. The great W.G. Grace, the Gloucestershire doctor who was the best and most famous cricketer of the Victorian age, described C.T. Studd as 'The most brilliant member of a well-known cricketing family, and from 1881 to 1884 he had few superiors as an all-round player. His batting and bowling were very good.... His style of batting was free and correct, and he scored largely and rapidly against the best bowlers of his time. He bowled medium-pace, round arm, with a machine-like delivery, and had a fair break from the off.'

By 1883 C.T. Studd was a household name, the idol of undergraduates and schoolboys, and the admiration of their elders. But as a Christian he was a nonentity. 'Instead of going and telling others of the love of Christ I was selfish and kept the knowledge all to myself. The result was that gradually my love began to grow cold, the love of the world came in.' Looking back afterwards he felt he had spent these Cambridge years in one long, 'unhappy backsliding state'. In fact, he had not been averse to singing 'Sankeys' round the piano, or to having a 'read and prayer'; he went occasionally to the Daily Prayer Meeting and, as S.P. Smith found, he was willing to take CICCU cards to freshmen. Moreover he was recognized as a Christian, and since cricketing prowess, high spirits, good looks and a kind heart made him outstandingly popular in the University, his identification with the Christian set was not worthless. But he never led another to Christ. Whereas, as he once wrote to Kynaston, 'Our cricketing friends used to call you "The Austere Man" because your life was true to God and you were true to them, for you were ever faithful in speaking to them about their souls', C.T. preferred the easier path. He admired his brother's 'courage and loyalty in the Lord Jesus Christ', and was kept by J.E.K.'s influence from utter betrayal of his convictions, but his religion was effete: 'mincing, lisping, bated breath, proper', he once described it, 'hunting the Bible for hidden truths, but no obedience, no sacrifice.'

During Moody's Cambridge mission in the autumn of 1882, C.T. Studd was in Australia with the MCC team which recovered the Ashes, returning in the spring of 1883. By then, S.P. Smith had passed through his great experience of consecration near Lowestoft. Two old ladies, who had known Edward Studd, had set themselves to pray that C.T. be brought to rededication, but their prayers seemed unanswered. At the end of the 1883 season C.T. was 'for the second year in succession accorded the premier position as an all-round cricketer. Some years have elapsed,' commented *Wisden's,* 'since the post has been filled by a player so excellent in all three departments of the game.' He was at the very height of cricketing fame.

At the end of November 1883, when S.P. Smith was at Brockham in Surrey receiving definite guidance to the Mission Field, C.T.'s brother George, closest to him in age and affection, fell seriously ill. C.T. came down from Cambridge in December to find G.B.'s life in danger. He was prostrate with grief and anxiety, and as he sat in the sick-room overlooking the street and narrow gardens, while carts and carriages rolled softly by over the straw specially laid down, he began to see life in its true perspective. At night-time, as he waited in the semi-darkness lest his brother should call, he 'saw what the world was worth'. As night after night I watched by the bedside as he was hovering between life and death God showed me what the honour, what the pleasure, what the riches of this world were worth. All these things had become as nothing to my brother. He only cared about the Bible and the Lord Jesus Christ, and God taught me the same lesson.'

In the first days of January 1884, Studd could say later, 'God brought me back'. Very humbly he reconsecrated himself to his Lord; and as if to underline that God's hand is in all the accidents of life, 'in his love and goodness he restored my brother to health'. As soon as George was out of danger, C.T. went to Moody's meeting at St. Pancras. 'There the Lord met me again and restored to me the joy of my salvation.'

Immediately, 'and what was better than all', Studd learned the immense satisfaction of spiritual work. He began to tell his friends of his decision, taking them to Moody or to evangelistic services in Cambridge, devoting himself to Christ with the same determination which he had devoted to cricket. 'The Lord was very loving and he soon gave me the consolation of saving one of my nearest and dearest friends. I cannot tell you,' he was often to say later, 'what joy it gave me to bring the first soul to the Lord Jesus Christ. I have tasted most of the pleasures that this world can give. I do not suppose there was one I had not experienced; but I can tell you that those pleasures were as nothing compared to the joy that the saving of that one soul gave me.'

Back in London for the Easter vacation, after his last term in Cambridge, he was constantly helping at the Moody Campaign. S.P. Smith met him there on Sunday, 23rd March, and they walked back together from St Pancras to Hyde Park Gardens having 'a nice talk'. The cricket season began and C.T. felt he 'must go into the cricket field and get the men there to know the Lord Jesus'. He had found 'something infinitely better than cricket. My heart was no longer in the game; I wanted to win souls for the Lord.' He took members of the Test team to hear Moody. One by one A.J. Webbe, the great batsman, A.G. Steel and Ivo Bligh, the Captain, afterwards Lord Darnley, told Studd that they accepted Christ, and they kept in touch with him for the rest of his life.

On 19th June 1884, the Moody Campaign ended. The combination of cricket and Christian work had kept Studd happy without thought for the future. But now he 'wanted to know what my life's work was to be for the Lord Jesus Christ. I wanted only to serve him.' Studd was impatient, and conscious of his powers and influence. It was hard not to consider himself an asset to the Christian cause and he expected that he would soon find his niche and make his mark. No clear guidance, however, was granted. He invited the opinions of his friends but they were contradictory. The more he strove to make up his mind the more impatient he became, and within a few weeks of Moody's departure Studd had worked himself into such an emotional tangle that his health gave way and he had to go into the country to convalesce.

During July, August and September, while S.P. Smith, Cassels and Hoste were preparing for China, C.T. Studd was recovering his balance, spending much time in Bible study and in prayer for guidance. His only decision was to read for the Bar 'until the Lord Jesus should show me what my life's work was to be for him'. As soon as he returned to Hyde Park Gardens early in October even this decision seemed wrong, and he was convinced that he must spend his whole time in Christian service. His inheritance was ample, 'God had given me far more than was sufficient to keep body and soul together.... How could I spend the best hours of my life in working for myself and for the honour and pleasures of this world while thousands and thousands of souls are perishing every day without having heard of the Lord Jesus Christ, going down to Christless and hopeless graves?'

Studd's mind worked in single tracks. Whatever he did must be done to the utter exclusion of other interests. Awakened as he was, he knew that nothing less than uninhibited dedication to the winning of souls would satisfy him. He 'began to read the Bible more earnestly and to ask God what I was to do. But this time I determined not to consult with flesh and blood, but just wait until God should show me.'

But the first thing God had to show him was himself. Towards the end of September a close friend invited Studd to a drawing-room Bible meeting. A passage was read. As they studied it someone mentioned a woman they all knew. 'Have you heard of the extraordinary blessing Mrs W. has received?... You know she has been an earnest Christian worker for nearly her whole life, and has had a good deal of trouble and sorrow which had naturally weighed upon her. But somehow lately God has given her such a blessing that although she has had so much trial it does not affect her at all now. Nothing seems to trouble her. She lives a life of perfect peace.' They turned to their Bibles again to see whether such a blessing was promised. Before they parted they were convinced that the peace which 'passeth understanding' and 'joy unspeakable' were offered to every Christian, and they had knelt down to ask that God should 'give us this blessing'.

Back in his own room Studd knelt down again, 'very much in earnest'. Someone had just given him a popular American book, *The Christian's Secret of a Happy Life*. *The Christian's Secret*, by Hannah Pearsall Smith, which was to become a best seller when published in England four years later, dealt in simple, practical terms with the very possibilities which they had been discussing at the Bible meeting. 'In order to enter into this blessed interior life of rest and triumph,' wrote Mrs Pearsall Smith, 'you have two steps to take – first, entire abandonment, and second, absolute faith.' As Studd read, sometimes on his knees and sometimes sitting in his chair, he began to see that he had not received the blessing because he had been 'keeping back from God what belonged to him'. 'I had known about Jesus Christ's dying for me, but I had never understood that if he died for me, then I didn't belong to myself. Redemption means "buying back", so that if I belonged to him, either I had to be a thief and keep what wasn't mine, or else I had to give up everything to God. When I came to see that Jesus Christ had died for me, it didn't seem hard to give up all for *him*. It seemed just common, ordinary honesty.'

Convinced that 'I had kept back myself from him, and had not wholly yielded', C.T. Studd went down on his knees and from the bottom of his heart said the words of Frances Ridley Havergal's hymn:

'Take my life and let it be
Consecrated, Lord, to thee.'

The next step was faith – a straightforward confidence that God had accepted his life because it was offered, and that what God had taken he could keep. Then and there Studd took up the position which was to be his chief characteristic to the day he died: 'I realized that my life was to be one of simple, childlike faith.... I was to trust in him that he would work in me to do his good pleasure. I saw that he was my loving Father and that he would guide me and keep me, and moreover that he was well able to do it.'

What S.P. Smith had discovered near Lowestoft in January 1883, C.T. Studd found in London in September 1884 – peace, security, overflowing contentment and a willingness to go wherever he was sent.

It was not long before light was thrown on the future. Until his recent experience no thought of overseas service had crossed Studd's mind: 'England was big enough for me.' But the call of the foreign field soon became insistent. It was almost a matter of mere mathematics – the percentage of Christless people to every witnessing Christian. Furthermore, the pioneer's blood was stirring in his veins. As for sacrifice, it seemed the wrong word to express the intensity of his joy in being put to God's work.

On Saturday, 1st November, Stanley Smith returned to London from his farewell visits to Cambridge and Oxford. His contacts had been informal – frequent, crowded meetings in the colleges, breakfasts and lunches with twos or threes, brief words at Bible Readings and prayer meetings. At about eleven o'clock in the morning of that Saturday, on his way home from Paddington Station to John Street, Stanley Smith drove up in a hansom cab to Number Two Hyde Park Gardens, to call at the Studds'. Both Kynaston and C.T. were in, and when Smith mentioned that he was going that evening to the CIM headquarters to a service of farewell to John McCarthy, a returning missionary, C.T. said he would join him.

At the service McCarthy, one of the founder members of the CIM, told once again the story of his call, nearly twenty years before, and spoke of the vastness of spiritual need in China, 'thousands of souls perishing every day and night without even the knowledge of the Lord Jesus'. As McCarthy spoke, C.T. Studd was convinced that God 'was indeed leading me to China'.

As McCarthy's address closed and they were singing *He leadeth me*, Studd for a moment thought of rising in his place and offering for China on the spot. But he felt 'people would say I was led by impulse'. When the meeting ended he slipped away by himself and prayed for guidance. Only one consideration made him hesitate: he cared not at all that to bury himself in China would end his cricket and snuff out his national reputation, that it might invite the disapproval of worldly friends; as for hardship, he relished the prospect. But he knew that his mother would be heart-broken. Should he repay her love by deserting her? Could he face wounding one to whom he was devoted? He opened his pocket Bible. A passage in Matthew 10 seemed to answer his doubts: 'He that loveth father or mother more than me is not worthy of me.' At that he 'knew it was God's wish he should go'.

Studd told no-one at the meeting. On the way home, as the two young men sat well wrapped up on the open top of the horse-bus clattering down Essex Road, Studd told Smith that he had 'decided to go to China'.

Stanley Smith was so delighted at the news that on reaching John Street, after parting from Studd, he decided, late as it was, to return to the CIM at Mildmay and break the news to McCarthy and to write to Hudson Taylor, who was away in the country. For Smith and his friends the night of 1st November ended in praise and thanksgiving.

For Studd it ended in conflict. He immediately reported his decision to Kynaston. Kynaston, who knew what it would mean to their mother and who could not forget Charlie's aberrations during the past four months, doubted the validity of the guidance. C.T. broke the news to Mrs. Studd. As he had feared, she was distraught.

The next two days were a nightmare. 'I never saw anything like Kinny's depression,' wrote Monty Beauchamp, who was round there on the Monday night, 3rd November, 'he says he has never in his life seen two such days of suffering and sorrow, referring to his mother.... All day she was imploring Charlie not to go up to Mildmay and at all events just to wait one week before giving himself to H. Taylor. He would listen to no entreaties from Mrs Studd or Kynaston, who looked upon him as a kind of fanatic.'

That Monday night Kynaston determined on one last effort: 'Charlie, I think you are making a great mistake. You are away every night at the meetings and don't see your mother. I see her, and this is just breaking her heart.' 'Let us ask God,' replied C.T., 'I don't want to be pigheaded and go out there of my own accord. I just want to do God's will.' J.E.K.'s advice and help had always meant much, and 'it was hard to have him think it was a mistake'. They knelt and put the whole matter in God's hands. 'That night,' said C.T. later, 'I could not get to sleep, but it seemed as though I heard someone say these words over and over, "Ask of me, and I shall give thee the heathen for thine inheritance and the uttermost parts of the earth for thy possession" (Ps. 2:8).'

This verse convinced him. On Tuesday, 4th November he set his face to Mildmay, called on Hudson Taylor and was accepted. The conflict was not yet over. As, once again, the horse-bus trotted down the dimly-lit Essex Road, the entreaties of his brother and his mother's weeping were uppermost in C.T.'s mind. Having held out so long, he was tempted to waver and withdraw his offer to the Mission. He alighted at King's Cross Underground Railway station, and stood on the platform waiting for the Bayswater train to steam in. In despair he prayed for a sure word of guidance. He drew out his pocket Bible. With a platform lamp flickering over his shoulder he opened and read: 'A man's foes shall be they of his own household.' With that his way was clear – and when Mrs Studd knew that C.T. was settled in his decision she withdrew her opposition and supported him warmly for the rest of her life.

A torch is lit

The announcement that Studd was going to China caused immense excitement in the universities.

Not only was C.T. Studd a household name, but the suddenness of his decision seemed to make it the more impressive. Smith had been stumping the country for Christ for nearly two years. Studd had been absorbed by cricket. 'We never thought he would go', was an Eton friend's comment. Moreover his sacrifice, abandoning cricket at the height of his fame, was the more apparent. Oxford undergraduates crowded to hear him.

'You have no idea how wonderfully the Lord helped and blessed dear Studd,' wrote Smith to 'My dear Mr Hudson Taylor' after the first meeting. 'We were simply so full of the joy of the Lord we could only wear the broadest grins on our faces for the rest of the night!'

They spent six days at Oxford, two others joining for

the last day. Curiously, in view of what was to happen, the later meetings were not well attended, and at one time Smith and his friends endured a sharp attack of depression and doubt.

At Cambridge, where Smith, Studd and Monty Beauchamp were to speak, the effect was marked. As one undergraduate said afterwards, 'We have had missionary meetings and we have been hearing missionaries talk to us from time to time. But when men whom everybody had heard of and many had known personally came up and said, "I am going out myself," we were brought face to face with the heathen abroad.'

Each day enthusiasm rose. Though some of the dons criticized Smith and Studd for their lack of scholarship, and the more flippant undergraduates wrote them off as eccentric, the Christian Union men were stirred to the depths. Smith won their hearts by his charm and shook them from complacency by the fervour of his call, supported by Studd in clipped, homely phrases. As the men listened to these 'spiritual millionaires', as one undergraduate described them, the very content of the word 'sacrifice' seemed reversed: and each man wondered whether he could afford the cost, not of utter devotion and worldly loss but of compromise and the loss of spiritual power and joy. Nothing less than the experience of these two men was worth having.

During this week the two brothers Polhill-Turner became certain that they were called too; both had been feeling their way, Arthur to give up (or postpone) ordination, Cecil to resign his cavalry commission. Cecil had already called on Hudson Taylor. When Arthur realized that Cecil might be joining the five others, he sensed a challenge that he, too, should join them.

Smith's and Studd's Cambridge mission had increased the 'extraordinary interest aroused by the announcement that the captain of the Cambridge eleven and the stroke oar of the Cambridge boat were going out as missionaries'. The news was in everyone's mouth, competing in public interest with the national anxiety for Gordon in Khartoum. These two young men, the world at their feet, seemed to be sacrificing so much so early to bury themselves in the back of beyond. And, by all accounts, they were doing it with gusto. 'S.P.' and 'C.T.' were daily discovering the depths and heights of grace. 'Dear Charlie is as full of blessing as an egg is of meat,' wrote Smith on 23rd November, while Smith spoke for himself of the 'glorious liberty Christ has won for me'. Both had told Hudson Taylor that their personal wealth was at the Mission's disposal.

Hudson Taylor had intended to set off early in January 1885 with a miscellaneous party including Hoste, Smith and Cassels. But as his son and daughter-in-law wrote in their biography, 'the unexpected happened, and God's purposes broke in upon these well-laid plans with an over-flowing fulness which carried all before it.'

The human agent was an elderly and noted evangelist living in Liverpool, Reginald Radcliffe, a close friend of Hudson Taylor. Radcliffe had noted Studd's and Smith's influence on students and had a particular desire to extend it to Scotland. With Hudson Taylor's permission he had written to Professor Alexander Simpson of Edinburgh, a distinguished throat specialist and layman, suggesting a visit by the two young men.

On 28th November, Smith and Studd left by the night train from Euston to Glasgow – Studd with nothing but the clothes he stood up in. His mother was very distressed, when Taylor asked her to send a parcel, 'at my son

Charlie's erratic movements and going off to Scotland without any clothes of any sort except those he had on. How or why he should wear one shirt night and day till the 9th of December is a mystery to me when he has a supply provided, and one has always been taught that "Cleanliness is next to Godliness".' She urged Taylor to place him, in China, with an older and sober minded Christian in steady work. 'I feel that he and Mr Stanley Smith are too much of the same impulsive nature and one excites the other.'

On 2nd December, Studd's twenty-fourth birthday, they spoke to Glasgow University students. After brief visits elsewhere they arrived in Edinburgh. Studd and Smith were not taking this tour in their stride. 'When we went round the students,' wrote Studd later, 'we were in a mortal funk about meeting them because we had never done anything like this. So we used to stay sometimes all night by the fire on the mat, sometimes praying and sometimes sleeping.' And thus in the meetings, as Smith could write, 'there was much power.'

At Edinburgh all was ready. But even Stanley Smith and C.T. could scarcely have expected the result.

A committee of professors and students had sent sandwich-men tramping the neighbourhood and had circulated printed notices. They had taken the Free Assembly Hall, a large building holding a thousand, and challenged their own faith by announcing that students only would be admitted.

Nevertheless they were afraid. This was the age of strident rationalism; Edinburgh University was largely medical and, despite the impact made by Moody three years earlier, Christianity was at a discount and considered 'only good for psalm-singing and pulling a long face'. 'There were two fears,' said one of the organizers, 'the first – that there would not be a meeting; the second – that if there should be, there would be a "row" – a very common thing amongst Scottish students.'

Studd and Stanley Smith spent the bleak December afternoon in their host's drawing room 'in prayer, till they got victory'.

In the University, as the evening drew on, 'the word went round our class-rooms, "Let us go and give a welcome to the athlete-missionaries".' Well before the hour the hall was crammed. As the committee and speakers knelt in the green-room they could hear the students 'singing their usual before lecture songs and beating time with their sticks', but Studd shamed the fears of the organizers by calmly thanking God for the result and, as one of them wrote, 'we felt there was going to be a great blessing.'

The two 'athlete missionaries' entered the hall and were warmly cheered. A divinity professor, Dr Charteris, a Chaplain to the Queen, took the chair. C.T. Studd spoke first, then R.J. Landale, an Oxford man returned from China, and lastly Smith. 'Stanley Smith was eloquent,' one of the students recalled years later, 'but Studd couldn't speak a bit – it was the fact of his devotion to Christ which told, and he, if anything, made the greatest impression.' Again and again he was cheered. 'The fact that a man with such prospects as he should thus devote himself and his fortune gave them an interest in him from the very first,' wrote the chairman. It was the age of ponderous homilies, and by the very contrast of Studd's happy, ungarnished story of spiritual development 'the students were spellbound'.

Landale's talk was on China, and Stanley Smith then began. Taking as his text 'They feared the Lord, and served their own gods,' he showed up, 'in words of burn- ing scorn', the flat, effete selfishness which so often passed for Christian service. He was heard in utter stillness. 'As he spoke,' said one of the committee, 'our hearts condemned us.' The atmosphere was tense with spiritual power. Smith swept on, his 'unusual powers of thought, imagination and utterance' roused to highest pitch by the response of his audience.

When he had done, the chairman announced that any who would 'like to shake hands with them and wish them Godspeed' could come forward after the Benediction. The committee expected that few would have sufficient courage in front of other students. To their amazement, 'no sooner had the Benediction been pronounced than there was a stampede to the platform.' Nor was it mere curiosity. 'They were crowding round Studd and Smith to hear more about Christ; deep earnestness was written on the faces of many.... It was all so evidently the work of the Holy Spirit.'

The meeting closed and Studd and Smith returned to their host's for a meal before catching the night mail to London. Shortly before half-past ten the two walked down to Waverley Station with a medical professor and several students, who were urging them to return before they left for China. At the station a hundred students or more were waiting. 'Speech! Speech!' they cried as the two men appeared. Studd stood on a seat and said a few words, resoundingly cheered. The quiet station had seen nothing like it since Gladstone's Midlothian Campaign five years before. A traveller asked what the fuss was about. 'Th're a meedical students,' replied a porter, 'but th're aff their heeds!'

As the train steamed out into the night Smith and Studd were waving from the carriage windows, some of the students running to the end of the platform, cheering and shouting goodbye, while others stood singing 'God be with you till we meet again.'

On the evening of 8th January 1885 the Seven were together for the first time on the platform of the Exeter Hall, supporting Hudson Taylor. Though nothing to what was to come, the hall was 'absolutely packed'. The Polhill-Turners both spoke of their call, and Stanley Smith wound up a long meeting with a comparatively short address. From that evening 'the Cambridge Seven' became a household name.

The next day Studd and Smith left Euston by the 1.30 p.m. express for Liverpool. Reginald Radcliffe met them, and they began the same evening with a meeting of young men. 'A most remarkable one,' wrote Smith. 'About twelve hundred there – packed: and such a time of power. Many received Jesus. Young men broken down; I hear there were seventy or more awakened. This is the Lord's doing.'

After meetings in six Scottish cities the two came to Edinburgh and found two thousand students were awaiting them, 'the largest meeting of students that has ever been held' in Edinburgh. 'I lifted up Christ crucified,' wrote Smith simply, 'and Charlie gave his testimony.' None there could afterwards forget, as Dr Moxey of the divinity faculty wrote, Smith's 'big muscular hands and long arms stretched out in entreaty while he eloquently told out the old story of redeeming love', or Studd's 'quiet but intense and burning utterances of personal testimony to the love and power of a personal Saviour'. More than half the hall stayed for counselling. On the Monday when they had spoken with equal effect to two further audiences, they promised to return after their engagements in Glasgow; and on the Friday they were back, to learn that all the signs of religious revival were about.

Their final meeting with the Edinburgh students proved the most remarkable. Many were in tears before the end, and three or four hundred stayed to the after meeting. At half past ten the floor was still 'covered with men anxiously enquiring 'What must I do to be saved?" One of the committee sought out the manager and obtained an extension of lease till midnight, and up to the end could be seen 'the glorious sight of professors dealing with students and students with one another.' As for Smith and Studd, they were utterly humbled. 'There were several conversions,' was all Smith could find in him to say, 'and many began to yield to God what had long been his due.'

Newcastle, Manchester, Rochdale, Leeds – through the smoke-grimed cities of the North, Smith and Studd moved in a triumphal tour, though the triumph was not theirs but Christ's. At Manchester on 26th January, 'a most glorious meeting,' wrote Stanley Smith, 'nearly all young men. Fully a thousand stayed to the after-meeting: and going away we did have our hands squeezed, a somewhat painful show of friendship!' At Rochdale, the next day, they had 'a most remarkable meeting. Quite the most remarkable.' Studd's comment was more picturesque. 'We had a huge after-meeting,' he wrote to his mother, 'it was like a charge of dynamite exploded among them.'

Wherever they went the effect was the same. Young men of all classes flocked to hear them. In the early 1880s wealth and position could command a respect untinged with envy, while the testimony of the greatest all-round cricketer in England, supported by a prominent oarsman, could impress where other men's words fell flat. And because of the imminent sacrifice of all that the world held dear, many could take from Studd and Smith what they would not from older men whose calling, however rightly, was conducted from cosy vicarages. Studd and Smith were the men for the hour.

They knew well enough that they were neither better nor more important than other Christian workers, but because they had yielded all they were given all. 'I cannot tell you how very much the Lord has blessed us,' wrote Studd to his mother, 'and we daily grow in the knowledge of Jesus and his wonderful love; what a different life from my former one; why, cricket and racquets and shooting are nothing to this overwhelming joy.' Furthermore, their conscience was stirred to the depths by the North, still in the throes of the industrial depression of the early '80s. 'Finding out so much about the poor in the great towns,' wrote Studd, 'has increased my horror at the luxurious way I have been living; so many suits and clothes of all sorts, whilst thousands are starving and perishing of cold, so all must be sold when I come home if they have not been so before.'

On Thursday, 29th January, Studd, Smith and Radcliffe came back to where they had started a fortnight before, reaching Liverpool early in the afternoon. After a brief rest at the Radcliffes', out at Waterloo, they came in for the final meeting at the YMCA. 'Packed, and an overflow pretty full.' The two were told afterwards that sixty young men had 'professed conversion on that one night'.

Shortly before eleven the two jumped into a cab for Lime Street Station. Symbolically, at the end of such a whirlwind tour, the cab horse 'ran away with us and bolted down Pembroke Place, though fortunately no damage was done'.

After reaching London in a cheerless drizzle in the dark of the early morning, and spending the day quietly at their homes, Stanley Smith and C.T. Studd joined the others on the evening of Friday, 30th January, for the CIM's final London Farewell at the Eccleston Hall. Hudson Taylor had left England the previous week.

From then on, except for a rushed visit by Studd and Smith at the weekend to Bristol, where the Colston Hall was not large enough for those who came to hear them, the Cambridge Seven were together – at Cambridge, Oxford, and a final public meeting at Exeter Hall, the historic London rendezvous of evangelicals – three meetings which burned the message of the Seven into the consciousness of the nation.

'When before,' asked one religious newspaper, 'were the stroke of a University eight, the captain of a University eleven, an officer of the Royal Artillery, an officer of the Dragoon Guards, seen standing side by side renouncing the careers in which they had already gained no small distinction, putting aside the splendid prizes of earthly ambition ... and plunging into that warfare whose splendours are seen only by faith and whose rewards seem so shadowy to the unopened vision of ordinary men?' Yet the crowds did not come to flatter or gape. 'Spirituality,' recalled Eugene Stock of the CMS, 'marked most emphatically the densely crowded meetings at which these seven men said farewell. They told, modestly and yet fearlessly, of the Lord's goodness to them, and of the joy of serving him; and they appealed to young men, not for their Mission, but for the divine Master.'

The Cambridge Seven attracted, not only by their birth and athletic prowess, and by the sacrifice they were evidently making, but because they were not cut to a pattern. Smith and Studd were ascetics, reacting violently from the comfort of their early lives. The Polhill-Turners, no less devoted, did not make such sharp distinctions. 'C.T. believed in rigid austerity,' wrote Cecil Polhill later, describing a journey in China, 'and no comfort of any sort, either of furniture or luxury in food were for a moment allowed. He would not allow himself even a back to a chair. My brother was mildly ascetic.... To me it did not matter one way or the other, all was good, and so we hit it off capitally.' Hoste and Cassels were both fastidious men, though going to the squalor of China with as much readiness as Cassels had gone to the slums.

At first meeting, Smith would seem severe, though affectionate and charming on closer acquaintance, but Studd's gentleness almost belied his burning words. Beauchamp, with his enormous frame and somewhat florid face, and his capacity to extract enjoyment from anything, was almost as eloquent as Smith; but Hoste and Cecil Polhill-Turner were shy and found public speaking a trial. Cassels, as quiet as Hoste, as good a speaker as Beauchamp, was in many ways the most mature of them all.

'*Exeter Hall* – last night, what shall I say? Such a meeting!' wrote the CIM Secretary to Hudson Taylor next morning. 'I question if a meeting of equal significance and spiritual fruitfulness has been held in that building during this generation. Its influence upon the cause of missions must be immense, incalculable.'

'It was a most magnificent success,' he went on. 'Exeter Hall was packed in every part, and people of note and title had to get in anywhere and be thankful if they got in at all.... That meeting will be the talk of all England wherever men meet who are interested in the cause of missions.'

Rain had been falling hard all evening, but 'long before the time announced,' reported *The Times*, 'the large hall was crowded in every part, and an overflow meeting of some of the many unable to obtain admission was held in the small hall.' 'Over three thousand,' Stanley Smith was told, 'and the overflow five hundred, besides hundreds going away.' Dr Barnardo and other well-known figures had to stand the entire time.

The meeting had been arranged for young men but they were lost in a miscellaneous mass of men and women 'of all sections of the Church and grades of social life.' Stanley Smith spoke first and longest and held his audience spell-bound. ' ....We do not go to that far distant field to speak of doctrine or theory, but of a living, bright, present and rejoicing Saviour,' not to offer 'the milk-and-water of religion but the cream of the gospel, and to tell what a blessed thing it was to have the love of the Lord Jesus Christ reigning in low hearts.'

When he reached his peroration the stillness was profound. 'How can one leave such an audience as this? It seems to me as if Christ has come right into your midst, and has looked into the face of you men and women, young, old and middle-aged. He would take hold with loving hands of each one, and looking into your eyes point to the wounds in his pierced side, and ask 'Lovest thou me?' And you would say, 'Yea, Lord, thou knowest that I love thee.' And what is the test of love? 'If you love me keep my commandments.' And what, Master, do you command? 'Go ye into all the world and preach the gospel to every creature."

Five of the Seven spoke more briefly. Then C.T. Studd rose. 'I want to recommend you tonight to my Master. I have tried many ways of pleasure in my time; I have been running after the best master – and, thank God, I have found him.' Unhurriedly, without flourish or effect, he told the story of 'how the Lord has sought and found me and led me back to himself.' The simplicity of the narrative, coming from such a man as Studd, brought the challenge of Christ to every man and woman present. 'What are you really living for?' he concluded, 'Are you living for the day or are you living for the life eternal? Are you going to care for the opinion of men here, or for the opinion of God? The opinion of men won't avail us much when we get before the judgement throne. But the opinion of God will. Had we not, then, better take his word and implicitly obey it?'

Next day the Cambridge Seven left London for China.

'There is enough power in this meeting to stir not only London and England but the whole world,' said the eminent Nonconformist who gave the closing address at Exeter Hall.

The interest was enormous. 50,000 copies of the China Inland Mission's account of the meetings were sold, and a revised edition a year later, with additional material sent back by the Seven from China, became a bestseller. In Britain, universities experienced a revival which spread to American colleges and led to the formation of the Student Volunteer Missionary Union, ancestor of the great evangelical student movements of the twentieth century throughout the world.

As for the Cambridge Seven themselves, their paths diverged but not one looked back, and a high proportion of their children (all the seven married) became missionaries in their turn.

Stanley Smith's life was spent in North China. He became a fine linguist and as fluent a preacher in Chinese as in English. In later years he endured severe trials and disappointments but worked on until the end, preaching and teaching until the night before he died on 31st January 1931.

C.T. Studd was the best known of the Seven in later life. His courage and endurance were unquenchable. In 1887, determined to live by faith alone, he gave away the whole of his fortune. His mother and family disapproved but when he married and had four daughters, they nobly paid for their education.

In 1894, broken in health, Studd and his wife left China, never to return. After six years in India and a period in Britain and America, where his words did much for the missionary cause, Studd set off in 1910 into the depths of tropical Africa, pioneering in defiance of illness, criticism and poverty. From his faith grew the Worldwide Evangelization Crusade, and though in later years he became a controversial figure, nothing could detract from the splendour of C.T. Studd's witness to Christ. Studd died at Ibambi, Belgian Congo, on 16th July 1931, over a thousand Africans seeing him to his grave.

The last of the Seven, D.E. Hoste, who had succeeded Hudson Taylor as leader of the China Inland Mission in 1903, died in London in 1946. But long after the later lives of the men who formed it are forgotten the Cambridge Seven will remain in the consciousness of the Christian Church – their splendid sacrifice, and their wholehearted devotion to the call of Christ; their intolerance of shoddy spirituality in themselves or in others; and their grasp of the urgency of the gospel to unevangelized millions overseas.

And, particularly relevant, not one of the Seven was a genius. Theirs is a story of ordinary men, and thus may be repeated, not only in countries of the West but in lands which were the mission fields of a century ago but now send missionaries themselves.

The gospel of Christ is unchanged, and his call is unchanged. The Cambridge Seven illustrate how that call may be heard: 'God does not deal with you until you are wholly given up to him, and then he will tell you what he would have you do.'

24. Rowland V. Bingham, 1870-1943
LEFT IN LAGOS

Sitting at the back of a newly opened church in Toronto in the early 1890s, a young man heard the great missionary statesman, A. J. Gordon, deliver his famous lectures on the Holy Spirit in Missions. Before the series ended the young listener, Rowland V. Bingham, was praying that the Spirit would call him to serve in some distant, lonely corner of the earth.

He went on with his obscure pastorate in the countryside near Toronto. The months passed without a clear answer to his prayer. Then he happened to address a small morning meeting in the city, where an elderly lady with a distinct Scottish accent invited him home for lunch, introducing herself as a Mrs Gowans, a widow. During and after lunch she told him of her son Walter, who had been certain that he was called to take the gospel to the neediest country he could find. He had pored over maps and statistics until one vast area in Africa had impressed itself on him as almost totally without Christian witness.

From coast to coast, south of the Sahara and north of the rain forest, lay a great, populated belt known in the nineties as the Sudan. Its eastern regions had been wrested by the fanatical Muslim Mahdi from the Anglo-Egyptian rule of General Gordon, murdered at Khartoum seven years before. The French were pushing into its north-western area, the British were probing from the Gold Coast (Ghana) and up the Niger from Lagos, but almost all the land lay under the rule of slave-raiding Muslim kings or animist tribal chieftains. Before Rowland Bingham left Mrs Gowans, he knew in his heart that he must join Walter Gowans to penetrate the Sudan with the message of the Lord Jesus.

On a fare scraped together by his farmer friends, and

with a college contemporary of Gowans', Tom Kent, whom he met in New York, Bingham sailed to England. Gowans had gone ahead, since the mighty British Empire, on which the sun never set, was the colonial power in the region, and it was a British missionary board who must send them. But, like Hudson Taylor when he tried to persuade existing societies to evangelize inland China, Gowans, Bingham and Kent met total refusal for inland Sudan: money was too short, they were told, and the climate was a killer.

The three young men decided to go ahead on their own; they had just enough money to reach Lagos, and the Lord would provide from there. On 4th December 1893, they were anchored off this fever-haunted port, which had as yet no harbour for big ships. Missionaries of the three societies which were working on the coast befriended them to the extent of introducing a tough old trader who rented them a home and, rough sinner as he was, went far beyond the claims of business to help them. But as for going inland, the three North Americans were told they were mad.

Rowland Bingham fell ill with the dreaded malaria which carried off so many in the 'White Man's Grave'. There was no known cure at that date, and at sunset the doctor sent a message to the Anglican mission home: he could not last the night. The newly arrived bishop, a burly New Zealander named Joseph Hill, came across to pray with Bingham, then gathered the missionaries to special prayer on his behalf. 'Do you believe,' he asked one of them as they rose from their knees, 'that we are going to receive that for which we have asked?'

'I do!' she replied. 'I believe that young man is going to be raised up.' And he was; but less than a week later Bishop Hill and his wife were both dead of yellow fever, he in the afternoon and she at midnight; of all the party of ten he had brought out only one survived.

When Bingham was strong enough to work again, he and his companions resolved that it was high time to leave for the far interior, for the central Sudan which, Gowan said, was closed only because no one would open the door. They sold almost all their belongings, including their watches, yet still had not enough to pay porters and boatmen – until the mail steamer arrived carrying a gift of $500 from a servant girl called Mary Jones: she had been left a legacy and sent it all to this new, untried, unnamed mission, together with a smaller amount which her mistress added.

By now Gowans, Kent and Bingham had realized that one of them must be left in Lagos to arrange for the despatch up-country of further supplies, for they had no field secretary or committee: the Lagos missionaries, in the kindest possible way, had washed their hands of them, yet they could not live in the interior without trade goods with which to barter, for money was unknown. Unless they engaged porters to carry rolls of calico and sacks of beads, knives, and other odds and ends highly regarded by the tribes, they would be reduced to beggary. Until they could establish a mission station, grow crops and breed cattle, they must depend on more trade goods sent from the coast.

Raymond Bingham, as the convalescent, was the obvious choice to remain behind, however disappointed he might be that he would as yet only see the Sudan interior by the eye of faith and prayer. Gowans and Kent waved goodbye and disappeared up the Niger River, beyond the invisible line which marked the frontier of Lagos Colony, into the distant north. They could not know that they were several years too early: both the pacification, which created Nigeria and ended the tyranny of slave-raiding emirs, and the momentous discov-

237

ery of the cause of malaria lay only a little in the future, but that little meant death.

Gowans and Kent reached a town about six hundred miles from Lagos. Its chief, a fetish worshipper, welcomed them partly because he hoped for a white man's protection from the powerful Moslem emirs whose armies ranged at will. Gowans decided to settle and begin preaching, using his newly acquired, little-tried facility in Hausa, the language most widely used in West Africa. Tom Kent set off to bring up further supplies of trade goods from the coast.

He had not been gone many days when the war drums sounded, the women and children ran screaming into the square, and the men rounded up their stunted cattle and drove them behind the walls of thorn and timber. A Muslim emir was approaching on a slave raid. For two weeks Gowans lived the life of the besieged, his health rapidly worsening, until the town fell to assault while the thatched circular huts went up in flames. The emir enslaved the survivors and drove off their cattle. He offered elegant courtesies to the white man but appropriated his trade goods, cannily offering slaves in payment, knowing they would be refused.

Gowans, expelled, reduced to penury, desperately weak, died of malaria on the way back to the coast.

Kent was ignorant of this tragedy when he reached Lagos after an appalling journey. Bingham nursed him back to health, and accompanied him as far inland as he could go while maintaining their contact with Lagos. Tom Kent went forward to rejoin Gowans – and did so literally, for he too died of malaria, a year and four days after the three young men had landed.

In 1895 Raymond Bingham, the last of the three, returned to North America to find reinforcement and to put the 'Sudan Interior Mission', as it was eventually named, on a secure footing. He did not manage to advance on the Sudan again for five years, but in that time he had gained further experience in pastorate and hospital, had won a wife, formed a Mission Council – with flimsy enough finance – and sailed joyfully in 1900 with two other young men.

They landed; the Lagos missionaries were as adamant as before that this was a fool's errand. And when Bingham once more, within three weeks, developed malaria and was told it was a choice of death in Lagos or survival by going back on the steamer which had brought him, they seemed proved right. 'It would have been easier for me, perhaps,' wrote Bingham in his autobiography, 'had I died in Africa, for on that homeward journey I died another death. Everything seemed to have failed, and when, while I was gradually regaining strength in Britain, a fateful cable reached me with word that my two companions were arriving shortly, I went through the darkest period of my life.'

The two companions had been persuaded to give up by the Lagos missionaries – and disappeared into oblivion.

Thus, seven years after Bingham had set out with such sure hopes from Mrs Gowans' parlour, his mission was a mere mockery. But Mrs Gowans' response to her son's death had been: 'I would rather have had Walter go out to the Sudan and die there all alone, than have him home, disobeying his Lord.' And Raymond Bingham, too, determined to continue to obey, whether it led to ridicule or death.

Most of his Council urged the disbanding of this Sudan Interior Mission that never was. One member backed Bingham. And four more young men offered. This time he sent them to healthier parts to learn the language before they all went to Lagos. Furthermore, he had met Frederick Lugard, who had recently defeated the slaver emirs and was on his way back to the central Sudan to form the peaceful protectorate of Nigeria. Lord Lugard, as he became, admired young Bingham and did all he could to encourage the missionaries. On his advice they made their first home away from the river valleys to avoid the mosquito for the short time remaining before quinine stopped malaria being a fatal disease.

The next seven years saw a growing Mission, one or two deaths – and no conversions whatever. But when Bingham died in 1943, the international, interdenominational Sudan Interior Mission was already numerically one of the largest, with strong national churches growing around it. Today, right across from West Africa to Ethiopia, despite civil wars, persecutions and the difficulties inevitable in a rapidly changing world, these churches represent a powerful witness to Jesus Christ. The printing press which Bingham had founded pours out Christian literature. The voice of Radio Station ELWA carries the message from coast to coast.

All, under God, because one man, left in Lagos, refused to abandon his call.

25. Mildred Cable, 1878–1952
Eva and Francesca French,
1869–1960 and 1871–1960
THE GOOD GOSSIPS OF GOBI

'We sat for hours leaning back against the Great Wall of China, as our cart was up to the axle in a mud pit.' All efforts by the two mules had failed. The three Western women in Chinese dress, with their faithful servant and the Chinese doctor's wife and little girl, could only hope that someone would pass by. Their incompetent carter, hired that morning to drive them the last stage, had given up.

At last they heard a movement behind the crumbling Wall. The head of an ox emerged, fixing 'wondering and meditative eyes upon us sitting there.' As the ox lumbered through the opening a man rode up on a donkey. The donkey stopped, transfixed at the sight of cart, women and ox, and 'sank peacefully to the ground as if in a state of mental collapse,' so that its rider had no option but to dismount and help them. The carter caught the ox; the traveller hitched his donkey to the mules; ox, donkey and mules heaved together, while the men and the ladies pushed. The cart squelched out of the mud.

Their large white mule, Lolly, and a beautiful little brown called Molly, drew them slowly forward in the teeth of a March wind, through a desolate countryside with distant mountains on both horizons. A sleet storm lashed their faces; the carter stuck them in the mud again; they feared they would never reach the city of Kanchow, in the remote north-west of China, by nightfall.

Suddenly they saw two horsemen galloping towards them – the Chinese Christian doctor and a friend. Dr. Kao greeted them with joy and then turned to the carter. 'Hullo, Old Sheep! You out of jail again?'

The cart was dragged out of the mud; the second horseman galloped back towards the city while the doctor escorted the four women and the little girl. Before dusk a relay of fine horses, belonging to a Mongol prince who was staying with the doctor, came out to their rescue and they rode through the gate of Kanchow into darkened streets, past flaring smithies and busy inns, to the doctor's compound 'and a longed-for cup of tea.'

The three Western ladies had embarked on a great adventure for Christ. They had already been many years in China. Eva French, aged nearly fifty-four when they reached Kanchow in March 1924, had joined the China Inland Mission before the Boxer Rising of 1900, in which she had nearly lost her life. She was Irish, and had been somewhat wild in her girlhood, but her temperament owed more to Calvin's Geneva, where she had been brought up. Mildred Cable, nine years younger, had joined her in 1902; she was a draper's daughter from Surrey, who had trained as a pharmacist. At great emotional cost she had broken off an engagement when forced to choose between marriage and the mission field, yet she was cheerful, always ready to laugh, and strongly drawn to pioneering. Eva's sister, Francesca, had come to China later, after their mother had died: she was between the other two in age and had some training as a nurse.

They spent nearly twenty years together in a flourishing mission station in North China, much loved for their gifts of spontaneous friendship with all whom they met. The Chinese called Eva the Grey Lady, Mildred the Blue Lady, and Francesca the Brown Lady. Towards the end of the Great War, which hardly touched life in China, the Trio began to feel an urge to break away and go where few or none had heard of Christ. Their thoughts centred on the remote provinces of Kansu, Sinkiang and

Mongolia. They had 'a secret consciousness of being in receipt of "Sealed Orders", marked *"To proceed to the Great North-west to a place at present unknown"*.'

And thus, in June 1923, to the tears of the large congregation, they set out on the long journey up the great Silk Road, with a first stock of New Testaments in Chinese, Turku and other tongues. Dr Kao, who had pioneered a Christian hospital and church in Kanchow, had invited them to begin their adventure there. By unhurried stages, evangelizing as they went, staying in the filthy inns which were all that the road could offer, they reached Kanchow in March 1924.

At Dr Kao's suggestion they first trained a band of young Christian men and women, and then travelled up and down the region, holding meetings in a tent which the young men would erect and dismantle. At that time – for a period all too short – the country was peaceful and the courteous people listened. But the Trio had no desire to settle. The Gobi Desert beckoned: the oases with their Tartars and Turkus; the trade routes leading from Tibet, Mongolia and Turkestan. Beyond Kanchow lay Suchow, the last walled city before the Great Wall and the desert, known as the City of Prodigals because of its fugitives from debt, justice, or stepmothers.

The Trio, accompanied by a pioneer band who would form the nucleus of a Bible school and church, were able to rent a delightful house in a garden with a glorious view of distant snow mountains in Tibet, but the Gobi made its presence felt when the wind swept in through their paper windows 'deluging us with grit as we lay in our beds. When daylight came, we found our room literally buried under a thick layer of Gobi Desert dust, and for forty-eight hours the fearful blast persisted.'

Suchow would be their headquarters: the Gobi Desert their field. No Europeans had traversed it since Marco

Polo, except a few destitute Russian refugees and the eminent explorer, Sir Aurel Stein. The Trio were as interested as Stein in the extraordinary contours and colours of the largest desert on earth; in the Cave of a Thousand Buddhas, and the lamaseries and temples of the great oases. They took copious notes which were later to be basis of their fame. But their plain object was to tell the scattered people of the Gobi about Christ, and to place in the hands of wayfarers, wherever they came from, the New Testament and gaily illustrated Christian books in a tongue they could understand.

Eva, Mildred and Francesca would plan carefully and set out in the cart drawn by Lolly and Molly at three miles an hour, to reach an oasis town, perhaps days away, during a fair or a religious festival.

'Lama, you look tired,' Mildred would say. 'Yes,' replied the man, 'I have walked eight months to get here. I have come from the east, seeking the land where the sun sets and where I can find God.'

Eva spoke to a temple priest: 'You have had a busy day!'

'Yes, and you also, I believe, and I have not had time to come and listen to you. What is it that brings you so far?'

'Have you ever heard of Jesus?'

'Yes, I did hear of Him once, in a temple, where the priest said that he believed in Jesus of Nazareth.' Mildred and Francesca came across, and a long and courteous discussion continued far into the night.

The Trio called their work 'Gossiping the Gospel', pointing out that the word *gossip* derives, like gospel, from the Anglo-Saxon word *God-spell*; a gossip was a *God's sip*, or 'Friend of the Lord', who talked about him to a pagan and then stood as the *gossip* or sponsor at the baptism which followed when the pagan had accepted

244

Christ. The Trio talked to any who came near their book table, such as the Chinese merchant commanding a long string of camels loaded with his merchandise. He bought and carried off, 'like a great treasure', a complete Bible in Chinese, 'glad to have a good read for the long lonely stages.'

Soon afterwards came a man from Mongolia on a swift camel, singing at the top of his voice. His large sheepskin garment probably hid a bag of gold dust, enough to buy their whole stock, 'but this time it is not money that we are out for. What we want of him is an unconscious act of colportage, so that when he leaves us and rides away his capacious saddle bags will hold many of those books provided for us by the Bible Society. Lamas all along his way will beg for a volume and offer hospitality in return.' Furthermore, his homeland and journey's end was closed to missionaries but the books could enter in his bags.

Mildred, Eva and Francesca were confident that 'the Glad Sound' (Chinese for the gospel) can 'take a hold on a man's mind so that it dominates his thought for life'. They could not go everywhere themselves but 'the Word of God is not bound'. And sometimes they rejoiced to find a heart already prepared. Near the celebrated Crescent Moon Lake they met a Tibetan lama on pilgrimage. 'He surprised us by saying that this meeting caused him no surprise: "This Jesus of whom you speak has appeared to me several times in a dream. I know that I have to believe in him." '

Back in Suchow, one winter day Mildred opened the door to find a small girl in rags, with cuts and bruises on her legs, holding out a begging bag.

'Where do you come from, child?' asked Mildred.

The girl merely pointed to the dog bites on her legs.

Mildred soon realized that the child, who looked about seven or eight, was deaf and dumb. 'What a poor mite!' she exclaimed as Eva came out to look, followed by Francesca with a bowl of soup which the child wolfed. Then Mildred bandaged her sores.

Next day a garishly dressed woman tried to extort money from the Trio for 'letting their dog bite her little daughter'. Their cook, who recognized the woman as a bad lot, told her roundly that household had no dog and that she should be ashamed of herself. The woman changed her tune and said she would thrash the child for misleading her, at which Eva threatened to report her to the mandarin: a well dressed woman had no business to drive her child to beg and be bitten by watch dogs which other beggar children would hear and avoid. The woman left quickly.

Mildred nicknamed the child *Gwa Gwa*, 'Little Lonely', and after enquiries by their neighbour, Granny Fan, discovered that the child was a slave, not a daughter. Some eight years earlier a Mongol chieftain, joining in the revelry at a festival in the Tibetan foothills, had slaked his lust on a peasant girl and ridden away with no further thought.

He had sired a girl, unwanted but beautiful, and at the age of three weeks easily sold in Suchow to a childless woman. But when the child grew she was found to be stone deaf and mute. Her foster mother, furious at the bad bargain, took away her pretty clothes, dressed her in rags and later drove her out to beg.

Gwa Gwa took to calling regularly at this house, where no dog bit, and where a bowl of soup and a hunk of bread, and kind smiles, were always to be found. But the Trio were due for furlough. Gwa Gwa instinctively realized that they would be gone a long time (though the Christians would see that she did not starve), and she followed their cart out of the city until Mildred, as miserable as Gwa Gwa at the parting, stopped the cart and gently persuaded her to turn back.

The Trio had planned their furlough in character. They would go home to England slowly across the Gobi Desert by their own cart, 'the Gobi Express' as they jocularly called it, gossiping the gospel at oases familiar or new, until they crossed the pass into Sinkiang, and thus to its capital Urumchi, eight hundred miles from Suchow.

At Urumchi they stayed with the veteran missionary George Hunter, and left Molly the Mule as his guest, then travelled faster by horse-drawn Russian *tarantass* along better roads, a further seven hundred miles to the Soviet border and the Trans Siberian railway.

They reached England in October 1926 and soon found themselves famous. The courage and endurance of those three women, aged fifty-nine, fifty-seven and fifty, caught the imagination of the nation. Mildred proved an excellent speaker, whether at missionary meetings or to learned societies, and their book, *Through Jade Gate and Central Asia*, became a best seller: it went into twelve editions.

They returned to Suchow eighteen months later in the summer of 1928. Gwa Gwa came round quickly, but the present of cloth they had brought her was promptly seized and sold by her foster mother. They decided to adopt Gwa Gwa as the only way to help. They bought her for a trifle and changed her name from Little Lonely to *Ai Lien*, meaning 'Love Bond'; but because Ai Lien was a difficult name to lip read they always called her Topsy. When they went on their next long journey within the vast Gobi Desert, lasting nearly a year, Topsy went too.

The political scene was now darker. The Muslim Turkus were rising in Sinkiang, while in Kansu and the

Gobi a youthful war lord, Ma Chung Ying, known as the Baby General, had taken arms against the weak Chinese government and was laying the province waste. As they travelled the Trio would find a once flourishing oasis town almost destroyed and the survivors starving. They passed grisly scenes of recent battles. At one place they were briefly arrested by soldiers or brigands (the distinction was slight), and though treated courteously were harrowed by the sight of flogged conscripts, whose festering wounds from the lash they washed and dressed.

They reached the extensive Tunhwang oasis. While they were there it was captured by one of Ma's armies and the women were forbidden to leave. For eight months they were virtually prisoners, though able to move freely within the oasis area, doing what they could to relieve the misery of the inhabitants as boys were conscripted, farms and grain looted until famine reduced even rich merchants to beggary. Typhus swept the oasis. 'Dogs and wolves had a good time outside the north gate,' wrote Mildred, 'for by ancient custom the bodies of all who died in the roadways were wrapped in matting and buried there in shallow graves.'

Then General Ma was wounded and Mildred was ordered to proceed to his capital, Ansi, four hard days' journey across the desert, to dress his wounds. The Trio refused to be separated or to leave Topsy behind. Singing *Guide Me O Thou Great Jehovah*, as they always did before each day's journey, they set out on a cold November morning with a party of prisoners.

When they stood in the presence of the famous general, 'We had expected to meet a dashing young warrior; we found a slim youth. There was a smiling, cruel sensuousness about him, and a shallow flippancy, yet he was reported to be an excellent horseman and a skilled athlete.' The Baby General, so callous in sending men

248

to death or torture, was a coward when confronted with iodine, but under Mildred's care his wounds healed rapidly.

As she prepared the dressings at a side table he would be enjoying his power. A frightened peasant would fall on his knees before Ma: 'Spare my son's life, Your Excellency!'

'Why should I spare his life?' sneered Ma, twirling a hunting knife but never looking at the man.

'He is my only son, Your Excellency.'

'The boy is disobedient and I have ordered the disobedient to be shot!'

'I promise he will never do it again, Excellency.'

'He has done it once and that is enough. I do not change my mind. You may go.' And the bodyguards hustled the man away before the General could fly into a rage and order floggings right and left.

When Ma was healed the Trio wanted to return to Tunhwang, and after much delay he consented. At their last audience Mildred looked the General straight in the eye. She produced a New Testament and a copy of the Ten Commandments, and solemnly bade him care for his soul. He took the books and stood motionless, listening, while the bodyguards marvelled at Mildred's courage. Without a word he saluted them and they retired.

Back at Tunhwang they planned to escape across the Gobi, putting aside every day a small store from the meagre rations of flour and fodder. Early one morning, when most of the town was sleeping off its opium, they drove out of the gate with Topsy, as if to visit a nearby farm. Once out of sight of the guards they changed direction: 'We turned our mules' heads towards one of the loneliest of desert roads, known only to local men.' They knew they must pass a military post on the edge of the oasis, but to their amazement they learned at the last farm that it was deserted: every soldier had gone on a looting raid. The Trio left the oasis still undetected and travelled hard, lying hidden at night. Once they were caught up by a patrol of Ma's men, who had noticed the cart ruts; but the Trio guessed that the soldiers were illiterate and foxed them by brandishing the majestic sealed passports of the Chinese government which Ma was fighting.

Mildred, who was often inclined to worry and doubt, wondered if they had done right to escape, but when a band of Muslim thieves had let them pass unscathed, and they had not been attacked by wolves, and had galloped through streams without the axle breaking, and had survived the nervous horrors of burned out towns and wayside skeletons, even Mildred became sure, as she lay awake exhausted under the stars, that 'He, watching over Israel, neither slumbers nor sleeps.'

They reached the safety of an oasis in the hot but lush Turfan Depression. The town was in government hands and they could relax. Mildred went to the stables of the inn to see that Molly and the other mule were being looked after. She did not return. Eva went to look and found her unconscious in the filth, bleeding from a vicious kick on the head by a tired donkey.

With the help of a kindly Chinese gardener who welcomed them to the shade of his mulberry trees beside running water, they slowly nursed her back to health.

'There is no denying that signs of wear and tear are evident, so we prefer to travel without a mirror!' But they added: 'The meaning and reality of Christ have become intense. He is Saviour, Guardian, Friend – way and end. We have lacked nothing.'

They finally left the Gobi when all missionaries were ordered out of the North-West in 1936 at a time of political disturbance. By then they had seen many Christian groups flourish, though sometimes persecuted; groups which were the foundation of the church in Kansu which survived the reign of Mao and all that happened after.

The Trio, with Topsy, devoted the rest of their lives to the Bible Society, which had been their strong ally throughout, and to lecturing and writing.

Their base was a little cottage near Shaftesbury in Dorset and there, when a schoolboy, I had tea with them and Topsy, the only subjects of these sketches that I ever met.

26. JOHN AND BETTY STAM
1916–1934   1917–1934
VICTIMS OF THE LONG MARCH

It was a prosaic, peaceful world, though locally there had been disturbances from bandits and Communists. America was immersed in the New Deal, England with preparations for the Silver Jubilee of King George V. Hitler was not yet a menace, and the League of Nations still had respect. War, bloodshed and murder were not much in mind, and as for new names on the roll of Christian martyrs, the possibility, in October 1934, seemed so remote as to be almost absurd.

A young American and a middle-aged Englishman were closeted with the district magistrate of Tsingteh, Anhwei province, a decayed little town a few hundred miles from Nanking. The American and the Englishman were missionaries of the China Inland Mission.

Martyrdom was far from the thoughts of John Stam, the young American, as he listened to his senior colleague asking the magistrate whether it would be safe for John to bring his wife and their month-old baby to live in Tsingteh. The magistrate admitted that there had been banditry, for the countryside was half-starving, but he was soothing in his protestations of security.

John Stam remarked that they did not want to meet the Communists, who had been passing through the next province during their famous 'long march' after defeat in South China.

'Oh, no, no!' the magistrate exclaimed. 'There is no danger of Communists here. As far as that is concerned, you may come at once and bring your family. I will guarantee your safety, and if there should be any trouble you can come to my *yamen*.'

A month later John and Betty Stam and the baby,

Helen Priscilla, made their home in the disused Tsingteh mission compound in the middle of the town, with a background of distant mountains.

John Stam was twenty-eight, a tall athletic New Yorker whose Dutch extraction showed in his fair hair and blue eyes. Betty, a year younger, had been born in China, daughter of an American missionary doctor. They had met at Moody Bible Institute in Chicago. Both were unusual personalities. Betty, for instance, could write verse of distinction. And John, in Chicago, had deliberately tested his faith, like the young Hudson Taylor at Hull eighty years earlier, by concealing his financial needs from his family and friends and depending only on God in prayer.

Betty had served her first year in China before John reached Shanghai. On 25th October 1933, a year to the day before the meeting with the magistrate, they had been married at Betty's home in North China. Two happy, unpretentious missionaries at the start of their lifetime of service, they were unreservedly dedicated to their call but aware of how much they had to learn, ready for the hardships and setbacks of Christian work in a foreign land, yet young enough to extract enjoyment from any situation. Their aim was simple: to 'talk about Him to everybody, and live so closely with Him and in Him, that others may see that there really is such a person as Jesus.'

Tsingteh was their first station on their own away from seniors. The opening ten days were much like any other missionary's introduction to a new location in China, with inquisitive Chinese crowding around so that privacy was impossible. The Stams visited the few Christians, preached in the little chapel, administered famine relief, and spoke on the streets to the chattering, restless press of peasants, soldiers, and townsfolk.

Early on the eleventh morning, 6th December 1934, Betty Stam was bathing the baby when a man ran in at the door. Out of breath and urging them to hurry, he panted that that the magistrate had sent him to warn that the Communists, whom everybody had thought to be beyond the mountains, were advancing on the city after a surprise flank march behind the government army.

John at once sent for coolies and chairs, intending to join the stream of refugees who were hurrying down the street to escape to the safety of the hills. Before the Stams had put together their few necessities, a distant burst of firing proved that the battle had reached the town, where the Communists quickly scaled the walls and opened the gates. As the chair-coolies loped into the courtyard the Stams heard that the magistrate had fled. They bolted the door, realizing that escape was now impossible. Scattered shots, the crackle of flames, and the screams of townsfolk in the street made this all too obvious.

John told the servants to kneel. He began to lead in prayer, but the prayer was interrupted by a thundering knock on the door. Red soldiers demanded admittance. John spoke to them courteously. Betty, as calm as if the soldiers were inquirers for the faith, offered them tea and cakes. These were brusquely refused. John was tightly bound and taken across to the communist headquarters. Betty and the baby were brought in later.

John and Betty stood together, bound, yet serene despite the suddenness of the catastrophe. The Stams had been allowed none of the mental or spiritual preparation which would have been theirs had these events occurred thirty years earlier, when the martyrdoms of the Boxer Rising were fresh in people's memory; or thirty years later, when the witness of Paul Carlson and the Congo martyrs rang round the world. The Stams faced death unwarned but their captors saw no trace of fear.

The Communists discussed the Americans' fate in their hearing. They were imperialists and should be liquidated. Moreover, the Communists detested Christians. To make an example of two Christian leaders should strike terror into the hearts of the rest. The Reds had no compunction about murdering Americans, for the affair would merely increase the embarrassment of Chiang Kai-shek's government in Nanking.

The one difficulty was what to do with the baby. Betty heard them say that it had best be spitted on a bayonet in front of its parents.

A bystander, an old farmer, protested: 'The baby has done nothing worthy of death!'

'Then it's your life for hers!' said the Red leader.

The Stams had never seen him before, and certainly had no claim on him, but their serenity and courage had gripped him. 'I am willing,' he said.

A moment later the man's severed head rolled across the floor.

The Communists abandoned Tsingteh, sacked and burning, and marched their prisoners to a town named Miaosheo. The looting and terror resumed while the Stams were left under guard in the postmaster's shop. The Stams had lived in Miaosheo and the postmaster knew them by sight.

'Where are you going?' he asked.

'We do not know where *they* are going,' replied John, 'but we are going to heaven.'

That night the Stams were locked with their guards in an inner room of a deserted mansion. John was tied to a bedpost, but Betty was left free with the baby.

Next morning they were ordered to leave the baby and to strip off their outer garments and shoes – though John managed to give Betty his socks. Then they were both bound tightly and led down the street while the

Communists yelled ridicule and shouted to the townsfolk, many of whom had heard the Stams preach here in happier days, to come and see these Christians die. On a little hill outside the town they came to a clump of pines. A Communist began to harangue the trembling crowd, pouring scorn and blasphemies on all that the Stams held dear.

He was in full tilt when a man stepped boldly forward.

The Stams recognized him as Mr Chang the medicine-seller, a nominal Christian who was known as 'rather unwilling to witness for the true and living God'. This once weak disciple fell on his knees and boldly pleaded for their lives. The Communists pushed him away. He persisted.

'Are you a Christian then?' they said.

Chang knew what his fate could be. 'Yes,' he replied.

He was dragged away to be butchered, and now it was John Stam's turn to intercede, for Chang. For reply John was ordered to kneel. People in that crowd said afterwards there was a 'look of joy on his face.'

The Chinese executioner, in time-honoured style, held the sword level with both hands, whirled round and round to gather momentum, and struck. Betty was seen to quiver for a moment, then she fell unconscious across the body. A few moments later her head too was on the ground and the Reds were driving the crowd away.

Two days afterwards, when the Communists had left to spread their trail of bloodshed and fire further across the province, an evangelist of Miaosheo named Lo, whose leadership hitherto had been indifferent returned with other refugees. Lo had heard rumours of the murder but found difficulty in obtaining facts because no one dared side with the Christians for fear lest the Reds return.

Following clues, he discovered the Stam baby, hungry but warm and alive in her zip-fastened sleeping bag in an abandoned house. He left her in the care of his wife.

Next he climbed the hillside where the headless bodies still lay, stiff and grotesque. He went back to the town and brought coffins, followed now by a crowd made braver through his courage. Lo and two other Christians, a woman and her son, placed the bodies in the coffins and bowed their heads in prayer. This formerly unsatisfactory half-hearted evangelist then turned to the crowd and told them that the Stams lived 'in the presence of their heavenly Father. They came to China and to Miaosheo, not for themselves but for you, to tell you about the great love of God that you might believe in the Lord Jesus and be eternally saved. You have heard their message. Remember it is true. Their death proves it so. Do not forget what they told you – repent, and believe the gospel.'

Many of the crowd were weeping as Lo set out on a hundred-mile escape through the Communist-held territory, with his wife, to bring little Helen Stam to the nearest missionaries.

In the years that followed, many millions of men and women throughout the world were to die by violence. But John and Betty were martyred in time of peace, when such an event seemed incredible, and they died because of their faith. As always, the blood of martyrs was the seed of the church. The shock of their death turned timid Evangelist Lo into a courageous preacher. The story of their steadfastness prepared their fellow missionaries in China for the testing times of the Sino-Japanese and Pacific wars.

The impact on the student world was enormous, for the Stams had been fresh from college. One of those who gave herself for missionary service as a direct result of reading about the Stams was an American girl who became Mrs Hector McMillan.

Thirty years later she escaped death by inches in the Congo, a few moments before her husband became one of the Stanleyville martyrs. As Ione McMillan had pledged herself to fill the gap in the missionary ranks left by the Stams, so her son, young Kenneth McMillan, as he lay wounded near the body of his father, pledged himself to return as a missionary to speak of Christ's love to the murderers.

27. Ernest Presswood, 1908–1946
TUAN CHANGE

On the Sarawak coast in East Malaysia a missionary tapped excitedly at the typewriter as she compiled an information sheet datelined 1968: 'Reports have been coming through of a great stirring among the churches of Indonesian Borneo.... Several Christians have had visions from the Lord which they have been told to proclaim to their people, and as a result hundreds have repented from sin and turned to the Lord. The spiritual stirring is influencing Murut and Kelabit churches on the Sarawak border.'

She glanced across the airstrip to the Bible School. They were just clearing up after the half yearly conference which two hundred indigenous pastors and leaders had attended. Some had walked eight days through the jungle, others had come by mission plane or river boat, and they represented an expanding, missionary-hearted church of many tribes in the mountains and jungles of former British Borneo.

It all went back to the pioneering of one forgotten North American, William Ernest Presswood who, because he died young a few months after the end of World War II and lies buried in Borneo, has been largely forgotten except by those who loved him. But his name is legendary among the natives of the interior; they call him Tuan Change – because so many were changed from a particularly evil darkness into the light of Christ.

Ernie Presswood was born in the prairies of Canada in 1908, son of English immigrants. In a Sunday school class which could boast of eleven who later were ministers or missionaries, he gave his heart to Christ, yet it was not until the Presswoods returned to England briefly in the early 1920s, and he heard Gypsy Smith, that he dedicated himself for service. His father next bought a meat and grocery store in Toronto, where Ernie trained as a motor mechanic. Then, after Prairie Bible School and the missionary institute at Nyack, New York, he joined the Christian and Missionary Alliance in the Netherlands East Indies during 1930.

About eighteen months later a most extraordinary rumour passed around the Murut or Dayak natives far up-country in the interior. As it was told to me in Borneo long after, by a Murut named Panai Raub, 'We were clearing the undergrowth for the new season's farming when we heard of a wonderful white man they called Tuan Change because he changed wicked natives and said they could have a new life. He was on an island off the coast.' They wanted to go down but were afraid of venturing where Malays, Chinese, and whites lived.

The Muruts, a large tribe scattered across the mountains of the British-Dutch border, were steeped in spirit-worship to such an extent that planting would be endlessly delayed for lack of an omen, or the half-grown paddy abandoned as the result of another. They turned most of the harvest into intoxicating ricebeer, sapped their tribal stamina by sexual malpractices, and frequently went head-hunting. They lived naked except for loincloths.

'When I heard,' Panai Raub continued, 'way up in the hills in the midst of all that drinking and fear of the spirits, about change and new life, I just could not sleep for desire. Two months later when we were felling the big timber we heard that Tuan Change was downstream. We all went to meet him, taking our sick.'

They found Presswood at Long Berang, a place above fearsome rapids which had needed considerable courage for a lone Westerner to negotiate, even with skilled boatmen. A huge crowd of Muruts, heads bowed, squatted round Presswood who was standing with eyes closed, arms outstretched to the sky.

'What is this?' thought Panai Raub. 'What are they doing?'

After praying, Tuan Change unfolded some pictures, and preached in Malay with one of the few educated Muruts to interpret. Panai Raub was right in front.

'I could hear every word. Some of the others could not. He preached on the Resurrection, with amazing effect on the crowd. Right from the beginning it hit me. I was just drinking it in. When I first heard the Word I believed.'

This was in September 1932. Next day Tuan Change left them and walked far over rugged jungle trails in great heat until forced back to the coast with a foot ulcerated by leech bites. He wrote home: 'What a time I have had. Physically it has been a hard one but the results have been *glorious*. I think around six hundred Dayaks were reached with the message.'

Ernie Presswood was now nearly twenty-five. He was a true pioneer, willing to forego the good things he enjoyed. He pushed himself relentlessly. 'His middle name could have been "hurry",' writes one who knew him well. 'It was always praying, reading, teaching, counselling, studying, and the little notebook always at hand.' He seemed austere, not quick to laugh though with a genuine sense of humour. He was a perfectionist and could be hard on those who had openly acknowledged Christ yet failed him, when Presswood would hide the compassion which ran strong within. His was a character that could be appreciated and admired by Muruts, who seemed so feckless then, yet subsequently disclosed the same characteristics of uncompromising dedication.

Presswood was kept at the coast by his bad foot until 1934 when he paid a second visit to Long Berang. 'I have been here two weeks, twice as long as I expected, the interest has been so great. From early morning till late at night I have been kept busy with scarcely a break. Pray much for me for the strain is very great. Thus far I have baptized a hundred and thirty and I expect there will be at least twice as many more.' After a third, longer visit he returned to America, married Laura Harmon from Pennsylvania, and in May 1937 they settled in Long Berang, having taken twenty nine days negotiating the rapids.

That Christmas there was a great baptism at Long Berang; one of those baptized was Panai Raub. The following April, Presswood could write of a 'morning service which the Spirit of God was manifest in a very real way. Waves of praise swept over us as we looked into the faces of these happy Christians.'

A few days later, when the Presswoods were still the only whites upriver, Laura had a miscarriage. Complications developed. There was nothing Ernie could do but see her die, and bury her in a coffin made from his own hands from one of the timbers with which they were building their home. Despite the sorrowing natives he felt desperately alone. 'Only those who have passed through such a heart-breaking experience can appreciate the distress.' Then floods swept down on Long Berang, carrying away much of their precious timber. 'Surely the Lord doesn't love me when he treats me thus, I thought: but he answered me so blessedly, "Whom the Lord loveth he chasteneth and scourgeth every son he receives...." The comfort and blessing that he has already sent upon my soul has strengthened me and given me courage to face the future.'

For Borneo, it was already proving a great future, for the revival was spreading right across the border. The Sarawak Muruts had been even worse than the

Indonesian. Officials of Rajah Brooke, the English ruler, estimated the whole community except the dogs to be drunk a hundred days in a year. After Tuan Change's first visit to Long Berang rumours of his good words had filtered over the border, and some Sarawak Muruts went to find an Australian missionary, Hudson Southwell, who returned with them in 1933. Several were converted, but Rajah Brooke reckoned the Muruts were irredeemable. He refused Southwell permission to settle, threw a *cordon sanitaire* round the whole tribe, and left it to die out.

Panai Raub and other baptized Muruts determined to evangelize their cousins. Presswood had not told them they should. He so preached Christ that converts caught the vision for themselves; long before it became accepted missionary strategy Presswood urged that a church should be self-propagating and self-supporting.

'The first village I came to,' Panai Raub says, 'just over the border, a big drinking party was on. I refused it: 'I do not drink now.' 'Why not?' 'Because I follow the Lord Jesus Christ.' 'Where did you hear about him?' 'From Tuan Change.' 'Does he live near this Lord Jesus?' They were very pleased and keen to hear. Even the old people who had been heavily involved in headhunting and the old worship brought the fetishes and burned them.'

Panai Raub was not yet literate and no Scriptures had been translated; he preached with the aid of pictures. On his next visit he found that drinking had been abandoned. Wherever he went 'there was not one house among the Muruts which did not want to hear.... 'Eternal life. *That's* what we want,' they would say.' After he left, a village would choose its own church leaders from those who showed the gifts of the Spirit.

Late in 1938 the Rajah of Sarawak heard that

something extraordinary had occurred. He ordered an expedition of inquiry, led by a government official and a missionary, who travelled among the Muruts from 12th December 1938 to 4th February 1939. The Government official reported that he was not popular with the Muruts because he smoked, drank whisky, and did not possess a Sankey hymnbook! After that missionaries of the Borneo Evangelical Mission were allowed to settle. Meanwhile across the border, Presswood undertook even more rigorous climbs to reach mountain villages, and by the time he left for his second furlough late in 1939 the Murut church was growing rapidly.

In America he was married again, to Ruth Brooks of Buffalo, N.Y., who returned with him in May 1940. He was appointed to head the Bible School at Makassar in the Celebes where the Japanese invasion engulfed him. Beaten, starved, forced to do coolie labour, kept in a pig house, he watched his brother missionaries die; even when giving a funeral address in a prison camp he was able to win men to Christ.

On 27th November 1945 the Presswoods returned to Borneo. Ernie discovered the grave of his successor, who had been bayoneted to death after surrendering to prevent reprisals on the natives. When the Presswoods went up-country, they found that the war had divided loyalties, caused disputes and much backsliding, even some rebuilding of spirit altars. 'Such things were disheartening to Ernie,' writes Ruth. But there were repentances, and much hunger.

Nor need Presswood have feared. The horrors of the Pacific War, the disturbances of the War of Independence, and the checkered growth of Sukarno's Indonesia could not quench so deep a movement of the Spirit. Over the Sarawak border a great forward movement began in the 1950s, with the Muruts as the spearhead bringing the gospel to other tribes, while the Borneo Evangelical missionaries translated the Scriptures into the different languages, ran a Bible School, and set up their own air service.

Ernie Presswood did not live to see it. At Long Berang on that first post-war visit of January 1946, a severe bout of sickness convinced him, physically weak from his sufferings as a prisoner, that he must return downstream to the coast at once, several days early, or die. The river was high but a legend among the Muruts that natives tried to stop him travelling is disproved by contemporary letters. On Ernie's thirty-eighth birthday the Presswoods set off, with seven boatmen and another passenger carrying a live pig to sell at the market.

At the first rapid they had to land and crawl among the leeches through the edge of the undergrowth. After that the going was easier. 'We continued shooting rapids for several hours and I found it fun,' writes Ruth. At the last and biggest, the boatmen climbed up the mountain side to reconnoitre and reported it safe to negotiate, so they floated out past a big boulder. They were struck by a ten foot wave. The next capsized them. Ruth could not swim and Ernie grabbed her. They were carried downstream three hundred yards, much of it underwater.

They scrambled ashore, safe except for the baggage which was nearly all lost, and finally reached the coast after a trying journey in an overloaded motor boat wedged among prisoners of war.

The drenching seriously affected Presswood's shattered constitution. But he had promised to attend a conference across the bay, and though feeling ill, and Ruth sick and unable to accompany him, he kept his word. Pneumonia set in and on 1st February 1946 he died.

His memorial is the vigorous evangelical church in Borneo.

28. Sir Wilfred Grenfell, 1865–1940
SANTA CLAUS OF LABRADOR

One Christmas morning in the early nineteen hundreds the people of a small isolated fishing village in Labrador were gathered outside their doors watching an unusual sight. A sledge was coming towards them across the frozen bay. But instead of the team of husky dogs it was drawn by a reindeer – an animal unknown in Labrador, though closely related to the wild caribou of the forests. The sledge drew nearer and the fishermen and their wives – descendants of the original British settlers – soon saw that the sledge carried their great friend, the Good Samaritan of the Coast, Wilfred Grenfell.

Crowding round him as he unloaded his surgical instruments for an emergency operation, they asked him how and why he had put a stag into harness. 'Milk! Milk! Milk!' he replied, at which they blinked, though they knew the doctor's jovial ways. After a little more leg-pulling, he explained that he had introduced a herd of domestic reindeer from Lapland as a substitute for dairy cows, which could not exist on the Coast, thus hoping to provide people with the fresh milk they sorely needed. Some of the stags he was using for transport. Marvelling at the doctor's unending ideas for their assistance, the rugged fisherfolk waited while he performed the surgery for which he had come, and then joined him for a simple Christmas service, lustily singing the old hymns and listening with bowed heads as Grenfell prayed extempore in the most natural, unaffected way.

Grenfell had already done much to transform the lives of the scattered fishing and trapping communities of Labrador. In the snowy wastes of the North he was a veritable embodiment of the Christmas spirit, bringing throughout the year good things for body and soul alike.

266

To him this was no matter for boasting, but just a response to one of his favourite verses from the Psalms, 'Teach me to do the thing that pleaseth Thee.'

It all traced back to a winter's day in the slums of East London early in 1885. Grenfell, a young medical student in his second year, a keen rowing man and rugby football player, and devoted to the sea and outdoor life, happened to wander into a large tent erected on a piece of derelict ground in dockland, near where he had been sent to attend a case. He found himself in a meeting of Moody and Sankey's second London campaign. 'It was so new to me,' records Grenfell, 'that when a tedious prayer bore began with a long oration, I started to leave. Suddenly the leader, who I learned afterwards was D.L. Moody, called out to the audience, "Let us sing a hymn while our brother finishes his prayer." His practicality interested me and I stayed the service out.' He left 'with a determination either to make religion a real effort to do as I thought Christ would do in my place as a doctor, or frankly abandon it.'

For some weeks he hovered; to come out for Christ in the 'coarse and evil environment' of the hospital medical school required more pluck than even Wilfred Grenfell possessed. Then he attended a meeting at which the speakers were the Studd brothers – it was a short while before C.T. Studd sailed with the Cambridge Seven. The fact that they were noted athletes made Grenfell hang on their words. 'I felt I could listen to them. I could not have listened to a sensuous-looking man, a man who was not a master of his own body.' At the end of the service the Studds asked all those who would give their lives to Christ to stand up. There was dead silence and no one stirred. 'It seemed a very sensible question to me,' wrote Grenfell, 'but I was amazed how hard I found it to stand up. At last one boy, out of a hundred or

267

more in sailor rig from a reformatory ship on the Thames, suddenly rose. It seemed to me such a wonderfully courageous act – for I knew perfectly what it would mean to him – that I immediately found myself on my feet.'

Grenfell scorned mere theorizing. He had no truck with people who talked pious and never lifted a finger to serve Christ or their fellows. At once he began work among the boys in his neighbourhood, running a Sunday school with such vigour that the staid parson, shocked by his introduction of boxing on weekday evenings, forced him to resign. He therefore joined up with a 'ragged school', which with East End boys in the 1880s required as much physical hardihood as spiritual zeal. To this he added lodging-house work and temperance campaigning in the worst of the slum saloons. Once the angry topers made preparations to beat him up and pour whisky down his throat: 'however they greatly overrated their stock of fitness and equally underrated my good training, for the scrimmage went all my way in a very short time.'

Grenfell's holidays were always spent sailing, with his brother and a few friends hiring an old fishing smack in the Irish sea. 'One result of these holidays was that I told my London boys about them, using one's experiences as illustrations, till suddenly it struck me that this was shabby Christianity.' After that, he always took some of them with him, and in subsequent summers he ran camping and boating holidays on the Welsh coast, with straight-from-the-shoulder talks on the Christian life to end each day.

From sailing holidays to service on the sea was a natural move. Shortly after he had qualified as a doctor and finished his hospital training, his great friend and teacher, the brilliant surgeon Sir Frederick Treves, told him that a recently formed mission (afterwards the Royal

National Mission to Deep Sea Fishermen) was looking for a doctor to help them among the North Sea herring fleet which stayed at sea for months at a time. They had 'chartered a small fishing smack, and sent her out among the fishermen to hold religious services of a simple, unconventional type, in order to afford the men an alternative to the grog vessels when fishing was slack.' Grenfell joined at Yarmouth, wondering whether he would be of any use among such men 'far older and tougher and more experienced than I.' But on the wheel of the Mission ship was engraved 'Follow Me and I will make you fishers of men.' 'That was a real challenge,' recalled Grenfell, 'and I knew then perfectly well that that was my only chance, anyhow.'

Fours years later, in 1892, he set out at the Mission's invitation to cross the far north of the Atlantic in a sailing vessel to see if he could help the fishermen of Labrador and North Newfoundland. The coasts would be wild, lonely and cold, though the expedition was only for the few summer months. But the venture seemed no sacrifice to Grenfell. 'I have always believed that the Good Samaritan went across the road to the wounded man just because he wanted to,' he once remarked. And besides, there was 'everything about such a venture as sailing to Labrador to attract my type of mind.'

After calling at St Johns they made landfall in Labrador. 'A seried rank of range upon range of hills, reaching north and south as far as the eye could see from the masthead, was rising above our horizon behind a very surfeit of islands.' At their first harbour they were bombarded with calls for medical help from ships and shore. That evening, when the last patient had left the spotless dispensary on board the mission schooner, Grenfell noticed 'a miserable bunch of boards, serving as a boat, with only a dab of tar along its seams lying motionless a little way from us. In it, sitting silent, was a half-clad, brown haired, brown faced figure.' After a prolonged stare the man in the boat suddenly said, 'Be you a doctor?' 'That's what I call myself,' replied Grenfell with the twinkle in his eyes which was to become so well known and loved throughout Labrador. 'Us hasn't got no money,' said the half-clothed settler, 'but there's a very sick man is here, if so be you'd come and see him.'

Grenfell was led to a small, bare, filthy hovel, crowded with neglected children. 'A very sick man was coughing his soul out in the darkness while a pitiably covered woman gave him cold water to sip out of a spoon.' The man's case was hopeless, and with his death starvation would be a grim reality for the whole family; government relief was a mockery because of the iniquities of the local trading system. Thus Grenfell was faced with something of the need of Labrador. As he put it, 'to pray for the man, and with the family was easy, but scarcely satisfying.' Grenfell knew that Christ would not have him leave it at that.

And thus year by year he returned to Labrador, to do what he could for their bodies and souls, and at last made his home on the Coast and stayed the whole year round. Among the bleak headlands and scattered islands washed by roaring seas in summer and gripped by ice in winter, wherever ship or sledge could take him, he carried the love of Christ, not in word only but in deeds. His frank speech laced with the merry yarns that the fisherfolk loved brought him right to their hearts. And they knew that he was as skilful and hardy a sailor as themselves.

He soon found that much of the misery of the Coast was caused by the grip of corrupt traders, aided by an outdated system of commerce. He proposed the creation of co-operative stores. The vested interests of the colony were enraged and made common cause to crush him.

Moreover the settlers who stood to gain most were afraid to join and when he persuaded them, 'not one shareholder wished to have his name registered, and one and all they were opposed to having the little building labeled as a store – so ingrained was their fear of their suppliers.' But despite setbacks and losses, Grenfell's scheme survived, and like the hospitals and dispensaries and schools which he built, helped to make the life of the settlers more tolerable and to open their hearts to the gospel.

On one voyage his little hospital ship had dropped anchor among a group of islands. 'Suddenly a boat bumped our side and a woman climbed over the rail with a bundle under each arm. On my chartroom table she laid the two bundles and proceeded to untie them.' They proved to be twin babies, 'blind as kittens'. The mother had four other children and her husband had been killed in an accident three months earlier. 'What ever are you going to do with the babies?' asked Grenfell. 'Give them to you, Doctor.'

When the ship was under way again, in a choppy sea, the babies howled so loudly that the helmsman 'stuck his head into the chartroom, which was directly behind the wheelhouse.' 'What are you going to do with those, sir?' he asked. 'Shh,' replied Grenfell, 'they're blind and quite useless. When we get outside, we'll drop them over the rail.' 'He stared at me for a second,' records Grenfell, 'before he turned back to the wheel. A few minutes later in popped his head again. "Excuse my being so bold, but don't throw them over the side. We've got eight of our own, but I guess my wife'll find a place for those two." ' Grenfell laughingly told him that he had already begun to form a collection of derelict children at his base at St Anthony's, to which these would be added.

And thus the work grew. As the years passed,

Grenfell's fame spread across North America and in Britain, and funds and volunteers flowed to his aid. After the First World War, in an age which tended to divorce social welfare from spirituality and in which many of the younger generation were ashamed of open profession of faith, Grenfell stood as a virile example of practical Christian love which counts service a privilege and spices it with humour and a refusal to be beaten. 'The King himself,' he once wrote, 'cannot win his battle without us, he having entrusted us with the task, ensuring victory if we "are bound to him".'

Grenfell was often near death as he made his way through ice and storms on sea and land. At Easter 1908, at the age of forty-three, he was caught with his team of huskies on a pan of ice during a sudden thaw and was rapidly drifting out to sea, to drown, or die by cold and starvation if the ice-pan held out. 'My own faith in the mystery of immortality is so untroubled that it now seemed almost natural to be passing the portal of death from an ice-pan. Quite unbidden the words of the old hymn kept running through my head, "Oh, help me from my heart to say, Thy will be done".'

He was rescued just in time. A full span of life was given him, for the good of Labrador and the glory of Christ; and he died in 1940 at the age of seventy-five, after only five years' retirement away from his beloved Coast.